Transforming
Our Painful Emotions

Transforming
Our Painful Emotions

Spiritual Resources in Anger, Shame, Grief, Fear, and Loneliness

Evelyn Eaton Whitehead
and
James D. Whitehead

ORBIS BOOKS

Maryknoll, New York 10545

Founded in 1970, Orbis Books endeavors to publish works that enlighten the mind, nourish the spirit, and challenge the conscience. The publishing arm of the Maryknoll Fathers and Brothers, Orbis seeks to explore the global dimensions of the Christian faith and mission, to invite dialogue with diverse cultures and religious traditions, and to serve the cause of reconciliation and peace. The books published reflect the views of their authors and do not represent the official position of the Maryknoll Society. To learn more about Maryknoll and Orbis Books, please visit our website at www.maryknollsociety.org.

Library of Congress Cataloging-in-Publication Data

Whitehead, James D.
    Transforming our painful emotions : spiritual resources in anger, shame, grief, fear, and loneliness / Evelyn Eaton Whitehead and James D. Whitehead.
        p. cm.
    Includes index.
    ISBN 978–1–57075–870–6 (pbk.)
    1. Spiritual life—Catholic Church. 2. Emotions—Religious aspects—Catholic Church. I. Whitehead, Evelyn Eaton. II. Title.
    BX2350.3.W48 2010
    248.8'6—dc22
                                                                                2009032332

In respect and gratitude
to our colleagues and friends over forty years
at the Institute of Pastoral Studies
Loyola University Chicago

With special thanks to

Robert Ludwig
Rachel Gibbons
Susann Ozuk

Contents

Part One
TRANSFORMING OUR PASSIONS

1. Emotions, Our Unlikely Allies	3
2. Befriending Our Emotions	18

Part Two
ANGER
An Emergency Emotion

3. Tracking the Tigers of Wrath	35
4. How We Deal with Our Anger	50
5. An Angry Spirituality	63

Part Three
GUILT AND SHAME
The Price of Belonging

6. Boundaries of Belonging	81
7. Guises of Guilt	93
8. Healthy Shame	108
9. Transforming Social Shame	120

Part Four
HIDDEN GIFTS
Grief, Loneliness, Fear

10. The Gift of Grief   135

11. Learning from Loneliness   147

12. Finding Fear as a Friend   162

13. The Christian Script for Fear   175

Conclusion
THE WAY OF THE PAINFUL EMOTIONS

14. The Way of the Painful Emotions   189

Bibliography   199

Index   207

Part One

TRANSFORMING OUR PASSIONS

The Chinese character for patience *(jen)* shows a knife poised over a heart: the willingness to hold still, in painful settings, until we know what we are feeling.

1

Emotions, Our Unlikely Allies

An emotion is a transformation of the world.
—JEAN PAUL SARTRE

To be human is to be aroused. Emotion ignites our best behaviors: courage in the face of danger, a fierce attachment to our children, the anger that resists injustice. Our emotions also impel us to our worst excesses: violent rage, sexual abuse, corrosive guilt. Even though we can hardly live with our distressing feelings, we cannot live without them. In their absence we may survive for a while, but we will not thrive.

The Puzzle of Feelings

"The fact was I didn't feel much of anything very cleanly or purely, if that makes any sense. It was as if I had been churned up inside, so that all my emotions were colored with one another and had become one muddy shade." A teenager in Richard Bausch's novel *Rebel Powers* reminds us how perplexing emotions are. Uneasiness leaves us upset and confused, but what are we feeling? A surge of indignation goads us to take action; what's the best way to respond? Or, unexpectedly, joy floods our heart; where does this surprising contentment spring from? In the chapters ahead we explore the puzzle of emotion. Our focus is the negative feelings of anger, fear, guilt, shame, loneliness, and grief.

What do we mean by *negative* emotions? Some emotions make us feel wretched. Anger's racing pulse sets us on edge. Shame taunts us with messages of our unworthiness. Guilt's recriminations preoccupy and dishearten us. Grief drains delight from our life.

And beyond the bad feelings within, these emotions have distressing consequences. Anger's fury can ignite violence and injury. Shame and guilt feed addictive behavior, as people seek relief—unsuccessfully—in the momentary high of drugs or sex or food. Fear weakens the immune system, shrinking our stamina and leaving us vulnerable.

Negative cultural messages reinforce these personal experiences. Conventional psychoanalysis links depression with neurosis; self-help gurus insist that guilt is immature. Anger makes religion's list of "seven deadly sins." And most discussions of shame cite it as a wound to be healed, the toxic residue of childhood abuse, a hidden dynamic in a host of harmful behaviors.

Under the weight of these negative assessments, we learn to link these emotions to inadequacy and weakness. Soon we *feel bad about feeling bad*. Whenever guilt arises or loneliness stirs, the inner judgment automatically sounds: "I should not be feeling like this!" Embarrassed by our negative emotions, we make haste to banish them. But banishing bad feelings seldom works.

Why Look at the Painful Emotions?

The drive to understand these painful emotions starts in personal need. All of us have been caught up in emotion's turmoil. Bewildered by some internal upheaval, we try to make sense of what is happening to us. If we are to live satisfying and fruitful lives, we know we must come to terms with these powerful forces. And the need touches the public world as well. Recent studies have uncovered the code of silence that encourages health professionals and other caregivers to ignore their feelings of sadness and grief. "Our profession has always been about helping others, and our needs have traditionally been lost in the shuffle," a spokesperson for the American Association of Critical-Care Nurses reports. "The tension between the grief that many professionals feel and the implicit code of silence their jobs demand often cause emotional and physical suffering." A nurse working with cancer patients adds, "Being professional has always meant this macho, stoic capacity to swallow everything." An inability to acknowledge the emotional distress that accompanies their work leads many human service professionals into burnout and exhaustion. Some highly trained practitioners leave the field. Others develop psychological defenses—cynicism, emotional withdrawal—that diminish their effectiveness and erode their commitment to the work. From both mental-health and economic perspectives, learning better ways to deal with painful feelings becomes imperative.

Benefits of the Negative Emotions

Anger   challenges us to right a wrong; calls us to decisive action to protect from harm something that we judge to be of genuine value.

Anger can lead to action in pursuit of *justice*.

Shame   affirms the necessary boundaries that support our sense of self; warns of the risks of premature exposure; protects the privacy that makes genuine intimacy possible.

Shame is one of the roots of *personal dignity*.

Guilt   reminds us of the shape of our best self; recognizes discrepancies between ideals and behavior; defends the commitments that give meaning to our life.

Guilt often supports our sense of *personal integrity*.

Loneliness makes an assessment of our relational world; questions the adequacy of our connections with others; feeling lonely can move us to take action to strengthen our relationships.

Loneliness can be an ally in our search for *intimacy*.

Fear   warns of possible danger; alerts us "ahead of time"; this serves as a way we carry the wisdom of our past experience into the future.

Fear is a component of *mature courage*.

Grief   ignites the dreadful feeling that something essential is perishing; prompts us to evaluate what must be held on to and what must be let go; moves us toward a future both uncharted and full of promise.

Through lamentation, grief opens us to *genuine hope*.

Social research uncovers even more compelling concerns about negative emotions. In their analysis of sexual addictions in *Lonely All the Time*, psychologists Ralph Earle and Gregory Crow show the link between addiction and unmanageable negative emotions. Subsequent research reinforces these connections: rapists often recall being intensely angry or feeling worthless over the days or even months leading up to the rape; many child molesters acknowledge a struggle with anger or intense loneliness and depression as part of the cycle of their distress.

Reports on drug use makes similar connections between negative emotions and addictive behavior. Although many adolescents experiment with alcohol and illegal drugs, only a small percentage develop debilitating drug habits that continue into adulthood. Social scientists wanted to know why. They found the primary difference was how young persons handled their painful feelings. Adolescents who used drugs primarily to get rid of disturbing emotions were more likely to accelerate their use over time. Many of these teens became seriously addicted adults. In contrast, young people who developed effective ways to deal with or move beyond bad feelings tended to give up drugs altogether or limit their use to social occasions. Here again, learning how to deal with painful emotions is the key.

The negative emotions raise special questions for religious folk: What do these feelings have to do with our life with God? Does feeling depressed separate us from God? Do people on the spiritual journey ever get angry or feel ashamed? Do we follow a God of desire or a God of control? Sorting out these questions helps us shape a spirituality of the painful emotions faithful both to our religious heritage and to our experience today.

Emotions Are Our Allies

Painful feelings make us miserable, but they often come bearing gifts. A negative emotion's gift sometimes comes in the self-examination it provokes. Emotional distress challenges familiar patterns—"something is not right!" Our regular ways of thinking and acting no longer work. Troubled and confused, we review our expectations, reexamine our values, raise questions about how our life is going. Our reflection carries the seeds of significant transformation; both personal and social change start here.

Frequently, negative emotions benefit us by compelling us to act. "I feel so bad, I just have to do something about it." Sometimes what we do makes things worse, so good judgment and tact are crucial. But by giving us energy to follow through on effective behavior, painful emotions can help make things better.

And sometimes our painful feelings' chief benefit is to apprentice us to mystery. Our emotions regularly remind us that life escapes our earnest control. And our feelings, especially those that bring pain, open us to deeper receptivity. Wrestling with our fear or anger, confounded by our grief or guilt, we savor a deeper awareness: "There is more here than meets the eye." A more profound appreciation of life's mystery invites greater acceptance of ourselves and other people, encouraging us to let go some of our own insistent demands and welcome life as it is. Our feelings help us be at home in the world, wooing us, in the words of T. S. Eliot, "to sit still . . . even among these rocks."

In the chapters ahead we examine in closer detail the contributions that the emotions of anger, fear, grief, guilt, shame, and loneliness make to our life and well-being. In the chart on page 5 we provide a preview of the benefits of the painful emotions when we welcome them as allies.

We extract these benefits of the negative emotions only with much discipline and many false starts. Each of these feelings easily escalates into a destructive sentiment. Unchecked, anger blossoms as rage and a thirst for revenge. Guilt mushrooms into obsessive self-punishment. Our healthy sense of shame succumbs to a crippling hesitance in social life. Grief, unattended, may degenerate into a self-absorbed lethargy. Shaping these unruly sentiments into accomplices of our psychological and spiritual growth requires determined effort. The conviction that our negative emotions may come as gift instead of affliction, sources of grace rather than disgrace, guides this book. When we can decipher their code, our feelings reveal us to ourselves. They become allies on the perilous adventure of our adult lives.

Culture's Case against Emotions

Human emotions are "probably always an illness of mind because both emotion and passion exclude the sovereignty of reason. . . . Emotion makes one more or less blind." This judgment of eighteenth-century philosopher Immanuel Kant survives today in two cultural biases: emotions seen as *private passions* and as *irrational impulses*.

Are Our Emotions Private?

Feelings seem uniquely our own. Guilt and shame are our most private of possessions; anger and depression happen "inside our own skin." America's cultural commitment to individualism feeds the temptation to see our emotions as private events. Weighed down by our bad moods, we retreat further, warning even our closest friends to "just leave me alone." Convinced other people just won't understand we retreat even further, searching out private remedies for private pain.

But emotions are more than private passions. In this book we explore an alternate perspective—emotions as social realities. The rules that govern our feelings are primarily social in origin; the behaviors that express our emotions have a social function. Our feelings do not exist for us alone; emotions are social strategies directed toward our interaction with other people. Feelings attune us to the web of connections that links us to one another. "Emotions," as Willard Gaylin reminds us, "are not just directives to ourselves, but directives from others to us, indicating that we have been seen; that we have been understood; that we have been appreciated; that we have made contact."

Our feelings also alert us to troubles in our social world. Even depression, that most interior of sufferings, is often the body's way of warning us about an intolerable environment. When a social structure begins to crumble, its demise registers in the unrest, fear, and grief of the body politic. Sometimes negative emotions announce interior troubles, but often personal distress alerts us to danger in our social life. As theologian Barbara Harrison insists, "When we cannot feel, literally, we have lost our connection to the world."

Do Our Passions Leave Us Passive?

Not only private, our emotions render us passive—so conventional wisdom tells us. Language and literature are filled with references to emotions as "passions" in the etymological sense: they *happen to* us. A person is *overcome* by guilt, *consumed* by anger, *paralyzed* by fear.

Each verb is passive, suggesting our surrender in the face of forceful feelings. "I can't help it," we plead. Indeed, considering ourselves victims of our emotions is consoling. If feelings are beyond our control, they are beyond our responsibility. In this understanding of emotional life, we don't have our feelings; they have us.

Social scientists and philosophers today pursue an alternate perspective. Philosopher Robert Solomon is a leading proponent of the view that we actively interpret and shape our emotions. In *The Passions* Solomon urges us to recognize "emotions as our own *judgments*, with which we structure the world to our own purposes." When we make judgments about what we are feeling, we are not merely recording objective physiological stirrings; we are making sense of our world.

John Cheever notes in his *Journals* that "we perform our passions." Emotions are more than automatic reactions that we undergo. We are agents in our emotional life, not simply victims. When we identify what we are feeling, when we decide how to respond, we "perform" our passions. This familiar example may help.

As Richard slowed at the intersection his pulse began to race. Traffic was already backed up at the four-way stop. One car would crawl through the intersection as the others waited like sheep. Then another would creep through a left turn. This was going to take all day! He cursed his misfortune, then began cursing the other drivers. "Where does all this traffic come from?" he steamed. "Why must these inexperienced drivers show up just when I am trying to get home? Will they never learn to deal effectively with something as simple as a four-way stop? It seems like the city's traffic system is designed to ruin my day."

For years Richard would become enraged at this same intersection. But this day, as he waited impatiently for a hesitant driver to clear in front of him, Richard was struck with a new awareness. "I had always assumed that other drivers were the cause of my anger," he reported to friends later. "It wasn't my fault they didn't know how to drive, that they were blocking my way home. Very gradually the light dawned: when I arrived at the corner, the road was empty of any emotion. Then I flooded the intersection with my anger. Suddenly the street was awash with the irritation and upset that I brought to it. I was not the victim of this emotion, but its perpetrator."

Are Emotions Irrational?

Traditional theories have made thinking and feeling adversaries. Dualisms of body/soul and flesh/spirit cast reason in the role of a cool, detached master of our unruly passions. But the vision of reason and emotion as natural enemies no longer fits the evidence. Willard Gaylin voices a conviction widely shared among social scientists engaged in the study of human emotions: "Feelings are the instruments of rationality, not—as some would have it—alternatives to it." Emotions, he continues, "are fine tunings directing the ways in which we will meet and manipulate our environment."

Roberto Unger expands the discussion of emotion's particular contribution. Although passion has often been judged "the rebellious serf of reason," our emotions enjoy a kinship with our deepest desires that reason will never understand. "Reason gives us knowledge of the world," Unger comments, but "it cannot tell us in the final instance *what to want* or *what to do*." Indispensable to the human journey, reason guides us as we analyze and clarify our experience. But reason alone does not rouse us to courageous or risky endeavors. Reason cannot ignite desire.

Likewise, reason "cannot provide the quality of sustained commitment that we need to pursue our most reasonable goals." Commitment springs from a source more visceral than cool cognition. Our dogged persistence in promises pledged is rooted in something deeper than rational plans and clear objectives. By tapping our desire, emotion sustains our commitment through dark days and dry seasons.

And "there are some revelations into our own and other people's humanity that we achieve only through experiences of passion." Empathy is a striking example of a passion that gives us a privileged glimpse into another's pain. This is a revelation that reason alone cannot muster. Our negative emotions, too, provide revelations. Guilt illumines selfish tendencies of which we would prefer to remain ignorant. Anger reminds us of cherished values for which we are willing to fight. And grief coaxes us toward a life on the other side of a painful loss.

Our feelings alert us to our desires; they sustain us in our commitments; they give us glimpses of who we might be. For Unger, the evidence of our lives shows "intimations of a richer interdependence between insight and impulse," confirming the links between passion and reason.

The A-I-M of the Emotions

Our friend and colleague James Zullo notes that every emotion involves arousal, interpretation and movement. Examining these three elements helps us track the critical components of emotional life.

Arousal points to what happens in our bodies. Feelings have their root in physiology. Bodily changes trigger and accompany emotions: hormones are released; muscles expand or contract; shifts in blood flow affect the oxygen supply to the brain. But the meaning of these physiological triggers remains notoriously vague. When my pulse speeds, am I indignant or afraid? Does this nervous stomach signal sadness or guilt? As my face flushes, am I feeling embarrassment or outrage?

Some few physiological arousals do appear solidly "wired" to certain emotions; for example, when feeling ashamed, the almost universal human response is to look down. But most arousals are at the same time emphatic and ambiguous. Typically, we notice our shortness of breath or an ache across the shoulders but are not yet sure what these stirrings signal. But by identifying a feeling—announcing "I'm afraid" or "I feel sad"—we make sense of a physical response. To know what we are feeling we have to give our arousal a name.

Emotions, then, involve *interpretation.* Distinguishing fear from anger—or anxiety from eager anticipation—is difficult, based on bodily responses alone, because our feelings are more than physical reactions. Not until we determine what our arousal *means* do we know what we are feeling. This example may help.

Lillian shared a big meal with a colleague on her way home from work. Arriving home, she collected her messages from the telephone recorder. The third message brought news Lillian had been expecting but dreading all the same. Her dear friend Anna called to announce her departure date. Over the past two months Anna had been weighing the decision to take a job in a distant city. The two friends spent many hours together discussing the pros and cons of the move. The new position was a definite career advance for Anna, one in which she was confident she would succeed. The biggest deficit in taking the job was its location. Anna, who was born and raised here, would have to move clear across the country. When Anna signed the contract, Lillian was genuinely happy for her. Over the three weeks since then, they had spent lots of time together working out the practical details of Anna's move. Hearing her friend's voice on the recorder lifted Lillian's spirits, but soon her good feelings were replaced by a more somber stirring.

To avoid this still shadowy distress, Lillian set about straightening up the apartment. Collecting the clothes for the laundry, dusting the bookshelves, she tried to turn aside a growing heaviness of heart. Sitting for a moment to rest, she felt her distress expand. Trying to hold it off, she occupied herself with the details of tomorrow's work schedule. But soon the feeling returned. Lillian drifted into the kitchen. Opening the refrigerator, she surveyed its contents. "I'm a little hungry; I think I'll have a bite to eat."

Most of us have played out such a scene. A disturbing feeling comes as a nameless malaise. At first we try to ignore it. When our vague distress doesn't go away, we name it hunger—a discomfort we know how to remedy. The fact that we've just eaten is irrelevant. Only after many trips to the refrigerator do we realize we have misnamed our distress. The loneliness and sorrow Lillian felt at the news of her friend's imminent departure will not find remedy in food. A very different kind of nourishment is needed.

Lillian's experience shows how social contexts and personal moods shape our interpretations. These interpretations are how we *make sense* of our mute physiological stirrings and create our emotional world.

Emotions stir as physiological arousals, then elicit an interpretation of their meaning, and then impel us to act. Emotions are feelings that move us; they generate *movement*. Delighted, we dance for joy. Grateful, we write a warm note of thanks. Distressed by guilt, we call a friend to apologize. Emotion's arousal issues an alert, preparing us to act. Primed for fight or flight, our body stands ready to rush toward the goal, to run from the danger, to repel the attack.

Sometimes dramatic action is called for: we dash into the burning building to save a child or fight to defend ourselves against a mugger's assault. More often, though, the appropriate response to emotional arousal is less clear and more complex. Should we challenge a colleague's racist remark now or wait for a less public setting? Is a simple apology the best way to resolve a growing rift with my spouse, or should we commit ourselves to a lengthier look at the troublesome issues between us?

In the real world of our social relationships, direct immediate action is not always useful or even possible. And what of those situations when better judgment warns that doing nothing is the right response? How do we deal with the intensity that lingers on? Physical activity often provides a release when we are caught in emotion's grip: going for a long walk or cleaning the house or working out at the gym. Sometimes relaxation helps: deep breathing exercises or therapeutic massage or the gentle luxury of a warm bath. Sometimes the best response is wonder, savoring the paradox of how strong and weak we find ourselves to be, how fragile is our hold on life. Then letting go.

The interpretation that we give to a physiological arousal often tells us what to do. If we decide we are hungry rather than lonely, we move toward the refrigerator. The resolution of this bad feeling, we tell ourselves, lies in food rather than companionship.

Sometimes the interpretation of what we are feeling is shaped by another judgment. If loneliness leaves the stoic in us feeling vulnerable, we will prefer to name this feeling hunger. If we have learned that anger is wrong or that fear is a sign of weakness, denial will be our response when these arousals stir. "I'm just a bit tired," we murmur as we turn away from our feelings and try to get on with our life. Sometimes this strategy seems to work: our disappointment diminishes or the anger dissipates. But powerful feelings seldom simply disappear. Often they find other outlets. James Zullo succinctly describes the result of trying to bury our feelings in our body:

> We think about our feelings and get migraine head-
>   aches;
> We swallow our feelings and get ulcers;
> We carry the weight of our feelings and get back
>   pain;
> We sit on our feelings and get hemorrhoids.

How We Hold Our Emotions

Christian life is about embraces—our experience of holding and being held. Faith begins in the embrace of a nurturing Creator; it expands in our companionship with Jesus Christ and the hold this person has on our life. Our fragile faith is tested and refined in a more disturbing embrace when—like Jacob in the Bible—we wrestle with a mysterious God who comes by night. Embraces build up the community of faith, where we hold some in affection and join with many in cooperation. As commitments mature, we hold one another accountable. And, unavoidably, there are times when we hold one another in the painful embrace of conflict.

But how do we hold our passions? Two opposing visions of spirituality contend to show us how. One approach to spirituality counsels that emotions are unruly instincts erupting with blind and selfish force. The remedy is to hold these destructive emotions off; that is, to hold them away and hold them still.

At the heart of this spirituality lurks the demon of dualism: the belief that the human person is split between body and soul, flesh and spirit. From this vision has grown the conviction that holiness demands a distancing of the fragile spirit from the body's violent passions. The belief that we must hold off our emotions is fueled by the nightmares we see in the daily news: terrorist violence, domestic abuse, civil war. When we abandon ourselves to strong emotions, we end by being held hostage by them. When we indulge our fear or wallow in regret, the journey of our life stalls.

The metaphor at the center of this spiritual tradition is *mastery*. Our unruly emotions are like wild animals that must be domesticated and controlled. The ideal of mastery powerfully attracted both Stoicism and Christianity. In the centuries-long quest for control we have not always noticed how often mastery leads to denial. We seem to have our anger under control: we seldom shout, we never hit other people, we try to smile in adversity's face. Only later do we notice that anger, seemingly mastered, seldom disappears. Instead, it goes underground, only to resurface in sarcasm and resentment. Not mastered after all, anger is just replaced by a more malignant mood.

A different spiritual tradition sees the negative emotions as ambiguous rather than destructive. Anger and fear and guilt are necessary disturbances, part of commitment's cost. These emotions are not irrational impulses but arousals and alarms that carry clues to our best aspirations. Admittedly volatile and dangerous, our emotions remain potential partners in our search for health and holiness.

This more optimistic orientation urges that we embrace our emotions with greater confidence. Rather than hold them off or hold them still, we embrace them in ways that tame and utilize their enormous energy. We cannot "master" our emotions because they are not our slaves. But we can learn to befriend these bewildering feelings. Befriending is a discipline that resists both the inclination to deny emotion and the temptation to abandon ourselves to it. Befriending begins in acknowledging what we feel, confident that our most frightening arousals are, finally, not our enemies.

At the heart of this spiritual tradition is the optimistic conviction that body and spirit are not hopelessly alienated from one another. Emotion and reason remain open to mutual influence. A partnership is possible between physical impulse and spiritual insight. Here spirituality is not about avoiding the flesh and its blind demands but about purifying and harmonizing our complex desires.

The *spirit* at the core of this spirituality is not a soul that is at odds with a hostile body or pining for release from the trials of the flesh. This spirit is the energy that springs from the breath-spirit *(ruach)* of the Jewish tradition and the vitality-spirit *(ch'i)* of the Chinese tradition. This spirit is the source of our liveliness and a link to our passionate Creator. Such spirit, so often wounded and scarred by our personal histories, is the energy in us that aspires to forge bonds of love and commitment and is willing to pay the price of guilt, loneliness, fear and grief. In the following pages we trace a spirituality that pursues *befriending* our emotions rather than *mastering* them. Resonant with the wisdom of both East and West, this spirituality honors the disciplines required to transform our volatile emotions into reliable virtues.

Reflective Exercise

At the end of each chapter we offer readers the opportunity to trace their own understanding of these painful emotions. While the reflections are designed for personal use, their benefit is often greatly enhanced by sharing with a friend or in a small-group setting.

In this first reflective exercise, we ask you to revisit the past week or so of your life. In a mood and place of quiet, recall the people you have been with, the work you were involved in, your predominant thoughts and moods. Then, make a list of the different feelings you experienced over the course of this time. Take your time with this.

Now go back over your list and indicate which of these feelings you experienced as painful or *negative.*

Finally, spend some time reflecting on these painful emotions: In your experience, why are these feelings *negative*? As you experienced these painful feelings, was there anything *positive* for you?

Additional Resources

Full publishing information for the books and journal articles listed here is given in the Bibliography at the end of this book.

Psychologists today approach the study of emotions from many different perspectives. Of particular interest are Paul Ekman, *Emotions Revealed: Understanding Faces and Feelings;* Carol Magai and Jeannette Haviland-Jones, *The Hidden Genius of Emotion: Lifespan Transformations in Personality;* and Richard S. Lazarus, *Stress and Emotion: A New Syntheses.* Catherine Theodosius examines the role of emotions in the professional work of nurses and other caregivers in *Emotional Labor in Health Care*; we quote from the article "When Health Workers Stop to Mourn."

A readable introduction to the negative emotions as positive resources is Willard Gaylin's *Feelings: Our Vital Signs*; the quotations used in this chapter are drawn from chapter 1. In *The Emotional Revolution* psychiatrist Norman Rosenthal draws on contemporary research findings to provide practical suggestions for "harnessing the power of emotions for a more positive life."

Philosopher Martha Nussbaum offers a comprehensive analysis of the emotions as cognitive resources in *Upheavals of Thought: The Intelligence of Emotions*; see also Antonio Damasio's *Descartes' Error: Emotion, Reason, and the Human Brain* and his *Looking for Spinoza: Joy, Sorrow, and the Feeling Brain.* Robert Solomon makes a strong argument for the emotions as strategies of a responsible life; we quote page xix of the "Introduction" in his *The Passions: The Myth and Nature of Human Emotions.*

Roberto Unger offers a provocative vision of the contribution of passion to human life in *Passion: An Essay on Personality;* see pages 101 and following for the observations quoted here. Richard Sorabji traces the influence of Stoicism on early Christian thought in *Emotions and Peace of Mind: From Stoic Agitation to Christian Temptation.*

For an excellent overview of the role of God's creative breath *(ruach)*, see Bernard Lee's *Jesus and the Metaphors of God*. For an exploration of the links between passion and grace, see James D. Whitehead and Evelyn Eaton Whitehead, *Holy Eros: Pathways to a Passionate God*.

2

Befriending Our Emotions

Language is the light of the emotions.
—Paul Ricoeur

A painful feeling stirs in a dark corner of our heart. Hidden in the shadows, protected from the light of speech, a negative emotion exerts its frightening force. We feel miserable. But is this misery fear or guilt or grief?

Words wrestle our feelings out of darkness, helping us befriend our emotional life. Befriending painful feelings doesn't magically take away the pain. But the effort of befriending opens us to a new relationship with our emotions; we no longer have to hold them off or hold them down or hold them still. Befriending points the way to the ordinary disciplines of emotional life—naming and taming.

Naming the Emotions

The first challenge is to name the emotions that stir within us. The need to name our passions is urgent and universal. Our ancestors in ancient Greece and Rome used names to personify the forces of the heart. Startled by the beauty of a poem or melody, they judged a *muse* had assisted the artist. An exceptionally gifted person was thought to be possessed by a *genie;* such a person was named a *genius.*

But malevolent forces, too, invade the heart. When people became furious, our ancestors believed, an enraging spirit—a *fury*—had invaded them. The Christian Bible recounts stories of demoniacs—persons possessed by some destructive power. Negative emotions erupted in these people, turning them into savages. To control the demon, one had first to find its name. Jesus confronted a deranged person who

18

had been chained among the tombs, demanding of the demon within him: "What is your name?" (Mk 5:9). When the demon had given up its name—"My name is Legion for we are many"—Jesus was able to cast out the harmful spirit. Muses, genies, furies, demons: powerful forces moving within us. Fear, grief, guilt, shame: volatile inner energies waiting to be named and tamed.

The discipline of naming our emotions offers a three-tiered challenge. First, what is this disruptive feeling? Second, what assumptions lie concealed in the names we assign? Does *anger* already imply an unacceptable feeling? Does *lonely* carry an evaluation of inferiority? In this second discipline we must identify the often hidden judgments accompanying the names we assign to feelings.

A third challenge concerns the origins of our emotions. We may know that we are angry but have no idea why. We may feel ashamed of our body but have no clue as to the source of this shame. Full naming includes awareness of the origins of our feelings. Consider the example shared with us by a friend:

Last year while my wife and I were visiting my aging parents, I drove the four of us to a business appointment. My father was sitting next to me on the front seat when we started our return. Unfamiliar with the quickest route home, I asked my father if we should turn at the next exit. When he didn't answer, I glanced over, and he seemed either unconcerned or lost. As we drove past the intersection (where we should, in fact, have turned), I was overwhelmed with anger. Barely controlling my rage, I managed to drive us home by another route.

Arriving safely at home, I asked my wife to go for a walk with me and we tried to puzzle out my sudden, surprising anger. Why did I get so enraged? We replayed the scene: I had asked my father the way home and he didn't know. There it was! All my life my father has been the one who knows the way home; for me, this is his very definition. I assumed this would always be so. And now, in his late eighties, he doesn't know the way home! An abyss had suddenly opened; one of the pillars of my security had suddenly collapsed. Consciously I knew I could find my way home. But the change in my father still startled me. As we talked, my anger rapidly dissipated. I began to see I would have to release my father from this covert contract—that he must always know the way home. Together we would find our way—and now with less anger.

The way of naming our emotions is fraught with peril. We frequently fool ourselves by assigning the wrong name or naively believing that simply identifying a mood brings its cure. Yet naming is the only way through the thicket of emotion. Humbly, allowing for mistakes and self-deception, we continue to name the feelings that surge through us. Naming our emotions, we are less their victims, even as we surrender the fantasy of becoming their masters. Gradually bringing these feelings to light, we see what we must do.

Naming the Deep Theme

Even knowing the name of an emotion that troubles us may not immediately reveal its source. We feel guilty, but why? Or certain situations enrage us for no apparent reason. Often the effort to name a mysterious feeling uncovers deeper themes. Recall Richard, whom we met in Chapter 1.

Regularly infuriated in heavy traffic, Richard accurately named his arousal *anger*. Right away he identified the obvious circumstances that contributed to his irritation—living in a heavily populated area, having to commute long distances regularly for his work, holding himself to the demands of a busy schedule. Yet having anger's name didn't do much to help him moderate its negative force. Attending a workshop session several months later, Richard discovered another provocation at play when he was behind the wheel. The workshop leader introduced an imaginative exercise, instructing Richard to fantasize the best possible experience of driving in traffic. A sudden vision came to him: a world in which all the traffic lights are green! In the fantasy synchronized switches turned each traffic light green as Richard approached the intersection. The fantasy expanded: as Richard moved through life, all roads opened up before him; traffic halts, crowds part, as he moves forward unimpeded and in control.

Exploring this fantasy Richard recognized the childish response still triggered in him by every stoplight: "This restraint should not happen to me! I should never have to be bothered by other people!" When this underlying theme emerged with such embarrassing clarity, Richard broke into laughter. The next time he felt anger surge as he approached a traffic light, Richard said aloud with great seriousness: "I should never have to wait!" At the sound of this outrageous demand, he laughed again and felt the anger dissolve. Identifying and exposing this hidden theme gave Richard insight into his anger and a perspective on how to change his behavior.

Noting his improved civility behind the wheel, Richard's wife presented him with a bumper sticker carrying the slogan "Be a Buddha of the Road." This has become a family mantra: confronting snarled traffic, inevitable car-pool delays, or the frequent inconvenience of road repairs, family members encourage one another with the chant "Be a Buddha of the Road."

When a perplexing emotion gives up some of its hold over us, we know we have found its name. Naming rescues our emotions from the recesses of our heart and readies us to embrace their power in our life.

Taming the Negative Emotions

Negative emotions carry both feelings of pain and the impulse to act. The painful feelings grab our attention first. If we focus only on the pain, we risk losing sight of the real gift of the emotion—its energy for change.

Releasing this gift requires taming our painful feelings. To start, we must see the pain for what it is—a bad feeling about something good. Pain is an alarm, a signpost, a signal for our survival. Our distress points beyond itself.

Psychologist Willard Gaylin offers a useful analogy: A negative emotion is like a fever—a distressing experience that has a positive purpose. The fever gets our attention; it signals something is wrong, often before we are otherwise aware of the problem. Sometimes training our healing efforts on the fever itself is important. We try to bring the patient's temperature down, especially if it is sufficiently high to be life threatening. We want to make the sick person as comfortable as possible, so that the body's own resources may be brought to bear on the healing. But we recognize that to focus our efforts exclusively on the fever is to miss the point.

A fever is a symptom of another, more serious distress. The high temperature indicates that the body is mobilizing its resources to attack an infection or repulse an intruding agent. So we turn our attention to tracking this deeper cause, wanting to direct our healing efforts at the source rather than the symptom. If we let the fever distract us from this more complicated process of accurate diagnosis and proper treatment, we may alleviate the pain in the short run, but our intervention may not be of any long-range help. In fact, the patient may get worse.

Like a fever, a painful emotion is an alarm, a signpost, a signal for our survival. The pain gets our attention, but the distress points beyond itself—alerting us to information we might otherwise miss, signaling something significant that we might otherwise take for granted.

Respecting pain as a signal starts the taming process. But often our painful feelings serve less as a signal than as a stop sign. Emotional distress debilitates us, bringing our life to a halt. Confronted by negative emotions, then, many of us respond by trying to get rid of the pain. The problem with this approach is that it seldom works. Instead, further isolation results; to avoid painful feelings we silence our inner voice and cut ourselves off from any experience or relationship that seems threatening.

Taming our negative emotions demands developing personal strategies to help us honor our pain without simply succumbing to it. Discovering what calms us under stress is a good place to start. Going for a walk or watching a sunset, seeking strenuous exercise or a relaxing massage, quieting ourselves in the receptive stance of meditation or prayer, in each of these strategies we learn to calm our distress long enough to discern its meaning.

But concentrating too intently on our emotional distress is risky. The first risk is that we will begin to wallow in the pain. Giving too much attention to our turmoil overshadows the potential gifts of the negative emotion—greater insight into our life and renewed energy to make things different. We let our pain drag us down toward helplessness rather than empowering us for change.

A focus on getting rid of our pain also makes us vulnerable to the "quick fix." Turning to drugs—prescription or illegal—to deaden the distress, we again short circuit the emotion's energy. No learning occurs; no effective action results.

To concentrate on eliminating painful feelings raises another risk—avoidance becomes our chief strategy. Sometimes avoidance works. Steering clear of situations that make us afraid, of people who shame us, of memories that reawaken our rage often makes sense. But as a regular response, avoidance exacts a toll. To avoid fear we settle for a lifestyle that includes few risks. To avoid anger we consistently turn back from asserting our opinions or our needs. To avoid guilt we build defenses of denial, protecting ourselves from self-scrutiny. To avoid shame we retreat from any closeness with others that might leave us exposed—our ideas, our hopes, our true self. In each case efforts to avoid painful emotions diminish our life. For most of us, this empty calm comes at too high a price.

Painful emotion comes in part as ally, provoking reflection and challenging us to act. So befriending the negative emotion rarely means avoiding the pain. Instead, taming enables us to embrace the emotion long enough to discern its message, long enough to evaluate its import, long enough to use its energy to fuel the action required. Taming doesn't imply domesticating our emotions, rendering them docile, housebroken, and spayed. Taming provokes positive action, focusing emotional energy into actions that can help us.

Taming begins in acknowledging what we are feeling. Its discipline leads us between the extremes of denying an emotion (I am *not* angry!) and succumbing to it. Here, as in the classic understanding, virtue lies in the middle: between refusing to feel anything and abandoning ourselves to emotion's immediate demands. This virtuous response takes many forms. We tame anger by learning to channel its force into fruitful confrontation. We tame the arousal of petulant rage or false guilt by developing techniques that dissipate their energy. Throughout, taming resists the temptation to cling to the feelings that bring us down.

Harboring Emotion

Taming warns us not to harbor painful feelings. The metaphor of *harboring* suggests an inlet—our heart—into which a feeling of loneliness or self-pity or jealousy floats, looking for a place to reside. A colleague tells this story on herself.

I was on the way outside to work in my garden when the mail arrived. One letter held an invitation to write a review of an about-to-be-published book, a collection of essays on marriage. Glancing through the letter as I walked toward the garden, at first I felt flattered. But as I began to pull weeds along the edge of the garden, I noticed that "feeling flattered" had suddenly been replaced by another emotion. Why hadn't the editors of the book asked me to contribute an original chapter? I wondered. I know more on the topic of marriage than many of these other people! Now, instead of being flattered, I felt offended. I was upset and— hating to admit it—envious of the writers whose work was showcased in the book. I turned back to my weeding, but before long this sour feeling returned. Envy seemed to be asking for safe harbor, a place to drop anchor for a longer stay. My tarnished pride wanted permission to pout. Again I dismissed the envy and turned back to the weeds. Ten minutes later the emotion reappeared, bobbing up and down at the edge of my harbor, asking again for attention. This time I decided to spend a few moments acknowledging my disappointment and nursing my wounded honor. Then, wishing them well, I sent these visitors on their way. No room in my harbor today. After a few minutes the gentle rhythm of pulling weeds restored my sense of peace.

Harboring indulges the negative emotions, expanding their claims and absorbing our attention. The metaphor of harboring helps us recognize our own complicity in feeling bad. A young adult friend gives an example. Chris frequently feels lonely, an emotion he dreads. But as he now recognizes, Chris often gives himself over to the feelings. "When I feel a mood of loneliness descending, I'll usually try to stay off by myself. I'll play romantically sad music. I'll turn off my cell phone so that no one can reach me. It's like I don't want to be distracted from my melancholy!"

Crossing the Bridge

Harboring an emotion, we cling to it. Instead of seizing its energy to face a challenge, we bog down. Rather than using the arousal to confront a threat, we mull it over. A harbored emotion becomes chronic, corroding our insides and spoiling our relationship with others. Author Michael Buckley describes such a prolonged attachment to anger: "The 'sinfulness' of anger may not lie in anger itself but in prolonged attachment to it; in the refusal, out of fear, to let ourselves back into the impermanent world of interrelationship, *across the bridge of sadness*" (emphasis added).

When we cling to feelings of anger or loneliness or guilt, we refuse this crossing. We choose, instead, to dwell in a private world of regret and self-pity. In Buckley's words this is a "refusal of grief, and thus of the possibility of going through and beyond both anger and sorrow." But what is this bridge of sadness, and how are we to cross it?

The bridge is constructed on all the disciplines by which we "make something" of our painful emotions. On one side of the bridge is raw pain, the nameless hurt we feel. Certain moods—sadness, shame, loneliness—seem to envelop us, absorbing attention and deterring us from action. But emotions are transitive. They are meant to move us, to impel us to face a threat or to seek forgiveness—to cross the bridge.

In *The Road Less Traveled* Scott Peck described the transformation of pain into suffering. Pain is the blunt and often mute experience of misery. We feel terrible, without knowing why. Or we know why—a child has died or a marriage ended—but we can do nothing about it. Stunned by pain, we are struck dumb; we groan but are rendered speechless. We can remain stuck in such meaningless pain, swallowed alive by grief or guilt. But pain like this tells us nothing, leads us nowhere. The only remedy seems to be medication to numb the hurt. Stranded on this side of the bridge, we register our pain in depression or sarcasm or self-pity. But as we struggle to name our distress, we start to cross the bridge. Meaningless pain transforms into suffering. Here *suffering* does not signify passive acceptance; it does not indicate that we relish our hurt or are willing to undergo more injury. Pain's transformation into suffering begins when we are willing, in John Bradshaw's words, to feel as bad as we really feel.

Recent studies of nurses who served in battlefield settings underscore the need to move pain into suffering. The nurses often felt they were not entitled to express their feelings of anger and loss; only the front-line soldiers had the right to such emotions. When nurses, and other medical personnel, return from battlefield duty, they often plunge into hyperactive lives, or depression, or both. As increasing numbers of nurses sought therapy, the medical community recognized in them the symptoms of Post Traumatic Shock Syndrome. Given the opportunity to acknowledge their negative feelings in counseling sessions and support groups, many nurses found their symptoms of frenetic activity and depression disappearing. The senseless pain of the war was being transformed and humanized into suffering.

William Stringfellow, lawyer, theologian, and poet, gives another description of the journey across the bridge from pain to suffering. He recalls his response to the death of Anthony, his life companion. At first, he is engulfed by grief, an emotion he understands "to be the total experience of loss, anger, outrage, fear, regret, melancholy, abandonment, temptation, bereftness, helplessness suffered privately, within one's self, in response to the happening of death." In case we have missed the point, he adds: "Grieving is about weeping and wailing and gnashing of teeth."

Stringfellow recognizes that regret and gratitude, anger and affection are all jumbled together in the initial shock of his friend's death. His own healing, and the ability to celebrate his companion's life, will require sorting out these emotions. For Stringfellow, this will mean the transformation of grief into mourning. "I comprehend mourning as the liturgies of recollection, memorial, affection, honor, gratitude, confession, empathy, intercession, meditation, anticipation for the life of the one who is dead." Again he adds: "Mourning is about rejoicing. . . . I enjoy mourning Anthony."

On one side of the bridge of sadness, stunning grief accumulates. Through rituals of memory and tears and thanksgiving, we can turn grief into mourning. Mourning is the "work" of grief. If we refuse the work of mourning, our grief will consume us. But when we mourn, we begin to transform pain into suffering—a sorrow that will enrich instead of cripple.

The final bridge we cross is our own death. Learning of our terminal illness floods us with emotions of anger, regret and even bitterness. Why me? Why now? What are we to do with the pain and panic of our own death? In *Intoxicated by My Illness* Anatole Broyard describes his efforts to become the main actor rather than the mere victim of his own impending death. Broyard suggests that "illness is primarily a drama, and it should be possible to enjoy it as well as suffer it." To savor an illness, we have to give it voice. "I would advise every sick person to evolve a style or develop a voice for his or her illness." This effort to actively embrace our approaching death "is another way of meeting it on your own grounds, of making it a mere character in your narrative."

By writing of his coming death, Broyard attempts what all literature aspires to achieve: sufficiently distancing an experience so that we can embrace it again as our own. Broyard turns his death into a drama, writing a role for himself. Having gained this perspective on death, he can step into the role and play it with vigor.

Being an active participant in sickness, even a mortal illness, we hold our hurt in a way that escapes both depression and self-pity. And, in the face of death, we win the only victory possible. In the words of Broyard's wife, "He did not conquer his cancer, but he triumphed in the way he lived and wrote about it."

Christians believe that the life and death of Jesus shows us how to cross the bridge of the negative emotions. The gospel calls us to take up our cross and follow Jesus. Too often in Christian history naive piety transformed this challenge into an endorsement of victimhood. The "good Christian" must accept his poverty or her abusive spouse; the virtuous person should put up with all manner of discomfort and injustice. But the invocation to take up the cross does not counsel passivity. It acknowledges, instead, that painful crises come to each of us and that we can *do something* about these troubles. We can grasp the pain and loss that come our way, and do with them what Jesus did. At the death of his friend Lazarus, Jesus was moved to tears and groans. Facing the end of his own life, he initially struggled, then finally embraced death without indignity or shame. Neither a stoic nor a victim, Jesus lived the delights and distress of his life to the full; he performed his passions. Following him, we struggle to find the way across our own bridge of sadness.

Befriending negative emotions is a lifelong adventure. Very gradually we uncover the origins of these forceful and frightening sentiments. Armed with their names, we begin to tame them: to distinguish between their healthy and destructive potential. Gingerly, we familiarize ourselves with anger and shame and fear. When we harness the energy of anger to challenge a wrong, instead of stewing in our resentment, we cross the bridge. When we recognize the source of our fear and take actions to confront the threat, we cross the bridge. When we learn to hold our hurt up to God in prayer, instead of harboring our grief and self-pity, we cross the bridge.

But what holds us back? Sometimes self-pity blocks the crossing; sometimes lack of support bogs us down. Refusing to risk this crossing mires us in lethal patterns. Harbored, resentment or guilt or regret eventually ruins us. Perhaps it is to this hazard the gospel points in the warning not to so love our life that we lose it.

What helps us across the bridge of sadness? As social creatures we rely on the encouragement of others. Friends and family members, mentors and pastoral ministers model how to tame our emotions of anger and loneliness and shame. We rely, too, on the rituals that society and religious faith provide: ceremonies of grieving and reconciliation that face us in the right direction and pace us on the risky journey across the bridge.

Finally, when we dare to cross the bridge, where do we arrive? In Buckley's words, we come into "the impermanent world of interrelationship." *Impermanent* is the crucial word here; we cross the bridge back into a world filled with loss and failure, a land scarred by sin and injury. We leave behind fantasies of perfectionism and of friendships that never change. If the world we reenter is impermanent, it is also inhabited by forgiveness. This is not a place of hatred or resentment, of bitterness or revenge. On this other side of the bridge our negative emotions become allies, helping us face the dangers and reconciliations that mark our path.

Christianity and the Painful Emotions

From our origins Christians have harbored deep suspicions about the world of feeling. As early as the second century two voices—one secular and one Christian—spoke out eloquently against passion, profoundly influencing our religious heritage. Marcus Aurelius, Roman emperor and Stoic philosopher, mused in his journal about "the puppet strings of passion." We identify easily with this image: an instant anger provokes us into injuring a friend; a spasm of fear collapses our resolve; a sudden sexual arousal blinds us to commitments already pledged.

The Stoic ideal of Marcus Aurelius was serenity, a dispassionate detachment that would rescue an individual from the maelstrom of emotions. By mastering our moods, he was convinced, we could find peace and equanimity. "It now lies within my power that there be no vice or passion, no disturbance at all, in this my soul, but I see all things for what they are and deal with them on their merits."

The emotion of grief overwhelms us only if we forget that loss and death are part of life's natural rhythm. "Do not be entirely swept along by the thought of another's grief. Help him as far as you can. . . . Do not, however, imagine that he is suffering a real injury, for to develop that habit is a vice." To this second-century Roman, grief is an indulgence and a waste of energy.

In the final paragraphs of his *Meditations,* the philosopher recalls the regret we all feel as our life comes to a close. As actors in a cosmic drama, we rebel against an early curtain: "'But I have not played the five acts, but only three.' Then Nature answers us: 'You have played well, but in your life at any rate the three acts are the whole play.'" If we would accept our fate, we would find no reason to grieve and no cause for anger. For Marcus Aurelius, the negative emotions are interior, fruitless disturbances. We do well to banish these passions that distract us from a calm and serene life.

Marcus Aurelius died in the year 180, just as a young Christian by the name of Clement arrived in the North African metropolis of Alexandria. As head of a Christian study center, Clement developed a spirituality linking religious and civic virtues. Stoicism provided Clement with much of the vocabulary for this task.

In his guide for Christian living Clement's instructions ranged from table manners (one should exhibit "no indecorum in the act of swallowing") to public bathing (permitted for purposes of hygiene but not for pleasure). Clement's ideal of quelling disruptive emotions was expressed in the Stoic term *apatheia*. For Clement, *apatheia* did not mean a lethargic apathy but a blissful deliverance from the interior whirlwinds of rage, panic, and grief.

Peter Brown, in his magisterial work *Body and Society*, reminds us of the special meaning of *passions* for Clement. These were distorted emotions that "colored perceptions of the outside world with nonexistent sources of fear, anxiety or hope; or else they bathed it in a false glow of pleasure and potential satisfaction." Emotions like sadness or sexual desire easily mushroomed into toxic vapors. "If undispersed by vigilant reflection, such vapors could mist over the entire inner climate of the mind, wrapping it in a thick fog of 'passions.'"

For Marcus Aurelius and Clement, passions were bodily impulses at constant cross purposes with our spiritual aspirations. Emotion and reason jousted for control of the person; the soul pined for a haven removed from the disruptions of anger, grief, and sexual passion. Clement, like many other writers, appealed to Plato's image of the charioteer and his horses: human reason must rein in and master the untamed horses of passion. This dualism of emotion and reason, of flesh and spirit still haunts Christian efforts to forge a robust spirituality of the emotions.

The negative emotions continue to scandalize Christians. Many of us still harbor the ideal that maturity means serenity and that holiness requires the mastery of emotions. The Christian community is challenged today to forge a spirituality in which our emotions are recognized as more than private passions to be silenced by private remedies. Instead, we need to reimagine our passions as social instincts that link us with one another and alert us to cherished values.

We must decipher the mysterious chemistry through which bodily impulses ignite spiritual insight and the alchemy by which reason and emotion embrace.

A Knife over the Heart

A spirituality of the painful emotions will be anchored in the difficult virtue of patience. As anger or fear or loneliness stir in our heart, threatening our calm and control, we are tempted to flee the emotion. The Chinese character for patience urges us to endure the threat until we learn its mission. The character represents a knife poised over a heart. Is this an assassin's sword or a surgeon's healing blade? Should I flee to avoid this sinister attack? Or should I stay, opening myself to a painful purification that may save my life?

Patience is the ability to hold still under threat until we can discern what is at stake. Patience demands neither passivity nor docility but a fierce attentiveness to what is really happening. The medieval philosopher Thomas Aquinas observed that patience girds us "to endure immediate injuries in such a way as not to be unduly dejected by them." Unlike the Stoics, Aquinas believed that sadness is an ordinary and honorable part of life. But he was aware that sadness quickly spirals into melancholy and depression.

Patience equips us to hold our hurt in a way that blocks this destructive escalation. For Aquinas, patience is one of the faces of fortitude; courage to live life to the fullest requires our willingness to face the sorrows and losses that accumulate along the way. In Aquinas's words, "in patience you shall possess your soul."

But something in the American character does not like patience. A culture of ambition makes it difficult for us to hold still. Patience seems to put a damper on the spontaneity and freedom we so cherish. Too much introspection unsettles our national soul. Faced with problems and scandals, political pundits encourage us—impatiently—"to put it behind us" and move on. A consumer society's dependence on impulse buying and the media's accommodation to short attention spans do not foster the development of patience. Advertising campaigns in which sports celebrities urge us to "just do it" celebrate athletes' spontaneous grace while ignoring the disciplined patience that perfected these skills.

Befriending the painful emotions demands patience. Patience prepares us to live our life wide awake, to taste our negative emotions rather than simply swallowing our pain. In the chapters ahead we explore the disciplines of patience that transform our painful emotions into positive passions for life.

Reflective Exercise

First, identify a feeling you have become more comfortable with recently. This may be a positive emotion, such as joy or confidence or compassion, or a more problematic feeling, such as jealousy or resentment or fear. Spend some time remembering what helped you befriend this emotion. Be as concrete as you can. Give some examples.

Then identify a painful feeling that you are sometimes tempted to harbor. Use your imagination to picture this emotion sailing into your heart as if into a bay of water. How do you permit this emotion to drop anchor; what attitudes or behaviors or beliefs encourage the feeling to linger in your heart? Why do you harbor this feeling; what is its *perverse payoff* for you? Concretely, what action can you take to resist harboring this emotion in the future?

Additional Resources

Daniel Goleman has sponsored a series of meetings involving the Dalai Lama and Western scholars in discussions about emotions. He reports the fruit of these conversations in *The Destructive Emotions* and in *Healing Emotions*. In *The Regulation of Emotion* Pierre Philippot and Robert Feldman draw together an important collection of essays by noted psychologists, reporting on current understanding and treatment of emotional distress. Elizabeth Norman reports on Post Traumatic Stress Disorder emerging among nurses who served in the Vietnam conflict in *Women at War: Studies in Health, Illness, and Caregiving*.

Thomas Buckley examines anger in "The Seven Deadly Sins." Scott Peck distinguishes pain from suffering in *The Road Less Traveled*, especially chapter 1. William Stringfellow charts his movement beyond grief in *A Simplicity of Faith: My Experience of Mourning*. Anatole

Broyard demonstrates his own assertive effort to name and tame his dying; we quote from pages 7 and 61 in *Intoxicated by My Illness*.

Paul Ricoeur explores the role of language in *The Symbolism of Evil*; we quote from page 7. In *Body and Society: Men, Women, and Sexual Renunciation in Early Christianity* Peter Brown traces the intriguing link between turning from sexuality and turning from society in monasticism and other forms of Christian asceticism; see pages 129–30 for his comments on the meaning of passions. Marcus Aurelius's *Meditations* is available in the Loeb Classical Library edition; we quote here from G. N. A. Grube's translation, pages 66, 79, and 129. In *Clement of Alexandria*, Salvatore Lilla discusses the early theologian's judgment that the passions "are the worst disease of the soul" (96). Josef Pieper explores Thomas Aquinas's understanding of patience in *The Four Cardinal Virtues*.

Part Two

ANGER

An Emergency Emotion

The Chinese character *ch'i* signifies vital human energy and this energy expressed as anger.

3

Tracking the Tigers of Wrath

Ch'i *is the driving and creative force of all human activities.*
—Xu Fuguan

It is dawn in China. In public parks and rural fields throughout this vast country, people young and old gather to pace themselves through the rhythmic movements of an ancient discipline called tai chi. The simple choreography of this classic exercise regime—part martial art, part oriental ballet—brings body and mind to alertness. The mysterious and healing energy of *ch'i* begins to flow.

In the elusive language of China, *ch'i* stands for spirit, energy, and arousal. The core figure in the written Chinese character is "rice coming to boil in a pot." This suggestive image—the water's agitation as the temperature rises, the necessary risk of boiling over in order to transform the dry seed into nourishing food, the abundant increase of the rice as it cooks—resists simple translation. China scholar Lee Yearley identifies *ch'i* as the physiological and spiritual energy that stimulates us toward vital self-expression. *Ch'i* is evident in our *animated* conversation, in our *spirited* pursuit of an ideal or goal. *Ch'i* also rises when our anger is aroused.

The Chinese language designates in this single word both the fundamental energy of our humanity and the volatile emotion of our wrath. The arousal that sometimes boils over in rage also fuels our determination. If we could surgically remove *ch'i* we might never get angry, but we would lack the critical energy on which courageous action depends.

Anger is the most frequent of the negative emotions. This familiar companion shows itself as a flash of irritation, a peevish complaint, a simmering sense of indignation. Unattended, anger's everyday arousal

35

may sink into a harbored resentment or sour into a longing for retaliation and revenge.

These angry feelings are almost always seen as negative. Culturally we're instructed that being angry isn't good—"Don't get mad; get even." Morally we've been cautioned that anger is one of the seven deadly sins. We've learned, too, that being angry isn't good for our health; anger raises our blood pressure, interferes with digestion, strains the immune system. We fear its social consequences even more. Anger sets us at odds with those we love. When angry behavior turns brutal, people are hurt and relationships destroyed. Rage stokes America's epidemic of incivility and violence. So we conclude that anger feels bad and has bad effects.

But that's not the whole story. Consider another experience that gives us pause: the common inability to become angry. Many of us have great difficulty with conflict. Eager to please, we flash uncertain smiles in the face of disagreement. Our hunger to belong works against any willingness to confront controversy. Summoning the energy to defend our values or to address an affront seems out of bounds. The memory of Jesus angrily driving the money changers from the holy place of prayer comes as a challenge to our own cowardice. This biblical image reminds us there are values worth fighting for and threats to which we must respond.

Three centuries before Jesus, Aristotle described anger as the force that enables us to face difficulty. The "good tempered" person is able to draw on this energy—to become angry when injustices arise. If too much anger threatens to erupt in destructive violence, too little puts us at risk as well. Deprived of this volatile energy we are unable to stand up to provocation; instead, in Aristotle's words, we "put up with an insult to oneself or suffer one's friend to be insulted." Such a lack of spirit undermines our engagement in life.

Thomas Aquinas, who brought Aristotle's thought into the mainstream of Christian culture, expanded this optimistic vision of anger. For Aquinas, feeling angry is normal: "It is natural . . . to be aroused against what is hostile and threatening." Anger's irritation serves us well since it stirs us to "repulse an injury and seek vindication." In the end anger's arousal may provoke courage, for anger is "a disturbance of the heart to remove a threat to what one loves."

Anger, then, is a signal serving our survival. Its arousal urges us to defend ourselves, our interests, our values. In Willard Gaylin's words, anger "arms and alarms," alerting us to threat and energizing us to act. And beyond self-defense, anger serves social transformation. As theologian Beverly Wildung Harrison reminds us, "We must never lose touch with the fact that all serious moral activity, especially action for social change, takes its bearings from the rising power of human anger."

Anger's Arousal

The body serves notice when we get angry. But, intriguingly, we don't all feel the same. Most people become tense, but others report numbness. People may break out in a sweat or develop chills along with goose bumps. Changes in skin temperature make some faces flush while others grow pale. Despite these different experiences, the underlying physiological process is the same. Our bodies are being readied for action. Adrenal hormones course through the body, putting us on alert. Heartbeat and breathing rates accelerate, blood pressure increases, skeletal muscles tense. The mind, too, is affected. Moderate hormonal increases sharpen our attention, but high adrenal levels sustained over a long time lead to confusion and exhaustion.

Physically, anger readies us to confront a crisis at hand. Digestion slows as blood supply is diverted from the digestive organs in order to bring additional oxygen and other nutrients to the muscles and the brain. These changes maximize strength, increase stamina, and heighten concentration—preparing us for an urgent response.

But the *feeling* of anger involves more than this set of physical reactions; being angry includes judgments about what these reactions mean. The hormones that put the body on alert can be stimulated by a range of factors: physical exercise or injury; drugs, like caffeine and nicotine; an environment that is stressful or unfamiliar; a family quarrel; or a traffic jam. Researchers report that similar states of physiological arousal occur in several emotions. So distinguishing fear from anger, or anxiety from eager anticipation, is not easy if we follow only biological cues.

Being angry involves a state of physiological arousal *and* an interpretation of what this arousal means. As an emotion, then, anger is a complex experience of arousal-and-interpretation. An example may help.

I am waiting in line in a crowded supermarket. Balancing several purchases in my arms (I was in too big a hurry to get a cart),

I wait for those in front of me to move through the check-out line. As I wait, the person behind jostles me. Edging forward, I bump the person in front, who responds with a sour look in my direction. I am becoming aroused, and the name I give to this feeling is annoyance. Blaming the check-out person, the rabble around me, and myself (for coming at such a busy time), I identify my escalating distress as anger.

Later that day, having survived the trip to the supermarket, I head out for the football game at a nearby university. As I approach the stadium, I fall in with the throngs hurrying to their seats. At the stadium itself I find myself jostled and moved along by the large crowd. There are smiles all around, along with chatter about the weather and comments about our team's chances for victory. I am aroused, and I like it. Here the jostling and the crush of people, similar to but even worse than at the market, stimulates me. This arousal, interpreted differently, becomes not anger but a delightful anticipation.

A state of arousal accompanies most emotions—not just anger. And whether this aroused state is named anger or something else depends not only on what is happening in the body but also on what is going on in the mind—on the judgments we make about our experience. Before exploring the judgments that are part of our experience of anger, we must recall its favorite sites.

The Arenas of Anger

Three social contexts account for our most frequent experiences of anger—close relationships, public exchange, and situations where justice is at stake.

Intimate Anger

> *Anger is not the opposite of love. ... Anger is a mode of connectedness and it is always a vivid form of caring.*
> —BARBARA WILDUNG HARRISON

Our close relationships teach us that anger and affection are no strangers. In fact, the people we love are most able to drive us crazy. Anger toward intimates is most frequent because we spend so much time together. Where lives intersect and activities overlap, we are likely to get in each other's way. Intimate anger is most significant because these relationships matter most; with spouse and family members, and among friends or work colleagues, angry behavior has far-reaching consequences. Expressing anger to someone close can make things better—or much worse. Intimate anger is most threatening because we know one another's vulnerabilities. We press on the bruises—the sensitive issues that wound one another, the hot topics that provoke our rage.

Maturity brings us to recognize anger as intimacy's inevitable companion—and even part of its strength. "Anger is aroused when a significant relationship is threatened," Dana Crowley Jack notes, "and its goal is to promote, not disrupt the relationship." Psychologist Rochelle Albin goes further: "Anger can be a constructive emotion that helps resolve hurts and differences between people, improves their understanding of one another, and gives their relationship a firmer base." But to reap these benefits, we must learn to handle anger well.

In close relationships, resolving anger often requires a direct approach—acknowledging our mutual distress, confronting together the issues that rankle, working out solutions we can live with, and learning to forgive. But many of us are reluctant to deal directly with intimate anger. Afraid of driving away those we depend on, we hesitate to admit anger toward people close to us. Yet experience shows that to talk it out and work it through often leads to deeper understanding and greater commitment in a relationship. Resolving intimate anger usually demands that we first acknowledge to ourselves that we are angry. Then we need to approach the other person involved, so that we can confront the concern together and work toward some practical solution.

Public Anger

> *Fear and anger were designed to serve as responses to threats to our survival. To our* survival—*not to our pride, status, position, manhood or dignity.*
> —Gaylin Willard

Anger surges in impersonal settings as well. Sometimes getting through the day is downright difficult: a car pulls ahead of us in heavy traffic;

a computer error on our bank statement resists correction; a loud party runs late in the neighborhood. Inconveniences like this multiply in a complex, fast-paced society. If we interpret these inevitable slights as intentional provocations—"they're out to get me"—anger erupts.

Taking action can reduce the arousal we feel in response to the assaults and strains of modern life. A commitment to reducing stress in our own lives helps: simplifying our daily schedule, learning to say no, enlarging our vision so that we see fewer people as enemies. Often we need to assert ourselves—returning defective merchandise, calling the contractor to ensure that a scheduled repair project is completed on time, negotiating with an adjoining property owner to settle a problem between us. Our intent in these transactions is not to deepen a friendship or to preserve a close working relationship. The more modest goal is a return to public civility.

Public anger is often a barometer of the other tensions in our lives. Recall how irritable we are on days when busy schedules leave us physically taxed and emotionally drained. The agitation that comes with continuing stress primes us for anger. Living through a bitter divorce or confronted with a threatened job loss, people find themselves responding with hostility in circumstances that otherwise they could cope with calmly. And current studies into the roots of urban violence point to more than the increasing availability of deadly weapons. Jeffery Fagan of the School of Criminal Justice at Rutgers underscores the links between violent young people and the staggering harshness of their daily experience. The cumulative stress from day-to-day interactions that regularly evoke fear and contempt results—for many inner-city children—in a state of heightened physiological arousal. Even small provocations can turn this arousal into a violent response.

Dealing with public anger means finding ways to manage the inevitable friction of social interaction—strategies that help us develop tolerance toward one another and learn to mediate our disputes. And paradoxically, resolving this public distress frequently requires a focus on ourselves. We need the discipline to overcome our impatience, turn away from provocation, and get on with our lives.

Justice Anger

> *Anger is the necessary handmaiden of sympathy and fairness.*
> —James Q. Wilson

Anger also flares in the face of injustice—unfair treatment of us or "our kind," actions that attack our sense of decency or fair play, situations that show contempt for values at the core of our own world view. When we are confronted by injustice, anger fuels our commitment to right the wrong. But anger at injustice can misfire, provoking behaviors that are self-destructive or that target the wrong enemy.

Dramatic examples were part of the US experience of urban violence through the 1960s and 1970s. The destruction and looting that accompanied widespread urban unrest during those years most often devastated the neighborhoods in which the rioters themselves lived. The biggest toll was taken on local businesses that provided basic services and jobs in the community.

At that time African American theologian Cornel West probed deeply into the roots of this kind of violence, finding them in the unremitting assaults that poverty and racism mounted on black consciousness. He concluded that "the accumulated effect of these wounds and scars produces a deep-seated anger, a boiling sense of rage, and a passionate pessimism regarding America's will to justice." West called for a politics of conversion to arouse disheartened communities from their collective depression and engage them once again in the struggle for social equality. In America's continuing struggle in pursuit of this national conversion, justice anger has helped to keep hope alive.

Systemic injustice seldom yields to short-term solutions. In these intractable settings anger needs to be both nurtured and tempered. Group support is critical. Emergency-response committees formed by local churches in distressed neighborhoods, nationwide chapters of MADD (Mothers against Drunk Driving), the movement of basic Christian communities in Latin America and the Philippines—these are places where the resilient anger of justice is forged. Supportive gatherings like this protect people from being overwhelmed by their feelings of frustration and rage. But the group's goal is not to get rid of anger but to keep its energy alive. Coming together renews conviction in the justice of our cause. In the safety of this setting, volatile emotions can be expressed, confirmed, and focused into effective action. Justice anger, carefully cultivated, sustains us through the lengthy processes of clarifying common goals, developing a plan of action, overcoming setbacks and celebrating even modest gains.

Identifying Chronic Anger

> *Bitterness is like cancer. It eats upon the host. But anger is like fire. It burns it all clear.*
>
> —MAYA ANGELOU

Anger is an emergency emotion—provoked by sudden threat, resolved by swift response. Anger's painful urgency compels us to act quickly in self-defense. After we respond to the danger, our body calms and the sense of urgency subsides. With the emergency met, we are released from anger's hold. We feel relieved, sometimes even renewed.

But things don't always work out this way. Our angry feelings sometimes resolve quickly, but often they continue to smolder. The emergency emotion deteriorates into a chronic mood; we experience ourselves as angry all the time.

In his discussion of anger Aristotle observes that "the bitter tempered . . . remain angry for a long time because they keep their wrath inside." Rather than seizing the opportunity either to act on this emotion or to turn away actively from its demands, these persons indulge themselves in anger. Feeling hurt or offended, they nurse their feelings in private. As Aristotle observes, "Because their anger is concealed, no one else tries to placate them." Since people who hide their anger often seem calm and in control, other people do not sense their wrath—at least not at first. But soon this private distress starts to corrode their public calm, and their anger leaks out in insult or contempt. Since the bitterness of chronically angry people seems so disconnected from any obvious offense, bystanders can't understand their anger. Often the angry persons themselves are unsure of the cause.

Chronic anger sometimes dresses up as resentment. Feeling resentful, we privately rehearse our grievances; we picture ourselves insulting those who have offended us, stopping them in their tracks with a cutting remark. We indulge ourselves in blaming others, but all the action takes place in the private theater of our heart. Robert Solomon suggests that resentment is anger defeated by authority. Resentful of powerful figures in our life, we feel too inferior to confront them directly. Resentment is anger ashamed to show its face. But this feeling does show its face—in the corrosive guise of sarcasm and bitterness. These actions release some of the pent-up energy of our internal rage but never relieve the hurt. Compelled to repeat our hostile remarks, we gradually pollute our own environment. Chronic anger slowly consumes us and drives our companions away.

Chronic anger assumes other disguises, as well. Passive aggression, in which we both comply with and show our frustrated resistance, reveals an unhealthy face of anger. The habitual use of irony may be the educated person's expression of chronic anger. The central figure in Wallace Stegner's novel *All the Little Live Things* uncovers his own mask of irony:

> Sympathy I have failed in, stoicism I have barely passed. But I have made straight A in irony—that curse, that evasion, that armor, that way of staying safe while seeming wise.

Resentment and sarcasm often result from our judgment that expressing anger directly is too dangerous. This leads us to examine how we appraise our anger.

Anger's Appraisal

Anger carries a moral claim: a wrong has been done that should be set right. This claim is not always accurate. Our immediate feelings may mislead us, and conclusions we rush to in anger must be revised later, when a calmer mood prevails. Since anger's appraisals are judgment calls, those judgments need to be tested. But testing our anger does not demand dismissing its claims out of hand. Rather we must learn to read, to review, to reevaluate the judgments our anger makes.

Injury Received

Anger's first judgment is of injury received. Physical injury makes us angry: we trip on a piece of luggage left in the aisle by a careless bus passenger; a neighborhood bully threatens our child with bodily harm. More often the injury is to our self-esteem. Insults and ridicule come as personal attacks, damaging our self-respect. Being belittled threatens to diminish us in our own eyes. But as self-esteem starts to slip away, another emotion often intervenes. Offended, we get angry. And our anger interrupts the downward spiral of self-doubt. Other interpretations arise: "I don't deserve this abuse." "You can't treat me this way!" Those who work with battered women, for example, report that this angry affirmation marks a turning point in a woman's recovery from the cycle of abuse.

Sometimes the injury is to our world view, our confident sense of how reality works. When people challenge our values, when events call into question our basic assumptions, when others flaunt the rules we honor, anger flares. The risk here goes deeper than "I may be wrong." These affronts threaten our meaning world, the certainties that help us make sense of life. What triggers the anger may be significant: recall the angry debate throughout this country triggered by the detention of terror suspects at the Guantanamo Bay Detention Center. Or they may be seemingly small: the anger generated in the 1960s over transgressions of dress code that seem trivial today, such as women wearing pant suits to the office or men letting their hair grow long. Whatever the trigger, anger is provoked when the established order and our own secure place in it are at risk.

Accusation of Blame

A second appraisal—anger accuses. Assigning responsibility is at the heart of anger. "More than anything else," James Averill remarks, "anger is an attribution of blame." Harm has been done and someone must be held accountable. We may fault ourselves (anger at oneself is a big part of feeling guilty) or someone else. Often enough we assign blame inaccurately; innocent bystanders—even inanimate objects—stand mistakenly accused. But finding a culprit is part of what it means to be angry.

Anger flares when we are frustrated; that is, when we are denied something we need; blocked from something we want; prevented from reaching our goal. Under stress we personalize the frustration, interpreting interference as a direct assault. "The careless bank teller is out to get me." "The evil genius who lives inside my computer has selected me for special suffering."

Harboring anger is hard without someone to blame. When we recognize no one is at fault, anger dissipates. We may still feel annoyed at the situation. We may still be inconvenienced by what has happened or irritated by what was done, but we are unlikely to remain angry. Consider a couple of examples.

In the shopping mall someone bumps you from behind, dislodging your packages and scattering their content. You turn with an angry rebuke to find that an elderly woman behind has tripped and fallen. Now your anger turns to concern. "Are you all right?" you ask, rushing to offer assistance.

In this situation you have been genuinely inconvenienced: you've been knocked about, packages are on the floor in disarray, plans have been interrupted. You probably feel annoyed, and all these people crowding around are just adding to the confusion. You quickly become impatient: why haven't the mall security guards arrived to offer assistance? You may even be looking for someone to blame: why doesn't the maintenance crew pay more attention to the floors on these wet days? But, judging that she is not really responsible, you are not likely to remain angry at the woman who actually bumped into you.

Anger loses its hold when we learn that the person we blame is not really the culprit. Another example:

My neighbor is late returning a borrowed chain saw. When I spoke to him yesterday, mentioning my plan to spend this afternoon clearing the yard of storm debris, he agreed to return it by noon today. Turning to the task this afternoon, I check the garage. The chain saw is nowhere to be found. My anger mounts. I fume. I think of the neighbor as being inconsiderate (and worse), and I rush into the house to give him a call. Just then my son Greg emerges from his room, the chain saw in his hand. My neighbor, true to his word, had stopped by earlier. Finding the garage door locked (I had assured him it would be open), he stopped at the front door and left the chain saw with my son. Greg, busy with his own schedule, brought it to his room, forgetting it was there until he heard my rantings in the yard. When I learn these details, my anger toward my neighbor disappears. I'm tempted to shout at Greg for not getting the saw to me sooner. Happily, I catch myself in time. Responsibility for this mixup is mainly mine. I'm the one who forgot to leave the garage door open. I'm embarrassed by my slipup and a bit angry at myself for all the fuss.

Assertive Response

A third appraisal: Anger urges us to act. Being angry brings a realization that we can, we should, we must respond now. In some situations this urgency serves us poorly. We act before we have considered the consequences—striking out in violence or take foolish risks. But anger's insistence also fortifies us for a more effective response.

Anger commits us to action. The links between anger and action are sufficiently strong so that if someone says "this makes me angry" but makes no attempt to change the offending situation, we doubt whether the person is really angry.

Being angry empowers us—body and mind. A friend captures the experience well: "When I am angry I feel strong!" Physically, anger generates energy. Being angry mobilizes our body for vigorous action, so we actually feel tougher. Psychologically, anger builds confidence. Being angry bolsters the sense that *we are right*. Doubts fall away in face of the conviction that our complaints are valid and our actions justified. The awareness that "I must do something" grows. Sometimes "doing something" goes only as far as letting off steam: we curse our lot or shout out accusations or stalk away, slamming the door as we leave. But "doing something" becomes more constructive when we move to remedy the harmful situation.

Anger provokes a passionate response: we stand up to the challenge, press for justice, try to instigate change. Such assertive actions make claims, inserting us into the thick of things. But anger's assertion does not necessarily lead to aggressive behavior. In fact, by drawing attention to the problem early and giving us time to work out a suitable solution before things get too bad, assertion usually works to prevent aggressive attack.

Aggression involves direct attack intended to bring harm. In his research into the everyday experience of anger, psychologist James Averill discovered that the links between anger and aggressive behavior are not strong. Even when they are angry, most people consider a direct attack on the blameworthy culprit to be a tactic of last resort. More typically, angry people try to communicate convictions ("This is important"), to defend rights ("I deserve better"), to indict misdeeds ("What is happening here is wrong"). Their anger prompts vigorous action to correct a bad situation. This kind of assertion brings feelings of personal empowerment. Violence is more likely to result in settings where people feel impotent, without effective ways to express their distress or to use its energy to make things better.

A Sense of Hope

Finally, being angry carries the conviction that something *can* be done. This hope makes anger a friend of transformation, an honorable dynamic in change and growth. Most therapists know anger is an ally; its energy fuels the hard work of personal change. Harriet Lerner, whose influential work has redefined the experience of anger for women, notes, "Anger should be used to define a new position in a relationship pattern, a position that does not mean self-betrayal." Many marriage counselors prefer working with couples who are angry. People who are angry with each other are still significant in each other's lives. Indifference is a greater enemy of reconciliation than anger, because angry people are still linked.

Anger signals social transformation as well. Angry people want things to be different; their anger says no to the status quo. Angry demands arise from the hope that change is possible. When people lose this hope, anger dies. This connection makes anger crucial in social change. People long oppressed become resigned to their fate. Passive in the face of their plight, they are reluctant to work for change. "What's the use. Nothing can be done. This is just the way things are." But anger brings a sense of entitlement: "We deserve better." Feeling entitled, people rally to action—standing up to challenges, pressing for change, instigating reform. So community organizers and other advocates of change do not shy away from the distress of anger. "We're trying to give people back their anger, because anger will give them back their hope."

Anger remains an unpleasant and unsettling emotion. It threatens our self-control and overturns our serenity. Most of us would much prefer to live without it. But anger is a necessary disturbance. When we are belittled, when our values are threatened, when injustice imperils our shared life, we must be able to be aroused against these offenses. Befriended and tamed, anger becomes the powerful ally of our responsible life in the world.

Reflective Exercise

Recall a recent time when you were angry with someone else. Spend a few moments bringing the incident to mind. What triggered your anger toward this person? Did you express your anger? If so, how? If not, why not? What happened as a result?

Now consider this incident in terms of *gains* and *losses*. Were there any *gains* resulting from this experience—positive results, benefits received, good effects? List whatever comes to mind. Were there any *losses* experienced here—negative results, harm inflicted, bad effects? Let your response range widely.

Next, recall a time when you were the target of someone else's anger. Let yourself be present to the experience again. As you see it, what triggered the anger toward you? How was it expressed? How did you feel? What happened as a result of this angry exchange? Then consider this incident in terms of *gains* and *losses*, using the questions in the paragraph above as a guide.

Finally, spend a few moments comparing your assessment of these two experiences with anger. What learnings can you take away from this reflection to influence your experience of anger in the future?

Additional Resources

Psychologist Carol Tavris provides a comprehensive and readable review of research findings in *Anger—The Misunderstood Emotion*. For significant contributions to the understanding of everyday anger, see James R. Averill, "Studies on Anger and Aggression: Implications for Theories of Emotion"; we quote from pages 1149–50. Theologian Barbara Harrison discusses the positive potential of anger in "The Place of Anger in the Works of Love; we quote twice from page 14.

Harriet Lerner writes perceptively about the benefits and abuses of intimate anger in *The Dance of Anger*. Looking especially at women's experience, she suggests practical ways to break unhealthy patterns of angry response. Dana Crowley Jack, in her larger analysis of depression, *Silencing the Self: Women and Depression*, examines the valuable contribution anger makes to the effort of personal and social change; we quote from page 41.

Willard Gaylin offers a comprehensive look at anger as an emergency emotion often at odds with the complex demands of contemporary life in *The Rage Within: Anger in Modern Life*; see also his discussion in *Hatred: The Psychological Descent into Violence*. James Q. Wilson urges recognition of the moral sensitivities needed to moderate current society's rampant hostility in *The Moral Sense*. Cornel West examines nihilism in black America in *Race Matters;* we quote from page 224. Maya Angelou's distinction between anger and bitterness is part of her interview in *Writing Lives: Conversations between Women Writers*. Wallace Stegner's comment on irony is found on page 12 in *All the Little Live Things*.

Lee Yearley examines *ch'i* as a "psychophysical energy" with "numinous qualities" that, in Mencius, is intimately related to righteousness and courage (see *Mencius and Aquinas: Theories of Virtue and Conceptions of Courage*, especially pages 152–54). For Aristotle's discussion of anger, see *Nicomachean Ethics* 1125B–26B. Thomas Aquinas's observations on anger are found in Questions 46–48 of Ia–IIae of his *Summa Theologiae*.

4

How We Deal with Our Anger

*Any damn fool can have rage. What takes guts is to take
the anger and rage and do something with it.*
—Salvador Villaseñor

Victor Villaseñor is the author of *Rain of Gold*, an epic account of an
extended family—his own—in Mexico and the United States over several generations. His work has won critical acclaim for its elegant
style, meticulous research, and universal sympathies. Recently
Villaseñor spoke of his own growing up in southern California in the
1940s and 1950s. The son of Mexican parents, Villaseñor felt the full
weight of the cultural message that Mexicans are not as good as other
people. At nineteen he spent a year in his parents' homeland. There
he came in touch for the first time with his own heritage. Villaseñor
was startled to see government officials, professional people, teachers, artists—all persons of color who looked and spoke like him.
Though he was badly dyslexic throughout his years in US schools, in
Mexico Villaseñor met a women who taught him to read, opening
him at last to the world of books. This exhilarating exposure to Mexican culture and literature nourished his confidence. As pride in his
Hispanic roots surged, Villaseñor felt growing anger over his early
experience in the United States. "I had so much rage and anger, I
didn't want to come back to the United States." Villaseñor recalls a
crucial conversation he had with his father at that time. "If I come
back, I might want to kill," the son declared. "You don't think I have
rage?" the senior Villaseñor retorted. "Any damn fool can have rage.
What takes guts is to take the anger and rage and do something with
it."

How do we deal with our anger? As Victor Villaseñor's father
knew, giving free range to rage seldom helps. An angry outburst may

momentarily vindicate our sense of honor, but at a heavy cost. We come away from the fray with people injured, relationships wounded, potential allies alienated. Regret cannot undo the harm done when anger turns brutal, whether in family life or in random social violence.

Most of us know from personal experience other responses that don't work: *denial* ("I'm *not* angry"), *guilt* ("I'm angry, but I shouldn't be"), *self-condemnation* ("What right do I have to be angry, since whatever is wrong is probably my fault?"), or *blame* ("No, it's *your* fault I'm angry"). These responses doom anger from the outset.

Dealing effectively with anger demands a different starting point. We might name it acceptance, but "acceptance" sounds so patronizing. The benefits—and risks—of anger inspire more than reluctant assent or begrudging tolerance. How do we *befriend* our anger? First, we honor it, then we evaluate it, then we tap its energy to help us act positively for change.

Honoring Anger

Anger is always ugly, but it doesn't always have to be bad.
—Hendrie Weisinger

Honor captures the *awe* and *respect* that anger provokes: Here is a formidable, even dangerous, emotion. Anger threatens the delicate web of social life. Unattended, its energy erodes relationships and risks degenerating into vengeance. But access to this energy is indispensable.

In the dictionary, *to honor* means both "to recognize" and "to respect." How do we honor anger? Recognizing that angry feelings are normal is a good place to start. Honoring helps us hold this formidable emotion as expectable, inevitable, allowable in our life—without rushing into actions we will later regret. Simply acknowledging "Yes, I feel angry" begins to release us from the burden of denial. The esteem implied in the word *honor* serves as an antidote for the wounded attitudes that many of us carry still, especially a tendency to punish ourselves for feeling angry. Instead of being besieged by guilt over an outlawed emotion, we learn we can accept our anger even as we struggle to decide what to do about it. Reaffirming for ourselves the difference between *feeling* angry and *acting* enraged takes us a long way in taming anger's power.

Anger announces, "Passion ahead; proceed with caution." Honoring anger helps respect this power. To honor anger we have to pay attention to what we are feeling. The effort of paying attention counteracts the impulse to respond too quickly. This discipline interrupts the urgency of our arousal, giving us time to consider consequences. Psychological research shows how paying attention helps people respond well to anger. Summarizing more than a decade of research on how people deal with their emotions, psychologist Leonard Berkowitz describes a pattern of reflection found among people who are able to regulate negative moods effectively. Berkowitz discovered that paying attention starts a significant process of discernment. When people first become aware of their anger, for example, "they are somewhat surprised or disturbed and this prompts a relatively high level of cognitive activity. They think about the possible causes of their feelings and even consider what may be the best way to act. These considerations then steer their behavior." When attentiveness does not intervene, Berkowitz found that "the hostile and aggressive tendencies created by the negative mood are less likely to be restrained and are likely to be expressed openly" in harsh language and violent actions. A commitment to honor anger encourages us to pay attention to our feelings. And paying attention helps us read anger properly and use its power productively.

Evaluating Our Anger

A friend recounted her experience with anger:

> Anger's always been hard for me to deal with. Some of my friends call me a hothead; I admit I'm likely to respond immediately if I feel slighted or if somebody takes advantage of me. And sometimes that's good, but sometimes not. Lately I've been getting a better hold on my anger. Something that works for me now: when I start feeling angry, I say to myself, "My anger is trying to tell me something." I keep repeating the phrase, like a mantra. This calms me down, but it also points me in the new direction. Instead of flying off the handle, I try to look more closely at what's making me mad . . . and why. And that's been a real revelation to me!

"My anger is trying to tell me something." Anger always carries information, but its message is seldom immediately clear. Befriending anger includes finding ways to retrieve this message. The first step is to interrupt our typical pattern of response. For some of us the automatic response is finding a scapegoat, someone to sacrifice to our rage. Searching out a culprit shields us from facing our own part in the problem. This stance warps anger's strength for self-defense into a strategy of self-delusion.

Or our customary response may be to give in when we are angry. Perhaps we've learned that anger is terribly unladylike, or seriously sinful, or patently immature. Or we may fear the consequences of our own or other people's rage. So we acquiesce, hoping that refusing to assert ourselves will make the feelings go away. "I don't want to upset anybody." "It's dangerous to demand my rights." "Protesting would be impolite." This compliant stance, too, subverts the revelation our anger may hold.

Therapists often recommend a simple strategy to help uncover our automatic response: keeping an anger log or diary. The practice of recording our experiences of anger—when it arises, how long it lasts, what thoughts come along with our anger, how we choose to express it—helps us recognize our own patterns of anger. Evaluating these patterns helps us decide what we might want to do differently.

"My anger is trying to tell me something." In befriending anger the response to be nurtured is readiness to learn. To learn what? Something about ourselves: the risks we sense to our self-esteem. Or the ways our personal histories have left us vulnerable to hurt. Or how events and circumstances trigger this vulnerability into rage. Since anger erupts when deeply held convictions are threatened, being angry can reveal the values we hold worth fighting for. Tracking our anger back to its source can also uncover a rift between our professed values and how we are really living. Anger here is an ally of our integrity, challenging us to make the changes necessary to get back on course.

Or anger may be trying to tell us something about our world. Being angry is a response to frustration. For many of us, the frustration is lack of time; our irritability stems from a sense that we're falling behind. We strain against the seemingly endless demands of work place and family responsibilities. For others, anger reveals the weight of other people's expectations. We live in a world where many people feel they have a right to dictate to us, setting goals we should achieve and faulting us for failing standards that are not our own. Our frustration may point to a troubled relationship: a valued colleague undermines our authority in public; a teenage son retreats into silence or verbal abuse. Or anger alerts us to significant settings that have become dangerous: a climate of racial intimidation pervades our neighborhood; the threat of sexual harassment erodes our confidence at work. Examined, our anger can give insight into how our environment has become hostile and start to show us the shape of an effective response.

"My anger is trying to tell me something." Discerning this message requires effort. We stop to reflect on what triggers our angry feelings; we interrupt a customary pattern of response to ask what needs to be questioned or challenged or set aside. Evaluating our anger inserts a pause in our arousal, leaving space for anger's wisdom to emerge.

Discern the Appropriate Response

Determining how to act with anger starts by focusing on our goal: what do we want to accomplish here? Sometimes the goal is communication; we want to let someone know how we feel. Sometimes the goal is change; we want to remedy a bad situation. And sometimes the goal is conversion; we want to turn away from our anger and move on. Each of these options involves a decision.

Seeing angry behavior simply as a spontaneous eruption beyond our control is misleading, because angry action always involves choice. Being angry is better understood as an interpersonal strategy, one of the ways we learn to deal with other people. For example, people decide *whether* to show their anger, *how* to express it, and *who* will be its focus—a spouse or a pet or a stranger on the street. Befriending anger means learning how to make the choices that transform our arousal into an effective response.

Many of us learned early that feeling angry is bad, a lesson that limited our choices to denial and repression. But when refusing anger's arousal deprives us of its energy, our composure comes at too high a price. For us, the chief discipline is to carry our arousal forward into effective action. But in many American families, children learn different lessons about anger. Early on the links between anger and violence are reinforced: by parents who, when they are angry, discipline their children by harsh physical punishment; by adults who characteristically handle frustration by lashing out; by violent arguments and assaults in the home. If this is our early experience, befriending means breaking the pattern that automatically links angry arousal to violent behavior.

Experimental programs are being developed in schools and rehabilitative centers and elsewhere to help violence-prone young people learn ways to break these links. From what has been learned so far, three strategies seem key. First, teaching young people simple ways to interrupt their anger—deep breathing, relaxing stretches, counting to ten, using their imagination to take them somewhere else. Second, showing young people how to find alternatives to their explosive response by introducing them to basic conflict-management skills—considering different ways to communicate their anger, learning nonviolent ways to be assertive, tracking the consequences of their actions. Third, helping young people find support for new ways of acting—setting up peer groups committed to change, encouraging them to identify people and situations to avoid, establishing adult contact persons to whom they can regularly report both their successes and mistakes. Obviously, troubled children are not the only folks who might benefit from these helpful strategies.

Expressing Anger

In close relationships letting the person who has upset us know of our distress often helps. Rochelle Albin notes: "Expressing anger not only provides relief for ourselves, it can also help other people see things differently. Expressing anger relieves hurt and can change things." In fact, theologian Barbara Harrison insists, "Anger expressed directly is a mode of taking the other person seriously." When anger arises, Harrison continues, "we have two basic options. . . . We can ignore, avoid, condemn, or blame. Or we can act to alter relationships toward reciprocity, beginning a real process of hearing and speaking to each other."

Telling friends or co-workers how their actions offend us may not be easy, but—if skillfully done—this honesty makes change possible. Our friends may not have meant to hurt us; they may not even have known we took offense. Aware now how their behavior affects us, they can take steps to act differently.

Communicating anger sometimes leads to more than changed behavior. Where people care for one another and for their life together, expressing anger can deepen intimacy. Letting others know our distress opens our inner world to them. Anger exposes us, revealing where we feel vulnerable. Telling others how they have hurt us risks giving them information that can hurt us more. But in a safe relationship, revealing our vulnerability—paradoxically—strengthens us. Having been angry with one another, and survived through that sweaty distress, strengthens the relationship as well.

Sadly, not all close relationships are safe, and not every angry statement supports positive change. Sometimes expressing anger just makes things worse. Psychologist Carol Tavris cautions that, contrary to some common-sense recommendations, "letting it all out" usually increases our rage. Anger dissipates when injustice is rectified, when a sense of personal control is reinstated, when self-esteem is restored. Giving vent to angry feelings can sometimes be part of this process, moving us beyond apathy and prompting us to get involved. But "getting it out of our system" usually does not dissipate rage; on the contrary, angry expression tends to increase anger—in ourselves and in other people.

Many angry people act on the supposition "if I just show how upset I am, the other person will change." But angry expressions make a clumsy tool for change. Since people under siege strike back, verbal attack is usually counterproductive. But expressing anger does not demand hostile behavior. We can let someone know that we are angry and why, without attacking them verbally or physically. To show the difference, therapists distinguish between a communication style that starts with information about self ("This is how I am feeling now. This is what I am going to do.") and messages that insult or blame the other person ("It's your fault, stupid! Look what you have done to me."). In situations where emotions run high, "I" messages make it easier to give and receive information. When our goal is to move beyond anger—toward understanding, toward negotiation, toward peace—these communication skills become crucial.

Acting with Our Anger

Anger moves us to remedy a grievance. Sometimes expressing anger is enough and just letting people know our complaint brings the change we need. But the world usually doesn't come around so quickly in the face of our displeasure. We have to do more than register our distress;

we have to strategize how to effect change. When our goal is change, the challenge is channeling anger into effective action.

Acting *with* anger means holding our anger in a new way. Rather than moving away from our arousal, we want to stay in touch with its urgency. In the face of entrenched bias or long-term patterns of abuse, change can seem impossible. Falling back into a resigned stance that "nothing can be done" or "it's not my job to make things better" is tempting. Resistance seems worthless. But giving in to this sense of futility saps our strength. Losing touch with our anger, we fall out of the loop of social transformation.

When apathy threatens, we need disciplines to keep our anger alive. Anger has a dangerous memory, committing us to action. By holding in mind the injustice we have witnessed, by recalling injuries we have received, by remembering our worth, we rouse ourselves to act.

But sustaining anger is risky to do by ourselves. Remembering anger also rekindles emotional pain. Fear of facing that force alone makes us reluctant to stir anger's ashes. Better, perhaps, to turn away from the evidence of personal malice or social inequity and get by as best we can. Finding support, then, can be one of the disciplines of anger. With companions who share our anger, we gain a sense of power that goes beyond what we can do alone. By providing a setting in which our distress can be acknowledged and then focused into action, a supportive group also protects us from simply being overwhelmed by the arousal we feel. The group helps us hold our pain so that we can draw on its energy for action.

When our goal is to remedy a bad situation, anger gives us steam to make things change. But being steamed up doesn't guarantee success. Channeling anger into effective action is the real work of change. Strategies of planning and problem-solving are key—being clear about what we want to accomplish, recognizing the barriers we face, gathering needed resources, enlisting allies to help. But anger remains an underlying energy of social transformation, fueling personal commitment and sustaining social resolve.

Cold Anger

The community organization movement shows how personal anger contributes to social change. Mary Beth Rogers followed the work of Ernesto Cortez and his associates in the Industrial Areas Foundation

(IAF). Committed to grassroots community organization in the tradition of political activist Saul Alinsky, IAF's goal is revitalizing democracy through active citizen participation. Its basic strategy is nurturing leaders within poor and working-class communities, leaders who then support their community's efforts to identify its needs and engage the local political structure in meeting these needs. Cortez himself worked closely with the development of Communities Organized for Public Service (COPS) in the Mexican American neighborhoods of San Antonio. His experience there, as in other IAF projects in New York, California, and Texas, convinced Cortez that a common energy motivates the most effective local organizers—personal anger.

The emotion Cortez looks for in leaders is not violent rage or hostile resentment but "cold anger," a disciplined impulse rooted deep in personal experience. "Most people feel uneasy with the prospect of using their anger, so they suppress it or deny it, only to have it appear hot and uncontrollable in inappropriate times and places," Rogers remarks. "Cortez works with the leaders he develops to get them to remember their personal anger, to understand its sources, and then to draw on it as fuel for the energy they need to confront those who hold power over their lives."

Cortez believes that social change happens when the injustices we suffer personally become a bridge connecting us with other people's pain. This shared pain, held collectively, transforms complaint into compassion. And compassion tempers our self-destructive wrath, forging cold anger as a potent resource that sustains commitment. To show this dynamic in action, Cortez turns to the story of Moses leading the Hebrews out of slavery in Egypt: "The memory of their oppression is so strong it is like a burning bush, a fire that never goes out, an unquenchable fire. That memory is powerful, has a force of its own. It's hallowed ground. That's what we mean by anger."

Letting Go of Anger

Acting *with* anger can be an appropriate, even virtuous response. But often enough we need to turn away from anger. When recalling a grievance spirals us into despair, our goal is to move beyond anger. When rage provokes us to respond recklessly, our goal is to dissipate its force. Later reclaiming this energy may be useful, but now it needs moderation.

Since we experience anger in both mind and body, both mind and body can help us let go. Moderate physical exercise—taking a walk, gardening, even doing laundry or cleaning house—channels energy away from angry behavior. Spending time in yoga or meditation lowers the body's physiological arousal, lessening the physical sense of urgency. Getting involved in activities that demand concentration and give us pleasure—such as pursuing a favorite hobby or preparing a festive meal—helps bring our body around and calms our emotions as well. And when we are angry, doing something generous for someone else almost always transforms our mood. Anger harbors the impulse to punish other people; helping people counteracts that urge. Hostility drains away, even when the recipient of our good deed is not the person who has angered us.

Reappraisal is another useful strategy for lessening anger's hold. A change in interpretation can be as effective in dislodging anger as a change in our bodily state. For example, our anger at being kept waiting dissolves when we find that our tardy companion had a compelling reason. Or we excuse an apparent insult when we recognize the strain under which the other person is living. Learning of new facts or extenuating circumstances helps us put our displeasure in wider perspective. Often this wider view diminishes our anger.

Laughter, too, helps us put anger aside. Humor reinterprets the meaning of events, setting our frustrations and failures at a new angle. Humor gives us perspective, helping us view differently the provocations that make us mad. And being able to laugh at ourselves lessens the impact of the assaults and reversals that are inevitably part of living. Taking ourselves less seriously lets us see through some of the petulant demands we make of life. So most of the time laughter heals anger. But humor is a tricky tool. Laughter can trivialize as well as relativize. And many of us have felt the force of humor used against us in efforts to make us feel foolish for our anger or to belittle our concern.

Forgiveness in Anger

Forgiveness, too, reinterprets anger. And it can be the gift of anger courageously faced. Forgiveness allows us to start again, to come to a sense of a new beginning. In forgiving we *choose* not to let the hurt we have experienced get in the way of a relationship continuing. The common sense adage is "forgive and forget." And for most of us, experience confirms that our efforts to forgive are helped by being able to forget. But forgiving is not the same thing as forgetting. Forgiveness knows that hurt has been sustained. But in forgiving we respond to the other person not in terms of the harm he or she has inflicted but in terms of who the person is beyond that pain. So the order of the adage is important, forgive . . . and then forget, lest the memory of the pain revive the anger and hostility between us. Social philosopher Hannah Arendt notes that "forgiving is an eminently personal (though not necessarily individual or private) affair in which *what* was done is forgiven for the sake of *who* did it."

Forgiving involves a decision, but it is not completed in the moment of choice. Forgiveness is a process that gradually allows hurt to heal as trust rebuilds. The process of forgiving does not bring us back to where we were, allowing us to go on as if nothing has happened. Something *has* happened, something profound. The fabric of our interwoven lives has been torn. Yet we can choose not to be defined by this rupture, incorporating it instead as part of an ongoing relationship. We hope the hurt will not become the pattern, but we sense its contribution of depth and substance to the design.

Forgiveness is not easy to extend or to receive. To forgive, we must face the offense and experience our pain. We have to test our anger to see if these feelings are justified. Submitting our anger to this kind of scrutiny, we may find that we have misjudged another's motives or overreacted to an event. Our commitment to being angry may tempt us to nurse our indignation and refuse to acknowledge our mistake.

The reflection that forgiveness requires often shows us ways we have contributed to the problem. In few situations is one person solely to blame. Most interactions are conjoint, with each of us part of the painful pattern that develops. But sometimes casting ourselves as the innocent victim seems safer than risking the self-knowledge that forgiveness demands.

Genuine forgiveness also robs us of our hurt; we can no longer harbor it for later use against the person. Instead, we must surrender the wound that has become a cherished, if bitter, possession. Letting this hurt go, we lose the painful advantage we had been savoring, but we regain the energy we have squandered in nurturing our vengeance. Forgiveness evens the score, undercutting the sense that we have something to hold over others. In forgiving, we start out anew, perhaps humbled (we know how fragile our relationship can be) but hopeful too.

If offering forgiveness is hard, receiving forgiveness can be more difficult. To accept forgiveness, we must revisit the harm we have done, acknowledging our responsibility or admitting our mistake. Asking forgiveness humbles us, so denial tempts us to resist. As long as we are in the right, we need seek no pardon. To accept forgiveness is to confess our guilt—not only to another but to ourselves.

Times exist when forgiveness is not our goal, or at least not the goal right now—situations in which the demands of justice or change take precedence over the restoration of a relationship. These are seasons when anger needs to be sustained, not set aside. But when reconciliation is the goal, forgiveness is a powerful ally. Often it is the only door to peace.

Sometimes, it seems we cannot talk enough or explain enough or regret enough to move beyond anger. The harm has been too heavy, the distance between us now seems too broad to be bridged. These times teach us that forgiveness is more than a personal achievement. We learn again that its power often comes as gift—a grace that, spent by our anger, we must await in hope.

Reflective Exercise

Consider your own experience in dealing with anger. Bring to mind a time you handled your anger well. First recall the circumstances: the setting, the persons involved, what triggered your anger, how you responded, the way things turned out.

Now spend some time with these questions: What did you like about the way you dealt with this anger? As you see things, what was most useful, productive, helpful? Then consider: What did you dislike about the way you dealt with this anger? Looking back now on that experience, what would you want to do differently?

Finally, what convictions do you bring from your own experience to add to this chapter's suggestions for dealing with anger?

Additional Resources

Significant resources are now available to support effective response to anger. See, for example, Ronald Potter-Efron, *Angry All the Time: Emerging Guide to Anger Control* and his collaborative work with

Patricia Potter-Efron, *Letting Go of Anger: Common Anger Styles and What to Do about Them.* Kathy Svitil's *Calming the Anger Storm* and Reneau Peurifoy's *Anger: Taming the Beast* each draws on research findings to develop practical strategies for acknowledging and managing anger.

For a fuller account of Villaseñor's compelling family history, see his book *Rain of Gold.* Leonard Berkowitz discusses the importance of paying attention to our anger in "On the Formation and Regulation of Anger and Aggression"; we quote from page 501. Rochelle Albin's comment on expressing anger is from page 83 of her book *Emotions.* Barbara Harrison's comment is from page 15 of her essay "The Place of Anger in the Works of Love."

In *Cold Anger: A Story of Faith and Power Politics* Mary Beth Rogers introduces the people and principles of the Industrial Areas Foundation (IAF) grassroots community organization effort; we quote from pages 190–91. Edward Chambers and Michael Cowan trace the history and strategy of the IAF from its founder, Saul Alinsky, to the present, in *Roots for Radicals: Organizing for Power, Action, and Justice.*

Kenneth Briggs's *The Power of Forgiveness,* based on Martin Doblmeier's compelling documentary film, provides a broad examination of the religious, psychological, and historical factors involved in personal and social reconciliation. Stephanie Dowrick reflects on the virtues that sustain human community in *Forgiveness and Other Acts of Love;* see also Lewis Smedes's helpful discussion in *Forgive and Forget: Healing the Hurts We Don't Deserve.*

5

An Angry
Spirituality

Yahweh is tender and compassionate,
Slow to anger, most loving;
God's indignation does not last forever,
God's resentment exists only a short time.
—PSALM 103

Passions abound in the capacious heart of God. In the story of the great flood, Yahweh's heart is awash in disappointment: "And the Lord regretted having made humankind on the earth, and it grieved God to the heart" (Gn 6:6). Jesus, the Son of God, suffered the full range of human emotions. He became incensed at his friend Peter; he wept at the tomb of Lazarus; he cried out with something like despair in his final moments on the cross. The Jewish and Christian scriptures show us a God immersed in all the passions that accompany commitment. The revelation seems to be that passions are the price of love. To be entwined in others' lives is to court sorrow as well as delight, to taste loneliness as well as communion, to come to grief as well as to gratitude.

Yet this revelation has been contested. For two thousand years Christians have argued about the place of passion in our lives. Is anger a natural enemy of spirituality? Are grief and loneliness distorted emotions that jeopardize our life of faith? Or are these painful stirrings wellsprings of our vitality, alerting us to endangered values and linking us to this passionate God? Early Christian thinkers, scandalized by the force of human emotion, gradually became convinced that the fleshly passions of anger, grief, and sexual arousal separate us from our spiritual Creator.

63

A Dispassionate God

"God himself, according to the scriptures, becomes angry and yet is never disturbed by any passions whatsoever." This surprising sentence in Augustine's *City of God* echoes the Stoic ideal of total serenity. Intimidated by their Stoic critics, Christian thinkers worried forth a strikingly unscriptural vision of a serene God, unperturbed by emotion, safely removed from the murky, compromising drama of human feelings.

In this portrait we are introduced to a God who loves us but does not need us, an "unmoved mover" who touches creatures with affection and forgiveness but is himself unmoved. Today we see more clearly that this portrait is less a theology than a defensive fantasy: the ideal of being able to care for others while remaining untouched by them; the aspiration to provide protection and correction without being made vulnerable to the perils of mutuality.

The Stoic ideal of a detached love developed into a theology of God's *impassibility*—God as unable to be stirred or aroused or made vulnerable. Such a doctrine was, of course, unbelievable, and most Christians simply ignored it in favor of a scriptural God of fierce feelings. But this theology did spawn a spirituality for Christian leaders. Many ministers and priests learned that to be like God they have to rise above their emotions; they should craft a life detached from the swirl of anger and fear and sexual arousal. A holy leader, this logic suggested, influences others with care and correction but remains unswayed by any passionate attachment to them. To be a good leader demands mastery of one's feelings.

Anger—
The Scriptural Account

The Stoic vision of a God of control diverges sharply from the biblical image of a God of desire. Throughout the Hebrew scriptures we encounter a God who is stirred by both anger and compassion. These twin passions are the compass that charts God's tumultuous interaction with humankind.

Images of God's anger abound. "Then Yahweh's anger flamed out against Israel. God handed them over to pillagers who plundered them;

God delivered them to the enemies surrounding them, and they were not able to resist them" (Jdg 2:14). The prophet Zephaniah pictures God as even more incensed: "For my decision is to gather nations, to assemble kingdoms, to pour out upon them my indignation, *all the heat of my anger,* for in the fire of my passion all the earth shall be consumed" (Zeph 3:1–9).

Hebrew scripture remembers God's passionate anger as a just response, triggered by the maddening inconstancy of the very people God has chosen. And this anger is constantly balanced by compassion: "God's bowels tremble with compassion and God decides not to give rein to the heat of anger" (Hos 11:8); "Yahweh is tender and compassionate, slow to anger, most loving; God's indignation does not last forever" (Ps 103). For those who espouse a dispassionate Deity, God's compassion presents as much a problem as does God's anger. In Hebrew, "compassion" and "womb" share the same root; this emotion is a gut-wrenching implication in the grief of others.

Anger enjoyed a privileged place in the community of ancient Israel. The prophets often relied on anger to fuel their indictment of the fickle Israel. Jeremiah, a truly irascible personality, announced Yahweh's ire—"My anger and my wrath shall be poured out on this place" (7:20)—and admitted that this fuming emotion had penetrated his own heart—"I am full of the wrath of the Lord and I am weary of holding it in" (6:11).

At this point in Judeo-Christian history, the prophets represented a potent political element within the religious community. Acting as a counterbalance to the authority of the king and the priests, the prophets raised painful questions about fidelity, stagnation, and change. Prophecy made anger legitimate within the household of Israel. Even when the prophets were dismissively ignored or violently silenced, their vocation gave witness to the honorable place of anger among our religious ancestors. Their continuing presence argued that dissent and conflict have a place among God's people.

Jesus belongs in this long line of prophets. Though piety sometimes prefers a memory of Jesus as meek and humble of heart, the Gospels recall an often angry person. The most familiar story recounts Jesus finding merchants setting up shop at the entrance to the Temple. Outraged, he trashes their display booths. "Then Jesus went into the Temple and drove out all those who were selling and buying there; he turned over the tables of the moneychangers and the chairs of those who were selling pigeons" (Mt 21:12).

The Gospels repeatedly recall Jesus' vehemence against those he judged to be hypocrites (see Lk 6:42 and Mt 7:5; also Mt 6:16). When some in the crowd baited him about bending the strict laws about activity on the Sabbath in order to heal a woman, he responded angrily: "You hypocrites!" (Lk 13:14). They were willing to water their ox or donkey on the Sabbath but self-righteously insisted that a suffering person go unhealed.

The Gospel of Mark recalls another time when Jesus' critics taunted him about healing on the Sabbath (Mk 3:5). Their narrow interpretation of religious laws infuriates him: "He looked around at them *with anger;* he was grieved at their hardness of heart." All three Synoptic authors—Matthew, Mark, and Luke—tell this story, showing their reliance on a common source. But at the mention of Jesus' anger, the stories diverge. Matthew's account (12:12) does not mention Jesus' angry look. Luke (6:10) repeats the phrase "he looked around at them," but without the adverb "angrily." Do we see here the first editorial attempt to dissociate Jesus from this questionable emotion?

If Jesus was angered by hypocrites and the self-righteous, he was—like us—also sparked to anger by his loved ones. Matthew's Gospel recounts a poignant memory of this "intimate anger." Shortly before his death Jesus prepared to go to Jerusalem, a decision he sensed was fraught with danger. Apprehensive—but convinced he must make the trip—Jesus shares his plan with his closest companions. His friend Peter, keenly aware of the hostile atmosphere in Jerusalem, warns him not to go. Jesus suddenly explodes in anger: "Get behind me, Satan! You are a stumbling block to me" (Mt 16:23). Harsh language for a dear friend, denouncing him as the devil. Jesus' anger reveals how vulnerable he felt in this difficult moment of decision. Fearful but determined, he looked to his friends for support only to find Peter offering him exactly the wrong advice. Jesus' anger flared to help him resist this tempting alternative and to keep to his painful decision.

The testimony of God's wrath, the witness of the prophets' rage, the images of an angry Jesus—these arousals show us anger as more than moral failure. But what about our own anger? For Jews and Christians, the biblical evidence seems to insist, anger cannot be rejected out of hand. The goal instead, as captured by the Psalmist and echoed in Paul's advice to the believers in Ephesus, is to "be angry and do not sin."

A Deadly Sin

In the second and third centuries the conversation about anger took a new turn. Stoicism's powerful influence in the Mediterranean world penetrated Christian belief and practice. Philosophers argued that the ideal of human life was serenity and emotional control. Human passions, whether sexual arousal, envy, or grief, were major obstacles to the achievement of self-restraint and calm. Marcus Aurelius, for example, saw anger as essentially an irritable byproduct of social life, a negative emotion we can well do without. Book Two of his *Meditations* begins with a musing that will sound familiar to the citizens of any large city today:

> Say to yourself in the morning: I shall meet people who are interfering, ungracious, insolent, full of guile, deceitful and antisocial: they have all become like that because they have no understanding of good and evil.

The passion most often inflamed in the course of such a day, whether in the second century or our own, is anger. Marcus Aurelius's remedy was the Stoic conviction that we are all part of nature's design, living and dying according to its script. Getting disturbed when others play their necessary role in this common, already-fated drama is more than foolish; it is a waste of time.

The solution, then, is to suppress the useless emotion of social anger. "Why be angry with a man because of his body odors or bad breath?" If someone jostles us at the gym (his example!), "we do not make a case of it, or strike back or suspect him in the future of intriguing against us." Even in instances of what we have called intimate anger, Marcus Aurelius counsels dispassion: "Though I was often upset at Rusticus, I did nothing excessive which I should have repented." Elsewhere he cautions against the company that anger keeps: "Never be downcast, or sneering, or angry, or suspicious." For Stoics like Marcus Aurelius, anger is simply a social irritant. To foster this feeling is a vice. In a life aimed at serenity, the disruptive passion of anger is to be turned aside, for "anger is a sign of weakness, just as much as grief."

Influenced by the Stoics, Christian thinkers soon identified anger as an unhealthy disturbance that was also sinful. Influential theologians—

Clement and Origen, Jerome and Augustine—interpreted Paul's concept of *the flesh* in terms of the Stoic vision of the passions. "The flesh," they reasoned, refers to all the impulses that distracted us from the pursuit of God; surely the human passions must be included here. Not surprisingly, when the first inventory of the seven deadly sins appeared in fifth-century monasteries, anger made the list. This tradition of early Christianity continues today. In his contemporary reflection on the seven deadly sins, Henry Fairlie argues that "anger may not always cause a deep wound, but *it must leave* a residue of hatred in the end, and a desire for revenge." If anger runs necessarily to rage, if vindication and revenge are indistinguishable, then surely anger is a lethal emotion.

Developments in church life contributed to the loss of a positive role for anger. In the course of the third century, for reasons that are still unclear to historians and theologians, the ancient tradition of prophecy suddenly withered and all but disappeared. For two hundred years after the death and raising of Jesus, a recognized ministry of prophecy survived in the community of faith. Individuals arose who carried on the dangerous but necessary mission of challenging Christians to purify their lives and remain faithful to God. But by the end of the third century this charism had atrophied in the community. Many Christians believed that the age of revelation had come to an end. God had now revealed all we must know for our salvation; henceforth we need only be faithful to an already available truth. In such a climate we would not need prophets.

The essential gift of prophecy survived in Christian life, but it had to find new abodes. Some bishops led with prophetic vigor, though their primary calling as administrators and preservers of the religious institution often put them in conflict with the radical demands of prophecy. Prophecy survived in religious orders as these flowered, first in desert monasteries and eventually throughout Europe. But the institution of prophecy—the official acknowledgment of an adversarial voice within the community of faith—had perished. Its demise undermined the legitimacy of dissent and cast doubt on anger's role. Now a good case could be made that religious orthodoxy required obedient conformity to the demands of those in authority. No longer did the church expect the outrage of ancient prophets or the angry challenge of Jesus to find an echo within its own life. Henceforth, opposition would be judged a moral failing and a sign of disobedience. The loss of the charism of prophecy effectively outlawed anger.

Reclaiming a Positive Vision of Anger

For a thousand years anger's sinfulness remained a dominant Christian conviction. Then, in the thirteenth century, the conversation about this emotion took a radical turn as Thomas Aquinas developed his vision of human nature. Newly available to the scholars of this period were the ancient texts of Aristotle, in which anger appears not as an irrational impulse but as an ordinary, indispensable emotion: "We praise a person who feels anger on the right grounds and against the right persons and also in the right manner." For Aristotle, anger is a healthy if volatile arousal that fuels a person's protest of a wrong or resistance to injustice. The good health of both individuals and societies hinges on the ability to become angry and express this emotion in a tempered manner.

Relying on the authority of Aristotle, Aquinas crafted a vision of human emotions that diverged from the Christian view that had prevailed for a millennium. For Aquinas, passions were not the distorted, compulsive emotions of Clement of Alexandria and Augustine, necessarily at war with reason and the spirit. Passions were healthy arousals, honorable parts of a human nature designed by the Creator. These powerful forces, when tamed, provide the vital energy that fuels human virtue. "Justice cannot be without passion, and much less other virtues."

In three chapters of his *Summa Theologiae* Aquinas used Aristotle's authority to reshape Christian attitudes toward anger. First, he shrewdly adjusted Augustine's conviction that "anger craves revenge." A healthy anger, Aquinas corrects, seeks a just vindication rather than indiscriminate revenge. Vindication and vengeance are not to be confused. Aquinas then reinterprets Augustine's judgment that "anger grows into hatred." The impulse of anger does not swell into hatred automatically or unavoidably but only over time—if and as we allow it. We can choose to block this destructive escalation. Anger and hatred are not linked lethally; hatred thirsts for evil, but a healthy anger desires vindication "for the sake of justice."

Aquinas carefully traces the links between anger and reason. If Christians had traditionally seen this emotion as a blind impulse embedded in "the flesh," Aquinas insists that anger remains open to reason's influence. Again, he depends on Aristotle's authority: "Anger listens to reason to some extent ... but it is not perfectly attentive."

Anger is compatible with reason, because it is natural and reasonable for a person to be stirred up to resist threats of injury: "It is natural . . . to be aroused against what is hostile and threatening." Anger fails only when it ignores reason's counsel in its pursuit of vindication.

In his second chapter (question 47), Aquinas anticipates contemporary research that uncovers the connections between anger and shame. "All the motives of anger are reducible to slight." When we are belittled or forgotten, or when our dignity is slighted, we are aroused to anger. Aquinas's reflections on the link between neglect and anger have a modern feel: "Neglect *(oblivio)* is an evident sign of slight; we take the trouble to remember things which are important to us." Likewise, when a special vulnerability or personal weakness is exposed, anger flares as a healthy defensive response. In his few paragraphs Aquinas develops an important insight: when shame diminishes us and our dignity shrinks, the arousal of anger enlarges us to protest our loss and prevent our being forgotten.

A Revolutionary Emotion

In his final chapter (question 48), Aquinas explores the effects of anger's physiological arousal. When we are offended, anger stirs as a counterirritant both to announce and to resist the injury. But this interior agitation has revolutionary potential; it may overturn our world and compel us to new behavior.

Anger is revolutionary in its ability to *expose* us. Again, Aquinas depends on Aristotle: "An angry person is not devious, but quite open." If we are aroused by anger, we may suddenly blurt out a conviction. Dropping our usual reserve, we show our emotional hand. Suddenly, everyone in the office or at the meeting knows how we feel. The spontaneous and precipitous openness that anger provokes may be harmful and a source of humiliation. But it may also be a fruitful revelation, to ourselves and others, of our own best beliefs. Aquinas interprets such impulsive self-revelation as a kind of ironic "magnanimity": "It is also partly an effect of the expansion of the heart, a function of magnanimity which is also produced by anger." Magnanimous people speak freely and openly show their feelings, unlike more secretive, defensive individuals. Anger, with its spontaneous "expansion of the heart," may compel us to be more magnanimous than we had planned.

When this arousal stirs us to resist an indignity and suddenly reveals our agitation to others, it sets us on a course of change. If we are not prepared to face the change that anger instigates, we do well to suppress this emotion. Contemporary analysts of anger have noted this revolutionary element in anger. Dana Crowley Jack, in her study of depression, underscores the lack of passion in depressed women and the radical implications of a rebirth of anger. This dangerous emotion "brings a clarity of vision and a requirement to act." The arousal of anger separates a person from the protective cocoon of depression, igniting the hope of a different way of living. Such changes are revolutionary because they require us to become assertive participants in our future. In *Composing a Life* Mary Catherine Bateson notes anger's gift to her: "Anger was an achievement, a step away from the chasm of despair."

In the Company of Conflict

Anger is revolutionary in the company it keeps. If anger is sometimes legitimate, so is conflict. Many Christians aspire to peace and harmony; we long for a calm life and an orderly society. But we do well to remember the essential role of conflict and even anger in our religious heritage. The saving journey of Jews and Christians is marked by long experiences in a hostile desert and a bruising exile, by a painful way of the cross. If harmony and calm are worthy goals, the path to these ideals is most often marked by struggle and conflict.

The ancient Greeks used the word *agon* to signify the "agony" or "contest" of life. Whether in physical contests or political debates or philosophical disputes, struggle was seen not as a scandal but as an essential means of finding our way. In the words of philosopher Alasdair MacIntyre, these ancestors recognized that "it was in the context of the *agon* that . . . truth had to be discovered." For these Greeks, true human achievement is not provided ready made; the genuine goods of life wait to be wrestled from the forces that repeatedly defeat them.

In an agonistic world of obstacles and antagonists, conflict is an unavoidable dynamic. MacIntyre reminds us of the centrality of conflict in every heritage: "Traditions, when vital, embody continuities of conflict." Differing visions collide in a richly pluralist society, but these differences need not be fatal. Our variety energizes us to reexamine our values; our disagreements compel us to clarify our shared goals. As Australian philosopher John Anderson has observed, "It is through conflict and sometimes only through conflict that we learn what our ends and purposes are."

Courage and Temperance

Anger often erupts as a raw, unruly emotion. To serve its best purposes, our passion requires refinement. Honing anger's arousal to the work of virtuous action is an angry spirituality's most practical task. Traditionally, this discipline's rewards have been named courage and temperance.

Anger enjoys its finest moment when it fuels the courageous pursuit of justice. Courage, of course, is not always angry. One person quietly and courageously faces terminal illness; another confronts a difficult job with a steady resolve. But sometimes courage rides anger's energy. The Spanish language hints at this link in the word *coraje* (righteous anger). Though the word names an emotion, it harbors the word *courage*. Just anger, it literally suggests, is a form of courage.

In his analysis of courage Alasdair MacIntyre notes its connections with care. When persons we care for or values we cherish are threatened, we rise to their defense. Courage, MacIntyre suggests, is this "capacity to risk harm or danger to oneself" in the expression of our care. The most universal example is the parent who spontaneously—and courageously—fights any adversary to protect a child. Anger fuels this dangerous mission of care.

For theologian Josef Pieper, the links between courage and anger lie in their overlapping intents: anger is "a force directed toward the difficult of achievement" and courage is our resolve in "facing the dreadful." Both dynamics embolden us to face painful challenges. Courage, Pieper reminds us, is not the lack of fear but rather the resolve to act in spite of fear. Conscious of their vulnerability, courageous persons still go forward for the sake of what they prize. As Pieper suggests, courage is the willingness to proceed in the face of threat and finally, "the willingness to fall, to die in battle."

Eastern wisdom, too, reinforces the bond between anger and courage. "There are some things that I loathe more than death; that is why there are troubles I do not avoid." These words of the Chinese sage Mencius anchor his vision of courage. To explore this ancient vision, historian Lee Yearley returns us to the mysterious energy of *ch'i*. As we saw in Chapter 3, this vital life force sometimes takes the shape of anger. For Mencius, the energy of *ch'i,* when joined to righteousness, becomes the fuel of courageous action. In Mencius's view, when we see an injustice, we do not simply evaluate its evil with a cool detachment; we get angry. This passionate arousal, in league with reason, rallies us to put ourselves at risk in confronting the injustice. Anger's passion, Yearley notes, "can generate the added impetus that allows a person to overcome fear or some other difficulty." Mencius's linking of *ch'i* and righteousness parallels the union of anger and reason in Aquinas. When nourished and nurtured, the vital energy of *ch'i* supplies one with an "assurance about one's goals, added energy to reach them" and helps "ensure that the tumultuous forces released by legitimate fears will be overcome."

But even in the service of courage, anger's force can go astray. Courage benefits from anger's power only if it is tempered. For many Americans today, *temperance* suggests mildness, reticence, and an absence of passion. Christian piety shares some of the blame, insinuating that the truly virtuous should absent themselves from passionate behavior. Such a conviction drains temperance of all vitality. And this hesitance about passion has a long history. In *Body and Society* Peter Brown illustrates that very early in Christian thought *chastity* came to signify abstinence from sexual sharing rather than lovemaking that blends tenderness and passion.

So it has been with anger. Christian temperance turned into a disciplined avoidance rather than a virtuous expression of this emotion. In a collective amnesia Christians forgot the angry prophets. Temperance seemed to demand "turning the other cheek" and following a Jesus who was seen only as "meek and humble of heart."

But in its truest guise, temperance serves as the companion of courage. The one virtue emboldens us to act, while the other moderates our self-expression. When we are angry, we must become sufficiently aroused to resist threat and injustice without becoming violent. The metaphor of heat helps us appreciate temperance's contribution here. Anger heats us up; we get "steamed" and threaten to boil over in hostile actions. We are in danger of losing our temper. Temperance helps cool the temperature, bringing our anger into a productive range. Avoiding the heat of anger is not temperance's only choice. We can act temperately *in the midst of* anger—moderating our rage and focusing its energy effectively. In metallurgy, "to temper" means to refine metal until it is both strong and flexible. A well-tempered piece of steel suits both a battle sword and a construction site. Our well-tempered anger, too, both protects and builds up.

Courage and temperance are not simply personal resources that we conjure out of heroic, individual effort; they are social strengths that are cultivated in encouraging environments. Ideally, we learn to be courageous and to temper our anger by watching our relatives, friends, and neighbors. If we come from injured and injuring homes, we may learn about boldness from sources where anger and rage are not distinguished and vindication looks very much like vengeance.

The Power of Wrath

"At the mention of anger, Christian awareness sees as a rule only the uncontrolled, the anti-spiritual, the negative aspect. But, as with 'sensuality' and 'desire,' the power of wrath also belongs to the primal forces of human nature." A generation ago Josef Pieper sounded the call for a recovery of the healthy resource of anger. "Wrath is the strength to attack the repugnant; the power of anger is actually the power of resistance in the soul."

A Christian spirituality of anger demands public acknowledgment of its revolutionary elements. By recovering our tradition of prophecy and the memory of an irritable Jesus, we may allow this emotion to take its place among us once more. This acknowledgment will compel us to recognize that conflict plays an unavoidable role in our shared life. We can argue about our differing visions of the Christian calling without insulting or injuring one another. We can even become angry with one another and still prevent this emotion from escalating into hatred. We can relearn the rules of civility and treat our adversaries with honor and respect.

Democratic societies have taught the world about the healthy role of the loyal opposition. We debate and oppose one another, but then we go forward as colleagues, not enemies. Embedded in the notion of a loyal opposition is the virtue of civility: the strength of combining antagonism with respect, of disagreeing without degrading our opponent. Critics ranging from Cardinal Joseph Bernardin to President Barack Obama have noted the withering of civility in America. When antagonists employ bitter invective and accuse one another of the worst motives, they erode the line between anger and hatred, and vindication becomes vengeance. Then the ordinary conflicts and unavoidable *agon* of social life become deadly.

A robust spirituality of anger faces a daunting future: overcoming our amnesia of irascible prophets and an angry Jesus; admitting conflict as a necessary dynamic in our religious life; disbelieving that violence can remedy our differences; recrafting civility as a political virtue; reinvigorating the ancient virtues of courage and temperance. Short of such a renaissance, we will be left with a moribund religious tradition of anger as a deadly sin and a cultural heritage of violence as the ordinary and inevitable voice of anger.

Reflective Exercise

Consider experiences of anger—yours or someone else's—in the public arena: in civic life, in politics, at work or school, within the church. First, list several instances when anger in these social settings was, in your judgment, detrimental or damaging. Concretely, what were the negative effects of these angry incidents? As you see it, what factors contributed most to making anger negative in these cases—factors in the combatants? factors in the bystanders? factors in the larger setting?

Then, list examples when anger in these social settings had a positive outcome. Practically, what were the good effects you noted? What factors—people, values, attitudes, behaviors, circumstances—helped anger produce these positive results?

Finally, list some of your own convictions about anger's place in public life and your convictions about anger's place on the spiritual journey.

Additional Resources

In *Transforming Fire: Women Using Anger Creatively* Kathleen Fischer offers spiritual guidance for discovering anger's positive potential. Dana Crowley Jack discusses the importance of personal anger in *Silencing the Self: Women and Depression*, page 140. Mary Catherine Bateson describes anger's gift to her in *Composing a Life,* pages 205–6. Thich Nhat Hanh provides a contemporary reflection on Buddhism's understanding of anger in *Anger: Wisdom for Cooling the Flames.*

Biblical scholar John McKenzie acknowledges anger as a core attribute of God in the Hebrew scriptures: the prophet Nathan was willing to provoke King David's anger with a story of injustice (2 Sm 12:1–14); Ezekiel announces God's wrath (8:18), as does the prophet Hosea (5:10) (see *The Jerome Biblical Commentary*, page 753). Theologian Phyllis Trible explains the literal link between compassion and womb in *God and the Rhetoric of Sexuality*, page 33: "In its singular form the noun *rehem* means 'womb' or 'uterus.' In the plural, *rahmim*, this concrete meaning expands to the abstractions of compassion, mercy and love. . . . Accordingly, our metaphor lies in the semantic movement from a physical organ of the female body to a psychic mode of being."

In *Ministry: Leadership in the Community of Jesus Christ* Edward Schillebeeckx chronicles the continuance of prophecy in the earliest Christian communities; see especially his note on page 145. For a discussion of the contemporary pastoral implications of prophecy, see "Prophetic Leadership Today" in James D. Whitehead and Evelyn Eaton Whitehead, *The Promise of Partnership: A Model for Collaborative Ministry*.

In *Body and Society*, historian Peter Brown traces the effort to interpret Paul's convictions about "the flesh and the spirit" in the new cultural contexts of early Christianity. See, for example, his excellent discussion on pages 48 and 418; Brown outlines Clement's Stoic understanding of passion on page 129. The quotations of Marcus Aurelius are taken from Grube's translation of *The Meditations,* pages 11, 46, 53, 9, 6, 118.

Josef Pieper explores the power of wrath, anger, and courage in *The Four Cardinal Virtues*. Lee Yearley discusses *ch'i* in relation to courage in *Mencius and Aquinas: Theories of Virtue and Conceptions of Courage*; see especially pages 152 and following. Henry Fairlie's comment on anger is found in *The Seven Deadly Sins Today*, page 87.

For Aristotle's discussion of anger, see *Nicomachean Ethics*, 1125b26–1126b10. Thomas Aquinas examines anger in questions 46–48 in the first section of the second part (Ia–IIae) of the *Summa Theologiae*. Aquinas's optimistic interpretation of the passions appears in question 59. There he carefully distinguishes two very different views of the passions: "If by passions we mean inordinate affections, as the Stoics held, then it is clear that perfect virtue is without passions. But if by passions we mean *all movements of sense appetite*, then it is plain that the moral virtues, which are about the passions as their proper matter, *cannot be without the passions*" (see page 96 in *St. Thomas Aquinas: Treatise on the Virtues,* translated by John Oesterle). This notion of virtues as bodily resources rather than purely spiritual strengths was alien to Augustine and much of early Christianity (see Paul Gondreau, *The Passions of Christ's Soul in the Theology of St. Thomas Aquinas*).

Alasdair MacIntyre examines the positive role of conflict in *After Virtue* (see pages 160 and 206); on page 153 MacIntyre quotes philosopher John Anderson on the revelatory role of conflict in society; on page 179 MacIntyre explores the link between care and courage. MacIntyre examines the revolutionary potential of temperance in "*Sophrosune*: How a Virtue Can Become Socially Disruptive."

Part Three

GUILT AND SHAME

The Price of Belonging

The Chinese character for shame *(ch'ih)* shows a heart next to an ear, the blush that reveals embarrassment or humiliation.

6

Boundaries of Belonging

He has no shame—that gift that hinders mortals, but helps them too.

—HOMER

In Homer's classic, the *Iliad,* the hero Achilles kills Hector in battle. His rage unsatisfied even by this bloody victory, he drags Hector's corpse behind his chariot around the walls of Troy. This dishonorable act—defiling the body of a defeated enemy—offends friend and foe alike. Outraged by his cruelty, even the gods are provoked to denounce Achilles: "He has no shame—that gift that hinders mortals, but helps them too."

At heart, shame and guilt are benefits—"gifts that hinder mortals, but help them too." Humans have an insatiable desire to be part of the group. We long to belong. We yearn to be chosen and to be included, sensing our very survival is at stake. Left alone, without the safety and nourishment of companionship, we are doomed. Shame and guilt are social dynamics monitoring our lifelong efforts to belong. Often working together, these painful emotions guard our social identity by warning us of personal transgressions that threaten to exclude us from "our kind."

The Journey from Shame to Guilt

Shame takes center stage in the first act of the human drama of belonging. For the ancient Greeks, shame was a social conscience, a warning that a person was trespassing a community agreement. In this same season of human history the sages of Hebrew scripture evoked shame repeatedly as a powerful guardian of their people's bond with God: "O My God, I am too ashamed and embarrassed to lift my face to you, my God, for our iniquities have risen higher than our heads" (Ezr 9:6). In China, Confucius linked virtue and proper conduct with this same emotion: "If you are led by virtue and conform to proper conduct, you will have a sense of shame and be good" (II,3).

Several centuries later, just before the time of Christ, the social consciousness of shame began to be accompanied by a deepening sense of personal responsibility—and its companion emotion, guilt. The concept of guilt was not unknown before this, but earlier the word referred predominantly to a legal judgment of wrongdoing; a person was *found* guilty by others. Gradually guilt came to describe a conviction of fault rendered by an interior judge. In this sense guilt arises as a personal awareness of our own failings.

In our own lives each of us recapitulates this cultural journey from shame to guilt. Moral philosopher Sidney Callahan recalls the dilemma parents face: "Children must be kept safe, be trained to be acceptable to the larger society, and be encouraged to flourish as unique persons. These goals . . . can be accomplished only when reluctant children are persuaded to do things they do not wish to do." At first persuasion comes from the outside, as parents and other caregivers enforce the rules of belonging—"this is how you must behave here." As children learn how to fit into family and neighborhood and society, they gradually internalize these once-external values as their own. Now when we fall short of what is expected, we don't need others to remind us. We have moved from disappointing others to disappointing ourselves! Ambiguous as such a transition seems, we must remember this development is an advance. We now carry our culture's ideals as our own. The best values of our family and faith and nation survive as we accept and internalize them. No longer acting simply to please others and avoid shame, we act out of personal responsibility and conscience. We have moved from shame to guilt.

The interior governor of guilt does not simply replace the social arbiter of shame; instead, guilt joins shame as another guide to our belonging. While both emotions are by nature troublesome, they remain resources we cannot do without. But injury to these interior resources easily throws us off stride. Then we carry constant concern about pleasing other people, worried that they might disapprove of us. Or we fret over whether we have ever done enough, afraid that we have somehow shirked our duty. These wounds twist shame and guilt, designed as guardians of our belonging, into tyrants. In Chapter 7 we will continue our examination of guilt; we turn now to the complex emotion of shame.

Shame as Grace and Disgrace

Nicholas was glad it was raining. He would be able to wear the yellow boots and matching rain hat that he had received last week for his sixth birthday. Throughout the school day he kept a close check on the boots that stood out like beacons among the drab rain gear in the coat room.

But on the way home after school disaster struck. Nearly home—only two blocks to go—he was stopped by three junior-high boys who started to make fun of his boots. They grabbed his rain hat and knocked open his book bag, spilling the contents. Nicholas himself slipped and fell on a muddy patch of lawn. Confused and frightened, he began to cry—evoking the older boys' mocking laughter. Kicking his hat into the mud, they ran off in search of other prey.

Nicholas gathered up his books and hat and trudged home. When he entered the house his eyes were red and he choked back tearful sobs. Sizing up the situation, his mother held him in a long embrace and then helped him off with his muddy clothes. "Are you OK, Nick? Can you tell me what happened?" Hearing her small son's tale of woe, she sympathized with his fright and humiliation: "Those big boys ganged up on you! That's terrible. You must have been really scared. I'm so glad you are all right now."

When his father came home later, Nicholas got to tell his story again and receive more solace. Then his parents spoke with Nicholas about what could be done to prevent his being frightened like that in the future. Perhaps he could walk to school and back with his older sister for the next few weeks. His parents could call the principal to see if other children had been victimized. Nicholas might change his route home to pass along streets where the school traffic guards were more in evidence. That last plan sounded best to Nicholas, and his parents agreed. Feeling battered but cared for, he went to bed early that night.

Across town a similar scene is played out. Terry, on his way home from second grade, runs into older bullies blocking his path. Here, too, the older boys terrorize the frightened younger one, dumping out the contents of his backpack and pushing him to the ground. Terry's tears draw the boys' scorn; they run away hurling shouts of "big baby!"

Like Nicholas, Terry slowly gets up and begins the trek home. As he walks, Terry recalls a recent family event. He heard his parents scolding an older brother who had been involved in a neighborhood fight: "Why did you let those kids push you around? You're old enough to fight back. No son of mine should let himself be treated that way. We don't take that stuff from anybody. And stop that whimpering! What are you, a sissy?"

Now, added to Terry's fright and humiliation is a painful realization: his feelings of confusion and embarrassment are unacceptable to his parents. This belittling incident should not have happened to him. More significantly, he should not have these feelings. Terry is ashamed of feeling ashamed. So he resolves to remain silent about his unfortunate encounter with the bullies. Nobody needs to know.

Exposed at the Boundary

Shame is about exposure. To be exposed, as Carl Schneider reminds us, means to be "out of position." The leader of a holiday parade or religious procession is suddenly embarrassed. Walking too fast, she has gotten "out of position" and stands exposed, out of step with the rest of the group. Most of us feel exposed when we stand out in a crowd—we seem too heavy or too dark-skinned to be found attractive, too poor or too assertive to be welcomed. Other social situations leave us feeling oddly exposed. A person dining alone in a restaurant may be a bit uncomfortable. Since eating is such a communal act, we sometimes feel slightly exposed or vulnerable when we eat alone in public. And at the scene of a death, we cover the corpse; leaving the deceased person exposed to casual view strikes us as somehow disrespectful. The English words *shame* and *chemise* share the same root; a *chemise* is a shirt or slip that covers us. With us, as with Adam and Eve in the garden, the experience of shame is one of exposure, and our immediate response is to cover ourselves, even to hide.

"Shame supposes that one is completely exposed and conscious of being looked at. . . . One is visible and not ready to be visible." These words of psychologist Erik Erikson catch the ambiguity of our social existence: we want to be seen, to be acknowledged and respected, but only when we are ready, only when we feel adequate to stand in another's gaze.

In adolescence we feel this ambivalence with a special poignancy. We desperately wish to be recognized, to be known and accepted for who we are. But we are petrified of being exposed. Our changing bodies, becoming more adult and more sexual, make us visible in new ways—whether we are ready or not. Sensing how vulnerable we are to other people's appraisal, we hesitate to reveal ourselves. "Not yet," our embarrassment cautions. Not until we can change our clothes or change our opinions or change our friends—so that we finally get it right.

In adolescence and well beyond, embarrassment is an ordinary part of our social life. We regularly find ourselves too close, too exposed, too vulnerable in our interactions with one another. At these critical and often painful moments, shame serves as a healthy warning system. By acknowledging this emotion and trying to understanding what has triggered our distress, we can learn lessons important for our life. In Chapter 8 we explore the benefits that healthy shame brings, but shame does not always come bearing gifts.

Recall the two young boys we met earlier. Nick's family members respond to his shame with attention, empathy, and grace. By acknowledging his confusion, they honor his pain. Their practical respect for his humiliation begins its healing. But Terry's experience is different. Anticipating how his parents will respond, Terry feels his embarrassment as disgrace. So he tries to bury the experience, hiding it from others and, if possible, from himself. Hidden from consciousness, unattended, this ordinary feeling of shame—his appropriate response to being belittled—begins to fester. When this pattern becomes a regular response, a healthy sense of shame deteriorates into a truly negative emotion—a debilitating feeling that poisons a person's life.

Nicholas's parents block his descent into destructive shame by acknowledging that the pain he feels is appropriate. He learns that this dreadful feeling—humiliation—is not a sign of his inferiority. Nick is as strong and capable as he should be at this age. The bigger boys took advantage of him; they, not Nicholas, are in the wrong here.

Terry, enveloped by a less healthy environment, senses that his feelings of shame signal his own inadequacy. If he were smarter or better or tougher, he guesses, maybe he would not have to feel like this. And he has no one to tell him otherwise. Knowing no other way to deal with this distress, he pushes the painful feelings away. What he takes from the experience is strong motivation to do whatever it takes to avoid feeling like this again.

The Perils of Childhood

As children we lack the strength to resist the intrusions of others; parents and others are able to do with us as they will. Robert Bly describes what can occur. If a grown-up moves to hit a child, or stuff food into the child's mouth, there is no defense—it happens. If the grown-up decides to shout, and penetrate the child's auditory boundaries by sheer violence, it happens. Most parents invade the child's territory whenever they wish, and the child, trying to maintain his mood by crying, is simply carried away, mood included. Bly shows how this vulnerability leaves children susceptible to a deeper shame. Each child lives deep inside his or her own psychic house, or soul castle, and the child deserves the right of sovereignty inside that house. Whenever a parent ignores the child's sovereignty, and invades, the child feels not only anger, but shame. The child concludes that if it has no sovereignty, it must be worthless. Shame is the name we give to the sense that we are unworthy and inadequate as human beings.

Being imposed on as children—whether physically, psychologically or sexually—throws us off balance. Unable to resist the interference of powerful people, we sense this intrusion is an indictment of our own worth. Acutely aware that others can cross our boundaries at will, we find trusting ourselves difficult. The healthy response of shame, bruised this early, turns toxic. Children growing up in such a hostile setting are likely to respond in one of two ways. Some of us learn that we have no defendable boundaries. Other people come and go as they will, without regard for our person or privacy. Intimidated by their power, our only hope is to please and placate these intruders. If we cannot escape their presence, perhaps at least we can avoid some of the painful feelings. As we grow up, we may become very adept in these "people pleasing" tactics. We seek out a service career—ministry, health care, counseling. Or we marry a partner we can care for full time. Our "self-less" behavior looks virtuous to us and other people, at least until we recognize its compulsive force. Then comes a stark confrontation with the underlying shame that propels so much of what we do.

A second reaction to early wounds is to build boundaries that cannot be trespassed. Acutely aware of our fragility, we erect barriers to protect ourselves. Gaining weight may be our defense. For boys, a weight gain often signals physical power. Working out in the gym, practicing martial arts, developing muscular strength means "nobody can take advantage of me now." But weight has a different symbolic meaning for girls. Our culture equates beauty with being slim; it condemns heavy women as unattractive. A young woman wounded by shame may gain weight to protect herself. In her experience, people coming close means threat. Fat, she hopes, she will be safe—even if alone. A colleague, the veteran of a fourteen-year struggle with an eating disorder, describes the strategy: "A shamed person eats compulsively to wrap herself in a layer of fat that will be a protection against letting anyone in to see her true self."

Such stout defenses have to influence our spiritual life. A workshop participant shared with us the influence of sexual abuse on her relationship with God. "My experience of the presence of God has always been pain. God is one who violently breaks through my protective shields." A deeply religious person, she found prayer increasingly difficult. Whenever she would start to feel God's closeness as consolation, she found herself blocking that awareness by "rebuilding the walls protecting myself-of-shame, retreating back into my worthlessness from a God whose very being proclaims worth." Puzzled by her strong ambivalence, she came to recognize that for her, "every connection is a violation. I am ashamed to be connected." Recognizing the threat that close contact held for her and acknowledging the "peril" of a God whose very presence announced her worth, she was gradually able to move to a new stage of healing.

An Unspeakable Emotion

In our ordinary bouts of embarrassment we are tempted to cover ourselves, to hide. More traumatic experiences of shame render us mute. Physical and sexual abuse in childhood can leave us speechless; we have no words for this assault, and its pain remains too raw to acknowledge aloud. This terrible feeling sinks into our soul as a paralyzing silence. Adult survivors of incest often report that they did not know their sense of worthlessness had a name; they just assumed this is how bad it feels to be alive.

In this way what begins as a social emotion—shame generated in interaction with others—becomes privatized. But shame suppressed does not stay silent. Instead, shame recruits other emotions to speak for it.

Some people may feel constantly afraid. All close contact threatens them; every conversation could expose their inadequacy; any interaction might end with them being taken unfair advantage of. Such fear no longer serves its healthy warning function, being a response to real dangers. Instead, they are anxious all the time. Enlisted by the hidden emotion of shame, their fear now stands on constant alert. Why they are so afraid confuses them. What they do know is that feelings of unworthiness erupt frequently, flooding them with pain. What causes these dreaded feelings remains hidden to them, so their attempts to confront their fear is seldom successful. They are left with the familiar fear that the painful feelings will return. But persistent fear is a costly survival strategy. To placate their anxieties, they shrink from life. They are tempted to avoid all risks, to hold all relationships suspect. Better to remain on guard, lest the fragile boundaries of their self-esteem be breached again.

In others, shame recruits the emotion of anger. A middle-aged man, for example, is constantly upset and irascible, easily provoked with no apparent cause. His silent shame finds daily but disguised release in bitter, hostile behavior. In such people's lives anger acts not merely as a hedge against humiliation but as a wall to block all advances that might expose them to others or provoke their self-contempt. Here anger loses its healthy purpose. No longer an emergency response, its arousal has been enlisted in the full-time service of shame. This, too, is a strategy of survival. But it takes its toll in damaged health and injured relationships.

Sometimes shame speaks through compulsive achievement. Self-doubt contaminates the confidence of the child who is constantly told "what you've done is not good enough." Bringing home a report card with four A's and one B elicits a parent's disappointed rebuke, "I know you can do better than that." A young pitcher allows only one run to score in the little league baseball game. His competitive father forgets to praise this accomplishment, urging him instead to try harder:

"Concentrate when you're up there on the mound! Next time you should make it a no-hitter." Sensing that he has disappointed his father, the boy intensely feels his inadequacy. Ashamed of himself, he vows to try harder. But how much is enough?

Children like this often bring to adult life an impressive drive to succeed. But even when success comes, they can seldom rejoice in their achievements. The inner critic is never satisfied: "You could do better next time!" As they push themselves harder, pleasure and gratitude drain from their life. Their energy for over-achievement is rooted ultimately in a profound sense of unworthiness, another name for shame.

In his award-winning book *A Bright Shining Lie*, Neil Sheehan tells the story of John Paul Vann, one of the most decorated heroes of the Vietnam war. Vann's bravery in combat impressed all who knew him. He defied danger, apparently unconcerned for his own safety or the odds against a mission's success. In addition, his energy seemed endless; on assignment, Vann regularly worked two eight-hour shifts every day over long stretches of time.

Sheehan's chilling account of Vann's early life gradually uncovers the links between his public valor and private shame. Growing up in a severely troubled family, Vann used daring to hide a deep-seated fear of inadequacy. His reckless courage and relentless vigor masked the shame that fueled his life—and finally brought him to his "heroic" death in a helicopter crash in Vietnam.

Healing Shame

Destructive shame hides in secrecy and silence. For healing to come, we have to bring our pain to light. As John Bradshaw observes, "We have to move from our misery and embrace our pain. We have to feel as bad as we really feel."

Many of us have begun this journey. Long hesitant, we finally bring our torment to a friend or counselor, hoping their wisdom will salve the pain. What we discover is that the simple act of saying our distress starts to diminish its hold on us. The pain does not automatically go away, but now it serves more as a stimulus to change than simply as self-punishment.

The healing starts within. Therapists describe their efforts to help clients recognize shame as a *learned* response. The profound sense of inferiority the clients carry is not a realistic assessment of their worth, but rather an interpretation they learned in a damaging environment. As adults, they can set aside these crippling self-definitions and learn to value themselves anew.

Experienced counselors use a metaphor to describe the healing process. Being severely wounded by shame is like living in a room with many doors, but all the doorknobs are on the outside. Others enter our room as they will; we have no say, no warning, no defense. The goal of the difficult struggle to acknowledge our shame and trace its origins is to return the doorknobs to their rightful position on the inside of the doors. Then we can determine who enters our world. Intimacy becomes safer, since we can decide who and when and how to be close. Sharing and self-disclosure are possible, even welcome, since we no longer see ourselves as victims.

Carl Schneider reminds us that healthy shame is about self-awareness. This emotion focuses our gaze on ourselves, inviting a sometimes painful—sometimes mellow—recognition of our limits and vulnerabilities. Like healthy guilt, the painful prodding of shame can deliver us from distorted ideals and the compulsions that feed on them. The bruising insight of shame sees through the props and deceptions, the roles and arrangements we have used to disguise ourselves even to ourselves. Healed, shame helps show us who we are. John Bradshaw describes this grace:

> The healing of the shame that binds you is a revelatory experience. Because your shame exists at the very core of your being, when you embrace your shame, you begin to discover who you really are. Shame both hides and reveals our truest self.

The healing of shame returns us to ourselves: limited, fragile, real. We are delivered from a desperate need to please others and the other addictions that had covered up and numbed the pain that had no name. More comfortable with our limited self, we discover that others are not the enemy. And we are eager again to belong.

Reflective Exercise

Adolescence is a season of embarrassment for most of us. Return in imagination to your own high school years. Spend some time remembering where you lived at that time and with whom, who your friends were at school and elsewhere, and the activities and events that filled your days.

Now, recall a time when you felt ashamed as a teenager, an experience of being painfully embarrassed. For example, you may have felt embarrassed about your body or ashamed of your family or of your religious or ethnic background. Once you have remembered a particular occasion, stay with that memory for a while, trying to recall the circumstances that evoked your embarrassment. Be mindful, too, of the range of other feelings that came along with shame here.

As you look back now on that experience, how did you deal with the shame or embarrassment? How successful were your efforts then? Do you sense any connections between that adolescent experience and your life these days?

Additional Resources

Helen Merrill Lynd's early work *On Shame and the Search for Identity* stands as a foundation of today's psychological interest in this issue. In *The Psychology of Shame: Theory and Treatment,* Gershen Kaufman offers an overview of contemporary theory and treatment of this pervasive emotion; see especially his chapter "Facing Shame over the Life Cycle."

Carl Schneider explores the significance of exposure on page 34 in *Shame, Exposure, and Privacy*; see pages 25–28 for his discussion of shame and self-awareness. Erik Erikson's definition of shame appears in his classic work *Identity and the Life Cycle,* page 71; see also the development of this theme in his *The Life Cycle Completed—A Review.* Sidney Callahan provides an illuminating discussion of the role of emotions in the development of mature conscience in her book *In Good Conscience: Reason and Emotion in Moral Decision Making*; we quote from page 75.

John Bradshaw gives an excellent, readable overview of the toxicity of shame in *Healing the Shame That Binds You*; we quote from page 237. Robert Bly discusses the potency of shame in the young child in *Iron John,* page 147. *A Bright Shining Lie* is Neil Sheehan's Pulitzer Prize–winning book examining the life of Vietnam war hero John Paul Vann.

In *The Mindful Path to Self-Compassion: Freeing Yourself from Destructive Thoughts and Emotions* Christopher Gerner offers guidance for confronting and moving beyond shame and other self-destructive emotions; see also Ronald Potter-Efron and Patricia Potter-Efron, *Letting Go of Shame*. Neil Pembroke examines pastoral strategies through which shame can be befriended and healed in *The Art of Listening: Dialogue, Shame, and Pastoral Care.*

7

Guises of Guilt

Guilt is the guardian of our goodness.
—Willard Gaylin

A rumor circulates these days that guilt is bad. How the rumor got started is easy to understand. Feeling guilty is unpleasant for all of us. And sometimes feeling guilty seems downright irrational; we are filled with remorse about an action that we know is not wrong or racked with guilt over situations for which we are not personally responsible. This ruinous mood recruits us to the chorus condemning guilt.

But there is more to it. Feeling guilty is a uniquely human response; without this "necessary disturbance" the species would be at risk. As psychologist Willard Gaylin says, "We are so constructed that we must serve the social good—on which we are dependent for survival—and when we do not, we suffer the pangs of guilt."

Guilt, then, is the price of belonging. In love and work we willingly forge bonds that give our life purpose and pleasure. And, being human, we sometimes fail these bonds. When we neglect these promises we have made or turn away from people to whom we are pledged, the emotion of guilt signals that something has gone awry.

Genuine guilt is a companion of commitment. But this positive resource sometimes is distorted into a destructive mood. A hardworking executive, successful at her job, struggles with an abiding sense that she is somehow blameworthy. She is filled with regret—but for what? This faceless misgiving seeps into her soul, sapping enthusiasm and joy from her life. A young man feels vaguely guilty about his sexuality. No particular transgression troubles him; rather, he is suspicious of any sensual delight and hesitant about the attractions he feels. His guilt is less about *doing* something than about *being* a sexual person.

93

In these examples the healthy emotion of guilt sickens into a mood of self-punishment. Psychologists and self-help authors rightfully condemn this kind of guilt and urge us to free our lives of its force. But guilt comes in many guises. Befriending this emotion demands distinguishing genuine guilt from the distortions that bear the same name.

Genuine Guilt

I left the house feeling terrible. I tried to put the argument out of my mind, but the feelings would not go away. Finally I had to admit it; I had hurt Angie very much. How could I have so ignored and then insulted her—the person I love most in the world! But I had. An hour later I went back into the house, found Angie and asked her forgiveness. We talked about my tendency to take her for granted, about her sarcasm, about how busy both our schedules have become. We talked about how we could start to change some of the ways we hurt each other. I left for work later with a whole range of feelings: gratitude that we were together again, sorrow for my repeated failure, mellowness about how difficult it is to love well.

When we injure a loved one, when we undermine our best values, we feel guilty. Genuine guilt is an arousal of the heart, an alarm that warns us of a wound we have inflicted. This healthy emotion has four characteristics. First, the alarm begins in the awareness that we have failed in a particular way. Genuine guilt focuses on concrete behavior, the actions and omissions by which we have hurt other people or ourselves. Second, we recognize that a significant relationship has been damaged—a relationship with someone else or with our own deepest values. Third, we admit that we are responsible; that our behavior is at fault. Finally, this acknowledgment impels us to action. Authentic guilt leads us to reestablish contact with those we have hurt and to renew the bonds between us. If shame makes us want to hide from other people, guilt, Gaylin suggests, "wants exposure."

Genuine guilt also motivates us to make amends. Its pain prompts us to apologize for injuries we have caused and to correct our behavior in the future. Without guilt's insistence we would be less likely to hold ourselves accountable to the commitments that shape our life.

Inauthentic Guilt

After ten years teaching history in a multi-cultural high school, Gregory applied for a professional leave and secured funding covering a full year's salary. Looking forward to the time on his own, Greg had planned a full range of activities—time for reading and possibly some writing, visits to libraries with important collections in his field, travel for fun with his wife and their two children. But about a month into the new schedule, Gregory felt increasingly uneasy and unproductive. "It took me a couple weeks to identify the mood. I was feeling guilty. I felt like I was letting someone down—but who?" The mood continued, taking up more of Greg's attention and exhausting him. "I had this growing sense of how selfish I was. Here I am on leave, while my friends and colleagues at school have to face the daily drudgery of their jobs. My wife, an emergency room nurse, doesn't get time away. If I were more generous, I wouldn't need this time off; if I were more creative, I'd already be making real progress on my sabbatical project. Some days I almost enjoyed being absorbed in this sense of guilt. The mood enveloped me. Sometimes I'd snap at Julie or the kids for keeping me from my projects, but most of the time I just felt depressed. There seemed to be no escape.

Guilt feelings signal that we have done something wrong. Genuine guilt focuses on the offending behavior and motivates us to change. Inauthentic guilt distracts us from the concrete details of what we have done by absorbing us in how bad we are. When the focus shifts from "I have failed here" to "I *am* a failure," guilt goes awry.

Joan Borysenko makes the distinction between these two tendencies:

Healthy guilt opens the way to increasing our self-awareness, resolving our difficulties, improving our relationships, and growing spiritually. . . . Unhealthy guilt keeps us stuck in a continual restatement of our presumed unworthiness.

False guilt distracts us from what we can do to make things better. When its arousal turns increasingly inward, guilt becomes a curse.

Genuine guilt is a social emotion, warning us of relationships we have injured and impelling us to make amends. To concentrate on ourselves as culprits obscures these social goals. This self-condemnation feeds a sense that we are helpless in guilt's grasp. Feeling unworthy derails us, diverting energy instead into punishing ourselves. Preoccupied by our personal distress, we lose sight of the social dimensions of our pain.

Cultural Metaphors of Guilt

Every culture introduces its members to the taste of guilt. We *learn* to feel guilty as parents and other authorities instruct us when and why to experience this painful emotion. The rules of guilt they teach have roots in cultural and religious traditions. In Western societies two biblical images have shaped the cultural vision of guilt.

The inhabitants of ancient Israel understood their religious failures as breaking the covenant with God. Our religious ancestors saw their life as a web of social relationships—in the family, among the different clans, with Yahweh. Within this sustaining network they survived and thrived as a people. Outside this vital web—in the hostile desert or among alien tribes—life was in jeopardy. Thus, to injure this network of belonging was to threaten death and deserve punishment. The meaning of life was knit together in the bonds that connected them as members of this believing community. The purpose of this people was summed up in its covenant with Yahweh; fidelity to this relationship meant life and blessings. To undermine or compromise these networks of life was to become guilty of sin.

A very different metaphor of failure appears in the Christian gospel. The New Testament word for sin *(hamartia)* means "to miss the mark." Calling to mind the picture of an archer aiming at a distant target, this image likens moral behavior to achieving a goal. In this metaphor life is portrayed as the pursuit of an external ideal more than as fidelity to a web of relationships.

"Honoring the covenant" focuses on belonging; "missing the mark" emphasizes achievement. Together these images have shaped Western culture's experience of guilt. The metaphor of covenant speaks strongly to those who place high value on relationships. Women, for example, are typically socialized to a strong sense of responsibility for establishing and maintaining the social connections of family and friendship. Understandably, then, many women feel guilt most keenly over injuries to their social network. Many men have been socialized to pursue personal achievement more than relationships. For men like this, "hitting the mark" expresses the sense of responsibility. Holding themselves accountable to performance goals, judging themselves according to external standards of success, these men feel guilt most keenly when they sense they have "missed the mark."

At their best these two metaphors of guilt are complementary. Every adult belongs to social networks; each of us seeks personal goals. So caring for our relationships and struggling to achieve our ideals are concerns shared by all, not tasks limited to one gender or the other. And acknowledging the truth of both these images often helps heal guilt's destructive force in our lives.

Some women, holding themselves responsible for making relationships go well, have considerable trouble with guilt. The web of family and friendship is a complex arrangement. Troubles anywhere in the extended network vibrate across the web. Defining boundaries of personal responsibility is not easy: "How can I ease the tension between my husband and our oldest son?" "Am I to blame for the failure of my daughter's marriage?" "Where does my responsibility for my aging parents leave off?" A woman, sensitive to the dynamics of relationships, often translates this sensitivity into obligation: "I have to fix it." If she cannot make things better, she very likely feels guilty: "I have failed the relationship."

We purify the metaphor of guilt as breaking the covenant when we recognize that not all covenants are holy. Sometimes we enter into contracts that are unhealthy. I must have decided somewhere along the way to be unfailingly friendly and never offend anyone. But being faithful to this false ideal—this covenant I have made with myself—has crippled my ability to face conflict and to speak out against the injustices I see. For me to mature, this covenant has to be broken. I know I'll experience pangs of guilt when I raise my voice or disagree with others, but I must do it anyway.

The metaphor of missing the mark allows for a more focused sense of responsibility and, thus, of guilt. In this image we leave home—and its web of responsibilities—to go to the archery range. This setting itself encourages us to set clear boundaries: the archer aims at a single identified target, ignoring other goals. And the athletic metaphor moderates our guilt another way, since the world of sport teaches us to incorporate failure into the game. Not every arrow hits the bull's eye, even for the champion archer. A baseball player who achieves a .300 batting average is considered a success, yet this is a person who fails 70 percent of the time! Basketball players who make just 55 percent of their shots are considered stars. Playing sports can teach us to learn from our mistakes rather than to blame or punish ourselves for them. Tennis champion Billie Jean King reframes the painful experience of failing: "For me, losing a tennis match isn't failure, it's research."

The metaphor of hitting the mark also awaits purification. Early on we inherit high ideals of achievement: to be as good in school as is our sister; to earn more money than our father; to become the doctor our parents have always wanted. Only later does the realization dawn: "These goals were placed on my archery range before I arrived with my bow and arrow. For years I have been shooting at somebody else's target!"

When Guilt Goes Wrong

My guilt pursues me like a small snapping dog. When guilt lunges at me, I back away. Then I throw out morsels—little achievements, duties done, good works accomplished—to placate the guilt and distract it from attacking me. But guilt just consumes my peace offerings and keeps on going! There must be a better way to deal with this little monster!

Guilt's destructiveness lies in its ability to tyrannize our life. Only slowly do we notice that corrosive guilt has seized control. A chief characteristic of destructive guilt is its drivenness. To overcome this sense of unease, we fill our days with tasks, duties, and good works. We become compulsive helpers, responding to every need that presents itself. And we find it almost impossible to say no. What criteria could we use to refuse these demands? No external criteria seem to work since the needs in our world are endless. What internal criteria can we rely on? Colds, flu, headaches, and exhaustion become the sole indicators of the limits of our responsibility.

When guilt goes wrong, we are bedeviled by the terror of letting other people down. We don't want to offend, to hurt feelings, to disappoint. So we comply indiscriminately to outside expectations. This destructive behavior enslaves us to conformity. Our eagerness to avoid offense is rooted less in personal principle than in a need for other people's approval. We salt our conversation with "should" and "have to," rarely examining the source of these requirements. Regretting our inadequacy, we apologize often. Even our generosity comes wrapped in apologies. Giving a friend a birthday gift, we make sure to include the receipt, convinced in advance that he or she will want to exchange whatever we have chosen for something else.

Destructive guilt often takes the form of perfectionism, an affliction sometimes confused with virtue. Calling someone a perfectionist may be meant as a compliment, meaning the person has high ideals, won't accept slipshod work, demands the best in life. And the addiction of perfectionism receives considerable support in an achievement-oriented society. Americans, for example, tend to admire the workaholic executive who keeps long hours and can master many tasks.

In fact, perfectionism is a compulsion driven by guilt, sapping our life of pleasure and enjoyment. This fretting preoccupation to get everything right refuses to accept our limited humanity. A friend, very successful in his career but harassed by perfectionism, tells this story on himself. After giving a lecture to forty professional colleagues, he checked their written evaluations to discover that thirty-eight participants had deeply appreciated the talk and two persons had found it only mildly useful. The rest of the day he worried about these two "lost sheep." What did they not like? Perhaps he could track them down, explain his lecture again, and they would be satisfied. The price of his punitive worry is that he takes little pleasure in his work. Guilt drives out delight. Obsessed with every limitation and upset with any shortcoming, perfectionists seldom permit themselves to feel proud, to rejoice, or to be grateful.

Compulsive guilt is a chain letter that must keep going! Every addiction—for attention or food or sex—has an endless hunger. We feed it more and more, but we always come up short because we are trying to satisfy an insatiable appetite. Destructive guilt's only remedy is to give up the driven quest for "getting it right" or "doing enough." Augustine, who knew something about compulsions and guilt, describes the moment of his conversion: "I let up on myself a little." For many of us, this is where healing begins.

Reaching for High Ideals

Seeds of unhealthy guilt may lie in the peculiar dynamics of our ideals. Early in our childhood, parents and teachers exhort us to be generous, to study hard, to do our work carefully. Society sets out lofty models for us to emulate: judges, nurses, astronauts, scholars, saints. In our teens and twenties we internalize these cultural ideals to fuel our own vocation.

These early ideals of achievement and service stretch us, expanding both ambition and generosity. But in our forties and fifties we face a different challenge. Now the task is to make these universal values fit our particular life. We need to personalize our ideals. Over the decades life instructs us in that mix of talent and limitation, of bravery and fear that is who *we* are. We wince, recognizing the unavoidable gap between our earliest ideals and how our life actually unfolds. Gradually we come to acknowledge that we are only *this* large-hearted, only *this* capable, only *this* wise—more than expected perhaps, but limited nonetheless.

When all goes well, this sober realization doesn't cause grave disappointment. Necessarily larger than life, our early ideals have done their work—enlarging and enriching us. Grateful for their contribution, we need not use them now to punish ourselves.

Keeping Guilt in Bounds

Authentic guilt operates within the boundaries of responsibility and forgiveness. Like powerful hands, these seasoned impulses hold guilt in check.

Responsibility

Our guilt extends only as far as we are responsible; without this sense of responsibility there is no guilt. Consider an extreme example—the sociopath who lacks the capacity for empathy and mistreats other people without remorse. A person like this, without effective emotional links to other people, is dangerously disconnected from society. The attachments and duties that bind us to one another forge a sense of shared humanity. Shorn of this sensitivity, people feel no responsibility for their social actions and hence, no guilt.

But most of us suffer a quite different affliction. We are more likely to feel *too* responsible. Trained to be dependable, we are alert to the troubles, shortcomings and failures that plague human life.

Christine gives an example:

A colleague came by my desk in the office yesterday and asked if I had a pair of scissors he could borrow.

"No," I said. Then I added, "I'm sorry."

And that's really how I felt—guilty, like I had somehow let him down.

Tony's example is different but his feelings are similar:

Last weekend when I was cleaning my desk at home I came across a stack of requests from worthy causes. I really feel bad when these appeals for money come in the mail. Financially, I'm not able to respond to more than a few. But I feel guilty about not sending money to the other groups. So instead of tossing away the other requests as they come in, I let them pile up on my desk! I know it's crazy, but throwing them all away once a year is easier for me.

How do we learn the limits of our responsibility? As children, our parents introduce us to the range of personal accountability, reminding us to keep our promises and to watch out for our brothers and sisters. As we mature our responsibility expands: we undertake new commitments and pursue larger ideals. But as our responsibility expands, we also learn about our limits. We cannot do everything or remedy all the woes of the world. Even as we take on new cares we must let go old dreams that no longer fit our life. Thus we learn about the boundary of our responsibility: the gray area where our duties end and the somber place where our ideals meet the limits of our strength and calling.

But the boundary, a signpost of both responsibility and guilt, remains permeable. In empathy we cross the line that separates us from others, now feeling their pain or sharing their joy. Empathy with another's sorrow makes us eager to relieve the person's pain. If we cannot improve the situation, we sometimes feel guilty. Compassion mushrooms into a false sense of responsibility: we *should* be able to change another person's life! Here a healthy impulse of empathy heads toward unhealthy guilt.

Women are culturally susceptible to this distortion. Social norms convince many women that their unique vocation is to care for their children, support their spouse, and listen to their neighbors' troubles. If her calling is to care for others, where can a woman draw the line? Facing this boundless responsibility overwhelms her. In such a cultural climate, care for others easily outranks care for self. So when personal illness or exhaustion compel her to pay attention to herself, she feels considerable guilt.

Maturity challenges us to forge a sense of responsibility that acknowledges its own limits: we are not alone responsible for the world. The limits of our responsibility, defined by our finite resources and by commitments already pledged, need not blind us to others' pain. But our calling is to solidarity, not to false guilt.

Forgiveness

Forgiveness is the complementary boundary that holds our guilt in check. Failing a relationship or commitment, healthy guilt impels us to make amends. And this same emotion moves us to ask forgiveness. A colleague writes:

> I feel miserable. Last week I let Sylvia down, breaking a promise I had made only the week before. On the weekend I stopped by to see her, told her how sorry I was, and asked for her forgiveness. We had a good long talk, setting things straight between us. When I left, Sylvia let me know I was forgiven. That evening I stopped at church on the way home and asked God's forgiveness as well. Today I still feel miserable. Thinking back on what happened I am so disappointed with myself. How could I have offended Sylvia like that? I know she has forgiven me, but I can't let go of the experience. It's almost that I *want* to feel bad for a while! Why do I hold onto this guilt?

Guilt fails us when we are unable to ask for forgiveness or remain convinced we do not merit pardon. Here, as when we feel responsible for the whole world, we make ourselves very important. In both instances we ignore a boundary designed to contain the dangerous emotion of guilt.

Embraced by an act of forgiveness, we are absolved of our guilt. Making restitution is part of seeking forgiveness: we give back the money or repay an emotional debt. But sometimes rebalancing is not easy. What restitution makes up for the abuse of an alcoholic parent or the injury of a violent spouse? Face-to-face reconciliation isn't possible with antagonists long dead. Some wrongs cannot be put right by repayments; then only the gift of forgiveness heals.

The Gospel of John tells a story of such forgiveness. A crowd, hungry for vengeance and public humiliation, surrounds a woman accused of adultery. They goad Jesus to condemn her as the law demands, but he seems strangely uninterested in their righteous fervor. Jesus questions the crowd's credentials for rendering such lethal judgment: "Let the one who is without sin throw the first stone." Confused and disappointed, her accusers drift away. Jesus does not condemn her. Instead he urges her to avoid her self-destructive behavior, and then he sends her on her way (Jn 8:7). His gracious attitude seems to dispel both her guilt and her shame. This is the surprise and renewal of forgiveness: the spell is broken. Forgiveness heals our history and dissolves our guilt.

A Question of Conscience

Erik Erikson describes conscience as "the great governor of initiative." In Erikson's vision of human development, children between four and seven are learning much about initiative. Now stronger in body and more capable in language and imagination, children express themselves more forcefully. But in a world with other people, taking initiative sometimes means intrusion: we collide with others, invade their preserve, interrupt their tranquility.

To survive we need to learn the limits of our initiative. We must develop the ability to recognize where we have gone too far and pushed too hard. This crucial ability to regulate self we call conscience. The reliable resource of conscience is the cornerstone of morality. Only if the values of our society are personalized in our conscience can we trust ourselves to distinguish between right and wrong. Erikson describes the fruit of this interior strength: "Only as a dependent does a man develop conscience, that dependence on himself which makes him, in turn, dependable."

Conscience has traced a tortuous cultural journey. Sigmund Freud argued that guilt is a necessary neurosis, the high price we must pay for repressing the primitive impulses of sex and aggression. As sociologist Philip Rieff explains, conscience, for Freud, "is furnished by social authority and remains, unreflectively, at authority's disposal." In this understanding conscience "civilizes" us by grafting society's demands onto our selfish psyches.

In an individualistic society like that in the United States, conscience can mean quite the opposite: independent private judgment, free of all social constraints. Here conscience becomes a privileged authority separated from the external demands of social institutions. Its interior autonomy legitimizes a boundless insistence on rights of privacy and self-expression.

Jewish and Christian wisdom has always envisioned conscience as more than social constraint or individual autonomy. Personal conscience originates in the cultural and religious values that parents and teachers instill in us. But for conscience to mature, we must personalize these ideals. Reaffirming some, rejecting others, we integrate our best hopes and beliefs in our particular calling.

Every conscience is social. In this reservoir of values the ideals of our family and faith survive and thrive. Our conscience is a repository and witness to the goodness we have inherited. But our conscience is social in a second sense. This interior strength not only serves our own life, but conscience is also what we hand on to our children as our best wisdom.

The Voice of Conscience

A dangerous but compelling metaphor for conscience is *voice*. This image is perilous because many of us experience unhealthy guilt as authority's threatening voice within us: "Do it this way or you will be punished." Psychologically disturbed persons excuse their destructive behavior by explaining that a voice told them to do it. Yet our healthy conscience acts like a voice, urging us toward certain decisions and warning us when we have failed our own best ideals.

Through our teens and early twenties we struggle to find our voice: the ability to express our deepest wishes for our future, to enact our best hopes with clarity and conviction. The ideals of teachers and mentors resonate in decisions that appear to us most personal. As the unique voice of our own conscience grows more confident, it harmonizes the many voices of those who have cared for us.

If conscience speaks, it also listens. Our voice becomes authentic and mature only if we listen well—to needs in our society, hopes in the immediate community, wounds in our own hearts. When we listen well, we feel the resonance of our good choices with those of our companions, and we hear these same friends challenge us when our decisions are harmful or ill-advised. In such a listening community the voice of conscience becomes a trustworthy resource both for us and for others.

Conscience is the gradually developed ability to hear the imperatives that arise around us, to be aware of the boundaries of our responsibility, and to voice our response. For our conscience to mature into a reliable resource we need to befriend our negative feelings. When we are smothered in shame or burdened by unhealthy guilt, our conscience cannot be trusted to make a right choice. Through the long discipline of naming and taming our painful emotions, we form our conscience and find our voice.

Even as we develop a finely tuned conscience, we can expect to suffer the lingering tremors of residual guilt. Despite our efforts to heal our perfectionism and trust our seasoned judgments, guilt may remain a companion on the journey. We abide in a world scarred with sin and injury. Some of us know the guilt that endures after a divorce. We see the harmful effects on our children of a necessary decision, effects that our sorrow cannot erase. Even with forgiveness this feeling of guilt endures. Or perhaps we are responsible for an accident in which other people have been injured. Our contrition does not give them back their health; regret and remorse continue. Survivors of tragedies recount their feelings of guilt. Why did they survive? They have no right to go on living. Each day brings fresh guilt. Despite time and forgiveness, guilt endures.

Original Guilt

Like original sin, guilt reminds us of the mystery of human malice. Its roots run deeper in us than we will ever fully fathom. *Original guilt* is the sorrowful responsibility that we share with others for our common inhumanity. This feeling is evoked by media accounts of atrocities inflicted in civil wars, by unending accounts of urban violence, by remembered images of torture or neglect, by the sight of the homeless and hungry in our streets. It is an experience of collective guilt rooted in the undeniable ways in which human beings continue to harm one another.

Initially, most of us are reluctant to share responsibility for the ancient and continuing injustice in human life. "I am not personally to blame," we protest, "for racism or poverty or terrorism." But maturity brings many of us to acknowledge that we belong to and are active members of this wounded and wounding species. We need less and less to deny our involvement in this shared history of sin and guilt. Such an acknowledgment needn't lead us to wallow in a mood of hopelessness. The painful recognition of original guilt can both rekindle our resolve to work for justice and bring us to a tolerance blessed by patient resolve. And this uncomfortable sentiment may turn us, as believers, to our God, who does not cease to forgive. Original guilt is a bad feeling that is good for us to know.

Reflective Exercise

Return to the two biblical metaphors of guilt: breaking the covenant and missing the mark. Consider ways these two images are part of your experience of guilt. To start, spend several minutes in a reflective mood, becoming aware of significant times you have felt guilty. You may wish to take some notes for yourself. Be gentle with this reflection; the goal is insight, not self-punishment.

Next, consider which image—missing the mark or breaking the covenant—best captures these experiences of guilt for you. Give some examples of how this is the case. Again, taking notes may help you stay with the reflection.

Then, focus on the two metaphors themselves. As you see it, how does the image of breaking the covenant heal or purify your own sense of guilt? Are there risks in this image, at least for you?

In your experience, how does the image of missing the mark heal or purify guilt? For you, are there risks in understanding guilt this way?

Additional Resources

Willard Gaylin offers his positive evaluation of guilt in *Feelings: Our Vital Signs*, see pages 40 and following. In *Guilt Is the Teacher, Love Is the Lesson*, therapist Joan Borysenko gives a clear analysis of guilt and shame and provides reflective exercises to help deal with these emotions. One drawback in Borysenko's approach is her severe dichotomy of religion and spirituality; she distinguishes a generic spirituality of healthy guilt from "religious guilt [which] is the most extreme form of unhealthy guilt" (27). For a more balanced discussion of religion and guilt, see Bruce Narramore's *No Condemnation: Rethinking Guilt Motivation*. Gerald May's treatment in *Addiction and Grace: Love and Spirituality in the Healing of Addiction* remains a valuable pastoral resource.

Erik Erikson offers a heuristic exploration of the developmental tension between guilt and initiative in *Identity and the Life Cycle*; we take his comment on conscience from page 84.

In *Freud: The Mind of the Moralist*, Philip Rieff distinguishes "the religious view of conscience as intelligent and reflective as well as passionate" from Freud's conviction that "conscience is furnished by social authority and remains, unreflectively, at authority's disposal" (299). *The Splendor of Truth (Veritatis Splendor)*, John Paul II's encyclical on morality, examines the "voice of conscience" as it echoes God's own voice within our own best desires (see especially pages 314–16).

In *Tragic Redemption: Healing Guilt and Shame* Hiram Johnson offers a moving account of his personal healing journey from guilt to grace. Psychologist David Burns distinguishes remorse that "stems from the undistorted awareness" of a wrongdoing, from guilt that, for him, includes the sense not only of doing wrong but *being bad* (see *Feeling Good: The New Mood Therapy*, pages 178 and following). Now a classic, Paul Tournier's reflection in *Guilt and Grace: A Psychological Study* abounds in wisdom concerning both healthy and unhealthy guilt. For important philosophical discussions of guilt, see Paul Ricoeur's *The Symbolism of Evil*, especially pages 100–150, and Richard Swinburne's *Responsibility and Atonement*.

8

Healthy Shame

We can remove our clothes, without removing our sense of shame.

—PLUTARCH

The emotion of shame embraces a bewildering range of feelings: the momentary embarrassment when we notice that the zipper on our pants or skirt is open; the deeper humiliation of losing our job and feeling like a public failure; the profound shame that still binds us many decades after an experience of sexual abuse.

Shame's status among the negative emotions is well earned. The threatening exposure of our vulnerability wounds us in many ways. How could shame be anything but a curse? How can these feelings of worthlessness connect with anything helpful? To heal this negative emotion we must recover our sense of shame as a positive and healthy sensitivity.

More Than an Emotion

Shame is about being seen. We long to be recognized, to be held in respect. We also fear being seen. What if we are judged inadequate? What if others see through us? What if, like Nicholas and Terry (in Chapter 6) we are discovered in our weakness? Shame names the sharp sense of humiliation that public exposure brings. But the word *shame* refers to more than bitter feelings of embarrassment. Shame also names the inner attunement we bring to our encounters with other people. Shame is the healthy sensitivity we feel as we come close to others. A gradually developed disposition, this positive resource alerts us to the vulnerable boundaries that both link us to and separate us from one another. When this sensitivity is violated, the painful feelings we call shame result.

Even these painful feelings serve as a positive guide to our belonging. A healthy sense of shame is the impulse of discretion that makes us hesitate as we draw close to another person. Is this someone we can trust? Should we risk telling this person about a concern that deeply troubles us? A sense of shame is the healthy apprehension we feel when we ask a friend about a recent divorce: Is this the right time? Or are we intruding on our friend's privacy? Our sense of shame generates the ordinary anxiety we feel as we weigh sharing something personal with a colleague: Is revealing ourselves to this person appropriate? Is it safe?

Healthy shame is about tact: literally, how to be in touch. Tact is the ability to gauge how close to come to another person, when to look away, when to allow extra space between us. Tact is the uncanny resource that allows us to draw close while leaving each other's integrity intact. Tact helps us develop a sense of tactics: strategies for approaching others and techniques of disclosing our heart without doing harm. Tactics may, of course, become mere tools of manipulation or attack. But in its best guise, tact serves our best hopes for intimacy.

A healthy sense of shame acts as a gyroscope, helping us keep our balance in the dizzying challenges of social life. It guides our approaches and helps us make mid-flight corrections. We appreciate this resource when we recall a common pitfall of many social occasions. A casual acquaintance approaches us at a party and starts to discuss some intimate details of his or her private life. Instantly an internal distress signal sounds: "This conversation doesn't fit!" Suitable, perhaps, with a psychological therapist or pastoral minister or close friend, here the disclosure is out of bounds. This person has come too close; the revelation tells us more than is appropriate for us to know. Our obvious discomfort responds to this boundary violation, alerting us to protect ourselves from this intrusion.

Composure

The little boy peeks out from behind his mother's skirt, then disappears. Again, he hazards a quick look, giggles, and returns to his safe hiding place. Who can resist the fascination of this game? As the child both hides and reveals himself, he gains our attention and recruits our affection.

Shyness is one of the charming dynamics of a healthy sense of shame, even among adults. A person holds back as we draw close, perhaps hesitating or blushing. As the person retreats, we are drawn forward; frequently we find this demurring to be attractive. The hesitance charms us and mysteriously charges the space between us with excitement. The author Milan Kundera describes the special allure of shyness:

> He had known her for a year now, but she would still get shy in front of him. He enjoyed her moments of shyness, partly because they distinguished her from the women he'd met before, partly because the girl's shyness was a precious thing to him.

But this natural shyness can become distorted and turn into a false modesty. We may learn to be *too* hesitant, *too* apprehensive as we approach the boundaries that connect us with others. If a healthy sense of shame attunes us to the real limits of our self, a false modesty makes us overly conscious of our fragility. What begins as modesty becomes a wall that seals us off from all threatening contact with others.

British psychologist Adam Phillips, in his enchanting book *On Kissing, Tickling, and Being Bored,* discusses this damaging withdrawal as *composure*. Infants have no composure—and need none. Oblivious of boundaries, the nursing baby assumes the breast is but an extension of its own body. But as the child comes to recognize the difference and distance between self and others, developing composure—"a calculated social poise"—becomes necessary.

As adults, composure is something we frequently regain rather than permanently possess. Recoiling from our overexposure to an emotional stimulus, we try to recover some quiet and control—we try to restore our composure. But we can become too good at this mode of "self-holding and self-protecting." Retreating from contact, we hold ourselves apart for too long. This withdrawal tactic generates "an appearance of self-possession" that communicates "a relative absence of neediness." But such rigid composure transforms our self-holding into self-hiding which, in its extreme form, "insulates the individual from ever allowing the recognition he seeks."

Phillips suggests that composure, this holding ourselves apart from others, may be linked to one of our deepest aspirations. More than simply an exercise of self-defense, composure may be "a kind of self-holding that keeps open the possibility of finding an environment in which the composure itself could be relinquished." Perhaps a person's best hope is to "create or find an environment in which his composure [is] of no use, and in which this fact [is] no longer a problem." As a strategy of healthy shame, composure protects our vulnerable boundaries. But, like shame, composure hopes for recognition. We long for the place and persons where our composure will no longer be necessary, where we might be, in the words of Genesis, "naked and unashamed."

An Erotic Sensibility

A healthy sense of shame guards the boundaries of our bodily self. And many of us experience the painful feelings of shame most powerfully in our bodies and our sexuality. Here we sense the fragile frontiers of our necessary and perilous exchanges with other people. Recall the excruciating embarrassment of a teenager removing clothes for a medical examination. In a season of high vulnerability, the young person feels the danger of exposing a body that is newly sexually charged. But even in acute experiences like this, shame remains a social instinct; others help us be more comfortable with our sensitivity. The professional respect with which the nurse or doctor uncovers our body teaches us important lessons. Without being embarrassed or embarrassing us, they model a finely honed sense of modesty.

Moral philosopher Bernard Williams reminds us that the Greek word for positive shame, *aidos,* is connected to the word for genitals. Literally, then, this emotion concerns our erotic life. Classical Latin employed the phrase *pars pudenda*—often translated as "private parts"—to designate the genitals. The different emotional nuances that are attached to *pars pudenda* illustrate our ambivalence about sexuality. A translation influenced by the Greek language renders the phrase as that "vulnerable part" of the body that deserves special respect. A translation more influenced by certain strands of Christian piety renders the phrase as our "shameful parts"—parts that are considered unholy, even disgusting.

At the time the Gospels were being compiled within the early communities of Jesus' followers, the Roman author Plutarch spoke eloquently of shame as an erotic virtue: "we can remove our clothes, without removing our sense of shame." Yet in both the Septuagint version of the Hebrew Bible and in the New Testament, the Greek word for healthy shame is virtually absent. In its stead we find the virtue of respect *(time)*, sometimes used with explicitly erotic overtones. In his first letter to the Christians in Corinth, Paul twice links this virtue to our bodiliness. "You were bought at a great price *(time)*; therefore glorify God in your bodies" (1 Cor 6:20). Our worth is rooted in God's having saved us, and the mutual respect this calls for must be registered in our bodies.

Paul evokes the imagery of the community of faith as the body of Christ. Like a physical body, a Christian gathering is composed of a variety of members, each blessed with unique gifts and possibly wounded by injury. Our integrity as a group of believers depends on the respect we have for each other, whatever our position in the body. Paul alerts his listeners to be especially sensitive to the weaker members: "Those members of the body that we think less honorable we clothe with greater honor; and our less respectable members are treated with greater respect. ... God has so arranged the body, giving the greater honor to the inferior member" (1 Cor 12:23–24). "Inferior member" echoes the erotic *pars pudenda* of every physical body, and the care and respect these vulnerable members deserve. Paul's metaphor about the body Christian alerts us to the "vulnerable members" of the social community today—the aged and the immigrant, the homeless and the sexually marginalized. The community of faith is charged to give special respect to these "less honorable members" of the body, to whom—Paul insists—"God has given the greater honor." We fail as a Christian body when we show disrespect to the vulnerable members of the human community, when our own behavior simply mimics the culture's condemnation and neglect.

Shame and the Development of Will

Healthy shame stimulates the development of personal will. Will is the capacity for sustained and self-directed activity: this inner strength is rooted in our confidence in who we are and finds expression in our determination to live out our personal convictions. To show how shame supports personal will we return to an early season of development, "the terrible two's."

As two year olds, children move beyond the all-encompassing dependence of infancy. Newly developed skeletal strength means we can stand and walk on our own. Muscular advances increase our capacity to control urination and defecation. And parents are eager to teach us how to use these newfound abilities. Now that we have the strength to get away, they are intent that we learn what we can and cannot "get away with." So instruction intensifies: what to eat, where to relax our sphincters, when to bathe, how to dress ourselves. In all these ways our caregivers are showing us how to belong, how to act so that we fit in this society.

As two year olds learn the lessons of belonging, they also awaken to the possibility of *no.* The growing child now has strength not only to walk, but to walk away—to escape parents' full control. The child can resist potty training or refuse to eat some strange-looking food. In these unavoidable early battles between parent and child, the struggle between belonging and autonomy is joined. As a child, we must eat and eliminate and dress according to the group's dictates, but we recognize that we must also be ourselves. Saying no lays down the gauntlet to the formation of the "ideal child"—a perfect reproduction of the parents' desires. In this early resistance, personal will is forged. And shame is the catalyst.

As parents struggle to shape the toddler's social behavior, they recognize that rational persuasion has its limits. The small child still lacks the cognitive ability to trace cause and effect, to see links between action and consequence, to weigh the merits of various choices. A more direct approach is demanded. Parents typically resort to shaming techniques to enforce their desires on their child. Cajoling (be a big boy!), name calling (you're just a cry baby), and threats of punishment and abandonment compel the child to act as expected, to behave as instructed.

Shame is the bad feeling that arises when children realize they have done something that significant people find improper. Even if we did it unknowingly (the parent discovers the child exploring his penis), even if the action was beyond our control (wetting the bed), what we have done is held against us. The distressing feeling of shame gets our attention. It signals that we have failed in other people's eyes; we have fallen short of their expectations. And these bad feelings provoke a new movement in the child's maturity.

The sting of shame confronts the child with the cost of acceptance: "this is what you must do to belong." Caught in the tension between belonging and autonomy, the toddler struggles to develop, in the words of psychologist Erik Erikson, "a sense of *self-control without loss of self-esteem.*" Without this tension between self-control and social compliance, the child's development is stunted. Only in the struggle do we learn how to reconcile inner desires with outer demands. Shame acts as an irritant, stimulating us to fight back. And from the resulting conflict, Erikson reminds us, "a lasting sense of autonomy and pride" may emerge.

If the force of shame overwhelms, children may capitulate and simply conform. They then set out on a course to always please, never offend, to fit in perfectly, making their parents proud of them. This shame-bound behavior puts them in lifelong jeopardy; always alert to what will please others, they abandon interior criteria of what is right for them. In the developmental schema of Erik Erikson, self-doubt swamps autonomy. Personal will, the root of an individual's sense of identity and purpose, fails its first developmental test.

But being damaged by shame early can produce the opposite reaction. The child rejects the demands of others and sets out on an overly autonomous journey. Insistent on doing it their own way, such people reject convention and compromise. Obsessed with independence, they develop a fierce determination to avoid any external influence. Severely irritated by shame, such children seek autonomy at too high a cost.

Healthy shame directs both conformity and resistance. In the no's of the two year old we see the first fruits of this stirring of independence. In this perilous season of balancing the yes to our parents' demands and the no of our own will, we begin the journey to self-confidence and self-esteem. Gradually finding the balance between conformity and independence, we come to a sense of our uniqueness, our peculiar identity and calling in life. This sense of self-esteem strengthens us in the face of social pressure and institutional shaming. It provides us with the daring to risk new ventures that have not been approved or sanctioned by social authorities. The interior strength of will equips us with the resilience even to fail at such efforts without being too ashamed and without having a particular failing mushroom into a judgment that we are a failure.

Shame is a dangerous dynamic in the process of socialization. This powerful emotion, if abused by those who are teaching us how to belong, may destroy our confidence and defeat the development of will. But when it is blended with affection and tolerance in early childhood, shame impels the toddler to craft a balance between belonging and autonomy. Through this important contribution, shame becomes a disguised gift on the journey toward adult maturity.

The Virtues of Shame

Shame is more than a momentary embarrassment or a destructive mood of inferiority. As a positive resource it embodies the crucial strengths of will and warrior. With proper care a positive sense of shame matures into a resident strength in us—a virtue. Bernard Williams, a moral philosopher and classics scholar, describes the development of the virtue of shame in Greece in the fifth century BCE. During this period the Greeks distinguished a servile shame that simply pivoted on public opinion and a healthy shame rooted in personal conviction.

In its most robust dimension a sense of shame gives a person "a sense of who one is and what one hopes to be." If guilt concerns what we have done, shame concerns who we are. Guilt addresses correctness, but shame addresses worth.

For Williams, shame's value derives from the internalized *other* whose gaze evaluates our actions. This *other* may embody only our parents' authoritative frown on our childish endeavors. But it may also mature into conscience, when our best inherited values, rather than tyrannical authority, serve as our interior guide. As Sidney Callahan observes in her study of conscience's role:

> In our internalized memory, we can carry our inner, unseen audience of beloved and admired moral tutors and exemplars, whom we do not wish to disappoint or morally betray, by betraying the standards of worth they have imparted to us.

A positive sense of shame flowers in a multitude of virtues, with humility the most basic. By alerting us to the limits of our strength and gifts, shame keeps us humble. Humility is a realistic and flexible sense of self that bends before adversity and even failure but does not shatter. A healthy sense of shame allows us to be humbled without being humiliated. Both of these words share the same root: *humus* (earth). We *hum*ans (same root) belong to the earth; contact with humility need not stain or shame us.

In our efforts of love and work we can expect to stumble. We are brought down to earth from our lofty ideals as we meet the limits of our courage and generosity. We bend under our commitments and are brought low in exhaustion. All this is humbling but not necessarily humiliating. We can taste defeat without losing our worth. Humbled by our limits and brought back to earth, we learn the crucial lessons that come as humility's gift.

A healthy sense of shame matures in the virtue of dignity. In dignity we recognize the value of our embodied selves. This virtue develops slowly as we come to a greater comfort with who we are—our gifts and limits, our strengths and enduring doubts. Dignity is the esteem in which we hold ourselves. And dignity is self-respect: how we see ourselves, our comfort with the particular person we are turning out to be.

If shame as a destructive emotion is a debilitating sense of inadequacy, dignity is an enduring awareness of our worth. As this inner resource develops, we are less susceptible to others' ability to belittle or shame us. This virtue guides us through troubling, even traumatic times.

Dignity is that sense of personal integrity against which the ploys of social shaming cannot prevail. Russian dissident Natan Sharansky has described the insight into humiliation forced upon him by the intrusive interrogations of the KGB:

> On that occasion, when I was stripped and searched, I decided it was best to treat my captors like the weather. A storm can cause you troubles, and sometimes those problems can be humiliating. But the storm itself doesn't humiliate you. Once I understood this I realized that nothing they did could humiliate me. I could only humiliate myself—by doing something I might later be ashamed of. . . . *Nothing they can do can humiliate me. I alone can humiliate myself.*

In the trauma of his crisis, Sharansky refuses to be shamed. Plutarch's proverb is proved true even in such straits: "we can remove our clothes without removing our sense of shame." A sense of dignity becomes so ingrained that it cannot be stripped away.

Forty years ago a gathering of gay and lesbian Catholics chose Dignity as the name of their new organization. Dignity members were keenly aware of how society's harassment stripped them of self-respect and instilled a profound sense of worthlessness. Shamed by civic and religious authorities, homosexual, bisexual, and transsexual men and women traditionally retreated into closets of silence and self-hatred. Such self-hatred often provoked behavior that seemed to justify society's condemnation. Now, with local chapters throughout the country and a national office for resources and coordination, Dignity/USA has lived up to its name, supporting lesbians and gay men in their liberation from the prison of shame into the world of self-respect, mutual support, and public roles of service and advocacy.

Chastity

Shame guards the boundaries of our sexual bodies. Dignity takes root in our body as the virtue of chastity. Chastity is the well-honed sensitivity that balances intimacy and solitude in our life, that guides our decisions about sexual expression. This virtue is not the same as abstinence or celibacy. Chastity is an inner sense of modesty that protects us as we attempt to both reveal and conceal ourselves. In the words of Carl Schneider, "The sense of shame is that space-creating hesitation that allows us to know one another without brusqueness or intrusion." Our matured sense of shame keeps the volatile energy of sexuality fully human, that is, respectful and mutual. Deprived of this seasoned instinct of shame, sexual excitement can erupt into abusive and obscene actions.

Chastity is the matured sense of shame that guides our exposure to one another. When we show ourselves to another person, we want this to be an act of revelation; we extend our heart as well as our body. Chastity is that healthy hesitance that helps love catch up with passion, so that they might go hand in hand in sexual sharing.

Humility, dignity, and chastity: virtues that shape the movements of our hearts and bodies. Guided by these resources we gradually become more graceful in our movements toward and away from others. A sense of shame becomes a grace—a skillful confidence in the dance of human interaction. But we think of shame more often in its negative guise—feeling ashamed or disgraced. When the grace of a positive sense of shame has been stolen from us, we are left unsure of how to act, of what we are worth. We move clumsily and awkwardly when we approach others. Susceptible to others' intrusions, we are easy prey to those who would take advantage of us. We live not in grace but on the edge of disgrace. Yet even here, will and warrior arouse us to reclaim the gift of a healthy sense of shame that safeguards our dignity.

Reflective Exercise

Consider some of the ordinary expressions of adult willpower: force-fulness, determination, self-control, persistence, self-confidence, stub-bornness, resolve. Then recall a recent experience of your own exercise of personal will; take time to bring the memory fully to mind.

Then reflect on these questions: How did this exercise of willpower enhance or strengthen you? Did this exercise of personal will challenge or distress you in any way? Did *shame* or *embarrassment* play any part in this experience—inhibiting you, threatening you, goading you to act, making you more sensitive to the context or consequences of your actions?

Finally, spend a few moments taking notes on your own sense of the connections between shame and will.

Additional Resources

We are especially indebted to Carl Schneider for his insightful exploration of the positive resource of shame in *Shame, Exposure and Privacy*; we quote from page 16. Historian Bernard Williams recovers the role of a healthy virtue of shame in *Shame and Necessity*. Williams is intent on rescuing the early Greek sensitivity to shame from its negative evaluation by many historians as "pre-moral" social conformity; see especially his discussion of "Shame and Autonomy" in chapter 4.

Erik Erikson discusses the development of will in *Identity and the Life Cycle*, pages 70–71. Michael Lewis advances the developmental approach in his positive treatment of shame in *Shame: The Exposed Self*. In *Transforming Shame: A Pastoral Response,* Jill McNish draws on psychological and theological resources as she examines the transformative potential of shame. Lewis B. Smedes explores shame's healthy dimensions in *Shame and Grace: Healing the Shame We Don't Deserve*; see especially chapters 4 and 8.

For Natan Sharansky's observation about humiliation, see his autobiography, *Fear No Evil*, page 8. Sidney Callahan's observation linking healthy shame and mature conscience appears in *In Good Conscience: Reason and Emotion in Moral Decision Making*, page 64. For Adam Phillip's reflections on composure, see *On Kissing, Tickling, and Being Bored: Psychoanalytic Essays on the Unexamined Life*, pages 42 and following.

9

Transforming Social Shame

"Do it this way," says shame, "or you'll be sorry."
—ELIZABETH JANEWAY

The puzzle of shame begins in the many meanings of the word. Shame names the discomfort we feel in the embarrassing moments of everyday life. But in some contexts shame carries a positive nuance; that is, a healthy sense of shame alerts us to one another's vulnerability, adding delicacy and respect to our social interactions. And in the influential vocabulary of therapy and recovery, shame identifies a corrosive mood of personal inferiority that defeats all achievement and delight.

The American inclination toward individualism disposes us to interpret shame as a private, negative feeling. But even this most intimate awareness is shaped by social forces. The environments of family, religion, and nation orchestrate our embarrassments. Healing shame's damaging force requires a grasp of the social dynamics that govern this pervasive emotion.

The Economy of Shame: The Measure of Our Worth

Complex, shadowy rules govern the experience of social shame. The economy of this emotion begins in the human concern for *earning* and *paying* respect. Respect refers, literally, to how we are seen by others. Playing by the rules, we hope to be seen in a favorable light. We earn respect by doing a good job at work, by meeting our commitments in friendship, by keeping our word. Eager to be well regarded ourselves, we show our respect for others. In childhood we learn the debt of respect we owe our elders. As adults, we gather at memorial services and funerals to pay our respects to the deceased and the survivors alike.

The economy of earning and paying respect inducts us into the world of respectability. Even as children we are keenly aware which homes in the neighborhood are respectable and which are not. We learn whether our own parents work in respected occupations. We sense the dictates of fashion—the class requirements of dress and demeanor, the special regard shown certain initials: MD, BMW, CEO. We suffer the perils of this economy, as well, when shifts in fashion leave us painfully vulnerable. Our house, our wardrobe, even our body size may suddenly lose value and no longer merit respect.

In this economy external evaluation measures our worth. When others approve of us, we feel appreciated: our value increases. But if others frown on our choice of friends or fashion or leisure activities, our worth plummets. Our value depreciates, catapulting us into an emotional—if not economic—depression.

Like respect, honor is a social measure of our worth. In the influential television series *The Sopranos*, the threat of dishonor cast a constant shadow. Ever vigilant against the loss of honor, members of these close-knit mafia families live with the specter of revenge; violent retaliation is demanded to restore diminished honor. The Spanish proverb says it clearly: the stain of honor is washed clean in blood. Honor and shame are blood relatives.

Even in our broader culture, seemingly free of the social code of honor and vengeance, the romance of revenge remains powerful. American honor sanctions violence in the service of injured dignity. Hollywood exalts this theme, and moviegoers' enthusiastic response to films with violent resolutions confirms that revenge earns respect.

The economy of social shame is driven by an interminable search for respect and honor. Love is the antidote to this economy. Its unearned affection reminds us of another measure of our worth. Our parents' gratuitous care does not depend on what we can achieve. Blessed by the enduring affection of friends and companions, we feel our value soar. Being loved teaches us to calculate respect differently. If we are fortunate, we learn our inestimable value does not depend on status or possessions. Our worth is rooted in something more fundamental than social conformity.

Yet, being human, we fall prey to the social dynamics of shame. Our desire for respect recruits us to dependence on society's constant approval. Every society takes advantage of this leverage to compel conformity. This brings us to the story of social shaming.

The Strategies of Social Shaming

The pain of shame reminds us that our behavior is in public view. People who matter to us are watching. If we measure up, we may be deemed acceptable—recognized as worthy to be "one of them." If these significant folk find our actions unacceptable, they may turn away their gaze. Now we risk being excluded—from their affection, from their protection, from the security of belonging to this elite group. As a psychological dynamic, then, shame seeks to ensure inclusion. As a social strategy, shaming attempts to enforce conformity.

The family table teaches us the price of inclusion. There our parents curb our preference for eating with our hands! They praise us for using the knife and fork properly and scold us for playing with our food. They instruct us in the rigors of delayed gratification: dessert remains untouchable so long as vegetables linger on our plate. If we don't comply, we risk being sent from the room "until you can show that you belong here with the rest the family."

These tasks of socialization—teaching table manners, encouraging potty training, urging us to share our toys—begin early. Parents start to shape behavior long before their infants and toddlers have a full range of cognitive skills. Before the appeal to rational persuasion can be effective, as we saw in Chapter 8, parents use other strategies in the service of socialization. Unilaterally, parents set the behavior standards to be met; they closely monitor the child's performance, rewarding achievement and discouraging resistance. Rules abound: Don't cross the street by yourself. Be sure to wash your hands before meals. Let your little brother play with that toy. Motivation is simple: "Do as I say . . . because I say so." At this early developmental stage, conformity is the goal. Children's external behavior is more important—to their safety as well as for their social acceptance—than is their agreement with the family rules.

As a strategy in group life, shaming outlasts infancy. Shame comes into play whenever external criteria are favored in evaluating personal experience. The threat of social shame conveys two messages: we will show you how to act here; you cannot survive apart from our approval and protection.

Social shame warns that if we do not fit in, we will be cast out; worse, we make ourselves outcasts. Recognition and respect (shame argues) are gifts of membership, benefits of belonging to the group. To be deprived of the community's resources and affirmation is to be disgraced. Literature and history are rife with instances of this shaming. An officer of the French Foreign Legion has his insignia stripped off his uniform; a woman accused of a sexual offense is clothed with a scarlet letter. While shaming supports human development during that short season before we are equipped for responsibility and conscience, its adult forms are almost always destructive.

Shaming and Naming

A chief strategy of social shame is to name a person as deviant. Names tell us who we are, assigning both identity and worth. When a beleaguered parent, discovering that a four year old has wet the bed again, scolds "bad girl!" the child hears herself identified negatively for something she could not control. With the taunt of "chicken, chicken," youngsters dare the new kid on the block to throw a stone at a street lamp. Intimidated by the chant and desperate to dispel its punishing claim, the child acts against his better judgment.

Deviant names stigmatize, marking the shamed person as not fitting in, as unworthy of membership in this group. This labeling strategy survives in our religious and political lives. Threatened by the assertive behavior of a woman new to the management team, the old timers label her a *bitch*. Eager to avoid this degrading title, she may decide to adopt a more docile attitude; the shaming strategy has worked.

Americans are especially vicious in sexual and gender slurs. Names like *pervert, fag, dyke, queer* stigmatize those whose sexual behavior hints they are not "one of us." Naming someone a deviant—whether the bed-wetter or the assertive woman or the homosexual—serves two purposes: to expose the person, and to threaten expulsion from the group. A derogatory name singles us out. Most of us have grammar-school memories of being asked to stand up in class or come to the front of the room. We cringed at the thought of this sudden exposure. What if we are asked something we don't know? What if the teacher decides to make an example of us? Behind this threat of exposure is the unspoken lesson: hidden within the group, we are safe. By fitting in and acting as others do, we avoid the embarrassment of exposure.

The dynamic of social shaming takes advantage of our enduring vulnerability. At the taunt of *chicken*, whether we are seven or forty-seven, we wonder: Am I really afraid to try something new and bold? Recoiling at the sound of *bitch*, we question our own strength: Perhaps I did come on too strong at the meeting; I'll have to watch myself next time. Assaulted again by the jeers of *dyke* or *fag*, we return to doubts we thought had been resolved: Is it OK to be who I am? If not, who shall I be?

If naming exposes us, it also threatens expulsion. Called to the head of the class, we stand close to the door, in jeopardy of being sent away. Every group develops exquisite tools to threaten its members with expulsion. We tell our child to leave the table until she can behave like the others. We send another child to his room until he "learns how to behave." The threat's power lies not in actual banishment; note that the children are still in the house. But their belonging is now in jeopardy.

Within some Amish communities a person who significantly offends against the group's rules is shunned by other members. Again, the offender is not so much driven away as threatened with psychological abandonment. Hidden in the threat of expulsion is the conviction that individuals cannot survive apart from the group. Perhaps this fear is rooted in millennia of survival in hostile climates where, deprived of the community's food and fire, the isolated individual would certainly perish. For several centuries Christian piety professed that "outside the church there is no salvation." Those separated from this saving community were doomed to eternal punishment, fire of another sort.

Belittling and Belonging

Social shame's second strategy is belittling. "You're such a cry baby!" we rebuke the youngster who is frightened by the dark. Calling the child immature, we hope to shame him into acting more adult, more "like us."

Ignoring and forgetting are other forms of belittling. Remember the day the teacher or camp director called the list of names and omitted yours? Suddenly you felt yourself diminished. In this important person's mind, you did not exist. Or recall in gym class, when sides were chosen for the game, and you were left standing on the sidelines, abandoned and belittled.

Belittling aims to reawaken whatever woundedness we still carry from childhood: memories of being left out or overlooked, fears of being forgotten. When it can evoke the trauma of abandonment, the strategy of belittling gains enormous power.

In civic and religious life belittling reappears in efforts to trivialize a cherished concern. The question of sexist language in the liturgy—constant references to "brothers" and "all men" that suggest God's people come in only one gender—is declared by some leaders to be insignificant. The message: You women should be ashamed of making so much of this unimportant matter. Raising a fuss here is just silly.

Laughter sometimes belittles. Humor, of course, plays many roles in group life. Laughing at our mistakes and poking fun at our worries reduces social tension. But humor is easily recruited as a weapon to keep others in their place. We make fun of people to "put them down," to expose them as inferior to ourselves. In the service of shame, humor turns to ridicule. We laugh at those foolish enough to try for a job that doesn't "fit" their ethnic background or social class. "They should have known better. Who do they think they are!" Here laughter hardly hides the hostility. And humor, steeped in bitterness, becomes scorn.

Shaming by Silencing

Silencing, like belittling, hopes to diminish a threat to the group's good order. Rather than instigating a dialogue to clear the air, silencing aims to quiet the voice that dissents. Exasperated parents shout at the troublesome child, "Shut up!" Irritated religious officials impose periods of silence on dissenting theologians. The intent here, as in all strategies of social shame, is to reinforce self-doubt. During this penitential silence, the offending parties will learn to modify their tone. And others tempted to speak out will be forewarned and forestalled.

The Transformation of Social Shame

Healing shame depends on the development of personal antidotes to these social strategies. Learning to trust our own instincts will attune us to the difference between personal goals and social conventions. Reinterpreting risk, we can embrace failure not as a shameful sign of personal inadequacy but as an acceptable scene in the drama of our vocation.

Cultivating the strength of will offers another antidote. Learning to be assertive helps us develop a flexible sense of boundaries: where we leave off and another person begins, where our rights intersect with those of others, where personal hopes put us in tension with people significant to us. Negotiating these interpersonal boundaries, we each craft our own balance of intimacy and solitude, of merger and independence. Gradually coming to trust our own instincts and to rely on our sense of boundaries leaves us less a prey to the forces of social shame.

An effective challenge to social shame takes more than individual discipline. Shaming strategies draw energy from deep cultural roots, the hidden assumptions and unspoken rules that govern our common life. Who is in and who is out? What shade of skin, what level of income, what beliefs and behavior are required to be included? Do outsiders have access to our bounty? Who has a right to belong? Invalidating the destructive strategies of social shame demands transforming these images of belonging. And in this social transformation of shame, religion can become an important ally.

Religion plays a highly ambiguous role in the realm of shame and belonging. Religious institutions have long employed shame and guilt to threaten their members. Despite its history of malpractice, Christianity can make a powerful contribution to the healing of social shame.

Christianity and the Healing of Social Shame

Religion, as a purifying force within human culture, invites us to reexamine our suppositions about social status and worth. As a society narrows its rules for who is included and who is highly regarded, religion challenges us to reform our criteria for inclusion and esteem. Religion's best contribution to the healing of social shame may be in undermining the conventional rules of belonging.

The prophets reminded ancient Israel that widows and orphans and the poor were not outcasts but members of the community. Yahweh's covenant with Israel had redefined the social indicators of status and worth. Because they are beloved by a compassionate God, the prophets insisted, these people are part of our family.

In the Christian gospel Jesus continues this critique of the human inclination to exclude the lowly and the marginal from the community. When he is told that members of his family had arrived to visit him, Jesus' response startles his tight-knit group of followers: "Who is my mother and who are my brothers?" (Mt 12:48). Then, following the lead of the ancient prophets, he redraws the boundaries of belonging: "Whoever does the will of my father in heaven is my brother and sister and mother." In a single stroke Jesus overturns the authority of traditional clan lines. The centrality of ethnic kinship, with its ancient grudges and concern with dishonor, is thrown into doubt. The concern for bloodlines, with its vigilance around shame and justification of revenge, comes into question.

Five times in Matthew's Gospel, Jesus challenges these "family values." The ancient commandment to "honor thy parents" is now balanced by the need to leave them in order to follow Jesus (see Mt 4:22; 8:22; 19:29). At his most antagonistic, Jesus warns his followers that he has not "come to bring peace, but a sword. For I have come to set a man against his father, and a daughter against her mother" (Mt 10:34–35). Christians have often preferred to ignore this questioning of family values that would compel us to welcome every kind of outcast into our midst.

When religion redraws the boundaries of belonging, it alters the criteria of our worth and our dignity. Reading the Jewish prophets or the life of Jesus, we momentarily glimpse a truth we find hard to embrace: our value is not rooted in our group's social status or our family's pride of place. Our worth springs neither from the superiority of our clan nor from our personal righteousness. Our value and dignity arise from our inalienable bond to a Creator who judges that all creation is *very good*.

This shift in the measure of our worth—from social status, civic pride, or moral uprightness to God's unconditional love—opens a novel remedy for social transgressions. When our dignity balances on the fragile respectability of our kin, we will be anxious to avenge all injuries. Apprehensive about losing respect, we ready ourselves for the ancient remedy. In a group dominated by a concern for its status and worth, vengeance prowls the borders of our belonging; any insult to our honor triggers the instinct for revenge. Neighborhood arguments, fights between gangs, wars between nations mushroom in our endless quest for respect.

But if our belonging is anchored in a more powerful source of worth, another remedy is available; forgiveness can replace vengeance. In place of an unending retaliation for injuries received, we can break this cycle with the novel and surprising act of reconciliation. We can surrender the obsessive pursuit of social respect and learn to give and receive pardon. This extraordinary gesture must appear foolish to the wise of the world. And to those still injured by a personal history of shame, forgiveness may seem intolerable, looking like more of the same passivity before others' intrusions and abuse. But forgiveness remains a possibility. When we are blessed with the ability to forgive, we feel the corrosive demands of shame and vengeance begin to dissolve. In their place is revealed a common humanity, both blessed and broken—the better measure of our worth.

Shame and Seeing Face to Face

Shame is both about belonging and being seen, about how we are regarded by others. At the beginning of Christianity looms the shameful public execution of a naked Jesus. This startling memory must indicate a special contribution of Christianity to the healing of social shame. The story of the Christian transformation of shame unfolds in three acts. In Act One, a couple wanders through an idyllic garden, "naked and unashamed" (Gn 2:25). Once upon a time, our religious memory tells us, we were fully exposed to one another and were not embarrassed. Adam and Eve lived, without protection or apology, face to face with God. But once they disobeyed their Creator, they felt suddenly exposed and rushed to cover themselves. Dis-covered by the eyes of God, they were asked the fateful question: "Who told you you were naked?" Henceforth, humans would need to protect their acute sense of shame with clothing and would have to shield themselves from direct contact with their Creator.

Act Two begins at this moment and continues through the Hebrew scriptures. For the ancient Israelites and many other religious traditions, the sacred was recognized as dangerous terrain. God's special haunts—whether on a holy mountain or in a temple sanctuary—must be marked off with special barriers. Humans must not come too close to this awesome and potentially lethal power. Moses is warned to "mark off the limits of the mountain and declare it sacred" (Ex 19:23) and that "whoever touches the mountain will be put to death" (Ex 19:12).

On Mount Sinai Moses pleads to see God's face but is told, "You cannot see my face, for a human cannot see me and live" (Ex 33:20). Another tradition suggested greater intimacy between Yahweh and Moses. When Moses would enter the Tent of Visitation in their desert encampment, "The Lord used to speak to Moses face to face, as one speaks to a friend" (Ex 33:11). Humans learned to cover their faces and shield their eyes in the presence of God. This separation of the sacred and the human was ritualized in the curtain that enshrouded the Holy of Holies in the Temple in Jerusalem, shielding human eyes from God's direct gaze. The altar railing in some Catholic churches lingers as a vestige of this conviction that sacred space must be marked off from ordinary secular territory.

During this long second act, humankind learned reverence for a mysterious and powerful God. Coming before God they bowed their heads, lowered their voices, bent their knee. A healthy sense of shame alerted believers to the vulnerable boundary that both links us to and separates us from God. Like Adam and Eve, we become acutely aware of God's presence and cover ourselves with reverential behavior.

In Act Three the death of Jesus erupts with revolutionary force into this long religious tradition of shame and reverence. Jesus suffers a humiliating public death. He is tortured and exposed and ridiculed. But, as the New Testament observes, "he disregarded the shamefulness of the cross" (Heb 12:2). The public shaming of his death did not humiliate him; he did not cast his eyes down in embarrassment or dissolve in despair. He confronted his death without losing face.

In his death the Christian story of shame mysteriously comes full circle: Jesus was naked and unashamed. But now the exposure is not the romantic nakedness of the primeval garden but the degrading exposure of a public execution. Yet the humiliating circumstances of this death did not humiliate Jesus. "He disregarded the shamefulness of the cross." Embracing his death, Jesus transformed the power of social shame. Christians celebrate this transformation in their devotion to the crucifix. What at first seems to be a shameful failure, something to be concealed in embarrassment, is raised up as a sign of suffering that has been healed.

The way that Jesus dies, the manner and dignity with which he embraces his suffering, saps death of its absurdity and its sting. The pain of death is not magically removed, but its degradation and humiliation are lifted. Because he has died this way, every other death becomes more tolerable, less absurd. But the mysterious transformation his death provides extends beyond physical death to every traumatic experience of shame. Christians who have suffered severe abuse in childhood bring their shame to prayer and religious liturgy. There they encounter someone who has survived profound social shame—Jesus, who has been humbled without being destroyed. Though ridiculed, his worth has not been lowered. Though exposed in all his vulnerability, he has not been found inferior. Rejected by society, he has been embraced by God. This extraordinary event encourages Christians to dare to expose their hidden shame to the Lord and feel its power dissolve.

In the account of Jesus' death in Matthew's Gospel we are told that "the veil of the Temple was torn in two from top to bottom" (27:51). This barrier between the divine and the human, so necessary since our expulsion from the garden, is pulled away. This sudden revelation of the sacred echoes the exposure of Jesus' body on the cross. The hidden is revealed and the secret made public. An ancient religious arrangement has come to an end, and with it the rules for public shame.

The author of the letter to the Hebrews interprets the tearing of the veil this way: we now have "confidence to enter the sanctuary by the blood of Jesus, by the new and living way he has opened for us through the curtain (that is, through his flesh)" (Heb 10:19–20). The message is the revolutionary gift of the incarnation: in Jesus we see God in the flesh, we meet God face to face. The traditionally necessary boundaries protecting us from God's awesome presence are removed.

We find a clue to the transforming power of Jesus' death in a similar fate recorded in the beautiful poetry of Isaiah. "A suffering servant" undergoes a death that is cloaked in social shame: "He was despised and the most abject of men, a man of sorrows and acquainted with infirmity. One from whom others hid their faces. He was despised and we took no account of him" (Is 53:3). But then the poet suggests the mysterious power of this suffering: "Surely he has borne our infirmities and carried our diseases. . . . Upon him the punishment that made us whole, and by his bruises we are healed" (Is 53:4–5).

What do Christians mean when we say of the suffering servant that "by his bruises we are healed"? Seeing Jesus face his death with courage and integrity powerfully affects us. When we observe that he is not humiliated by the shameful circumstance of his suffering, we wonder if we need be so ashamed of our pain. His disregarding of the shamefulness of his death encourages us to see our shame differently, to begin to question the need to conceal and hide our woundedness. Perhaps we too can expose our shame to God, to a counselor, or to a close friend. When we are so empowered, shame begins to lose its control over us. We begin to disregard the shamefulness of our own injuries and can say, "By his bruises we are healed."

The success of social shaming insures its survival. Threats of ridicule or rejection will continue to enforce conformity and guarantee compliance. But other resources, companions of psychological maturing and religious faith, can equip us to explore alternate measures of our worth. Our Christian heritage, despite its frequent complicity in social shaming, offers us opportunities to redefine belonging, to convert our thirst for vengeance into a willingness to forgive and to heal our shame.

Reflective Exercise

All of us have experienced social shaming; many of us have used shaming as a strategy ourselves. Begin this reflection by recalling a recent occasion when some technique of social shaming was used against you. The setting may have been your work site, your extended family, the civic community, or the church.

First, identify the shaming strategies involved. Were you belittled or excluded or silenced or mocked or the recipient of another form of shaming? Give examples to show concretely what was involved.

How did these shaming techniques affect you? Can you recall the threat you felt? How did you respond—your thoughts, emotions, actions? What resources helped you deal with or resist this effort to shame you?

Finally, in what ways has your religious experience been a help in your efforts to heal the effects of social shaming? In what ways has it been a hindrance?

Additional Resources

In *The Many Faces of Shame* Donald L. Nathanson offers a broad synthesis of current research perspectives on shame; see especially chapter 8, "Shaming Systems in Couples, Families and Institutions." See also his *Shame and Pride: Affect, Sex, and the Birth of the Self.* June

Price Tangney and Ronda L. Dearing discuss the social dimensions of shame in *Shame and Guilt: Emotions and Social Behavior.* Carl Schneider speaks suggestively of the significance of Jesus' death for the transformation of shame in *Shame, Exposure, and Privacy,* see page 115. Elizabeth Janeway offers wise and provocative counsel for dealing with social dynamics of shaming in *Improper Behavior: When and How Misconduct Can Be Healthy for Society.* In *Vital Involvement: The Experience of Old Age in Our Time,* Erik Erikson, Joan M. Erikson, and Helen Q. Kivnick trace connections between early personal experiences of shame and later life experience.

For an example of silencing used as a strategy within the religious community, see theologian Charles Curran's discussion of his personal and professional experience in *Faithful Dissent.* In his discussion of spirituality, *Taking a Chance on God,* John McNeill looks at shame's relevance to the religious experience of lesbian, gay, and transgendered Christians; see also his reflections in *Sex as God Intended.*

Part Four

HIDDEN GIFTS

Grief, Loneliness, Fear

The Chinese character for change *(hua)* includes biological alterations, cultural changes, and spiritual transformations.

10

The Gift of Grief

I am worn out with groaning,
*   every night I drench my pillow*
and soak my bed with tears;
*   my eyes are wasted with grief.*

—PSALM 6:6

"No one told me grief feels so much like fear." C. S. Lewis, stunned by
the death of his wife, offered this lament. The pain of grief sounds
the alarm, inviting us to face a threat we would rather flee. Grief is
intensely personal; we feel it in our bones. And this emotion is acutely
social; our familiar way of being in the world is in jeopardy. When
we are faced with a profound loss, we recoil. This cannot be happening. This is unfair. Beneath these reactions stirs fear: will I survive?

For most of us, the powerful emotion of grief arrives not as a single
sentiment but in a bubbling emotional stew. This volatile mix includes
shock, disbelief, and anger along with fear, guilt, sadness, and shame.
In grief, these searing feelings surface unpredictably—sometimes alone,
often in strange combinations—stirred by the haunting realization
that a part of our life is being stripped away. We find our way through
the desert of grief by sharing our stories of loss and by visiting again
and again the classic accounts of this mysterious dynamic. So we begin with a story shared from the life of a friend.

Fifteen years ago, after a terrifying night fearing that the eight-
month baby I was carrying had ceased moving, I heard the shat-
tering words "fatal demise." The emergency-room physician
explained that in most cases like this, labor begins within a few
days. All we could do now is wait. So my husband and I went
home to explain to our young daughters that I would be going

135

back to the hospital soon. But I was crying, we explained, because the baby was not well enough to be born alive and would not be coming home with us then.

A week passed, and my doctor examined me in his office. "For some women," he explained, "labor takes as long as several weeks to begin." It seemed as though I would never stop crying. I was afraid the labor would begin, bringing its physical pain without the reward of a living baby. I was afraid the labor would not begin, leaving me suspended in this state of life and death.

At home, a sense of isolation deepened my distress. We had moved to this new neighborhood only a few months earlier, and now I dreadfully missed the friends we had left behind. The mother of one of our children's new friends came by. I hardly knew her, but she listened to my anger; I was angry with myself, angry with the doctor, angry with God. A few days later she returned with a wonderful gift—a list of twenty people who had offered to pray with me. When I went into labor, I was to call the person who had signed to pray at that particular time of day, that person would call the next, and so on. Throughout the hours of labor I would be held in prayer, supported by these new friends and acquaintances. The presence of that prayer list, attached to the refrigerator door, helped me through the anguish of the next weeks. When labor did begin, I contacted a person on the prayer list even before the doctor.

In the months following the stillbirth of our son, I would withdraw in the evenings to reflect on the events and feelings of the day. The week of his due date was so painful; I just held still and let the emotion wash over me. For months I had carried new life; for three weeks I had felt death and carried death within me. I had been the cradle and the tomb for my son. Now I had the painful work of mourning his loss. Many days I longed to hold and nurse a baby instead of holding and nursing these feelings of confusion and understanding, of anger and forgiveness. But in the midst of mourning, surprisingly, I could feel new life arising.

For the next year my husband and I discussed the wisdom of opening ourselves to another child. The night we decided to say yes to the possibility of conceiving a child, I became pregnant. On Palm Sunday our son was born. I held this new life in my arms, fully aware of the Paschal Mystery, which links all those who have died and all those who are fully living.

As an emotion, grief registers significant loss. But the term *grieving* names more than this normal-yet-painful emotional response. Grieving also identifies the healing process of befriending loss. The process carries us through the tasks of mourning: reconciling with what is ending, recognizing how the past still continues with us now, and responding with hope to what lies ahead. But this process seldom proceeds in a straight line. Instead, propelled by grief, we careen among endings, beginnings, and the losses these entail.

Traditionally in American culture the bereaved have been counseled to turn away from grief. Facing loss, the goal has been to master our feelings, to forget the past, to pull ourselves together, and to move on. This refusal of grief has a long heritage in Western culture. Marcus Aurelius, who was both Roman emperor and Stoic philosopher, judged that grief was a weakness—a fainthearted refusal to accept the reality of loss. For stoics, both then and now, grieving does us no good.

The Gospels provide a different scenario. When Jesus learns that his friend Lazarus has died, he rushes to the family's home and meets the mourners assembled there. Seeing the family and friends weeping, Jesus "was greatly disturbed in spirit and deeply moved. He said, 'Where have you laid him?' They said to him, 'Lord, come and see.' And Jesus began to weep" (Jn 11:33).

Throughout the Gospels we find Jesus moved by grief. Recognizing that his deepest hopes for Jerusalem and its people will not be realized, Jesus sits looking over the city, filled with sorrow and regret. Alone and abandoned by his closest friends the night before his death, he wrestles with the apparent defeat of his life's mission. Grief is not an emotion Jesus avoids; he embraces its demands, facing his losses and struggling to find his way through sorrow to hope.

Grief announces loss, but it promises more than annihilation. The pain sounds an alarm, alerting us that something significant is being stripped away. Grief's alarm is meant to be a signal pointing out the path to healing, not a detour that stalls us in place. And when we are well supported, the distress itself can spur us along the necessary path of mourning.

The Path of the Grieving Process

Everyone's journey through grief is unique. So predicting a grieving person's experience is risky business. And attempting to assign—for ourselves or other people—certain stages to mark our progress often just adds to the pain. But we can recognize some common elements, some patterns that seem to describe the movement of effective grieving.

Grief often arrives first as shock and denial. As the certainty of the loss sinks in, denial dissolves and we struggle to cope with the painful truth that now confronts us. In time we may come to embrace this new reality, now transformed through the disciplines of grieving. To complete this journey through grief toward recovery, most of us need help to recognize what has been lost, to respect and express our pain, and to honor loss in life-affirming ways.

Recognizing What Has Been Lost

In the early stages of shock people need help accepting the loss as real. But we resist recognizing loss because a deeper question haunts us: without this cherished—or at least accustomed—part of our life, how can we move forward?

Accepting loss as real is more difficult when we are not yet sure what is ending for us. And even when we can clearly identify the circumstances that have changed, these public facts do not always explain the depth of our personal loss. Another friend shares her struggle to name a loss that was deeper than its public face. She writes, "Grief caught me unawares. Only gradually did I come to recognize and name what was really at stake."

> When Monica left home for the first time to begin her freshman year in college, she was nervous about being on her own. At the end of her senior year in high school Monica had been diagnosed with an eating disorder, anorexia nervosa. She started seeing a therapist, who recommended that she continue working with a counselor while she was away at college.
>
> Toward the end of the fall semester of Monica's junior year in college, I received a telephone call from her counselor. Monica was experiencing an emotional breakdown. The counselor recommended an immediate sick leave, so that Monica could receive in-depth help. When she felt ready to return, and with her doctor's approval, Monica would be welcomed back to school. This telephone call produced an icy dread, as grief caught me unawares.

With terror and sadness my husband and I set off to rescue Monica from the setting that had nurtured her, we thought, for over two years. Monica returned home, and we set about the challenging task of finding the help she needed. Community support was difficult for us to find in this time of grief and loss, because we were reluctant to share details of her return. At heart, we were ashamed of what had happened, seeing it as a failure both for Monica and for our family.

One unlikely ritual allowed us to begin to bless this loss. On a cold January day Monica and I returned to gather things from her dormitory room. With the other residents away on semester break, the dorm was quiet as a tomb. For several lonely and shame-filled hours, Monica and I packed her books and clothing and removed posters from the walls. As we started the drive home, I was exhausted and heartbroken; my dream of being able to protect my daughter from pain was shattered.

At home I tried to be open to what was happening for my daughter but my attempts were halfhearted. My job, as I saw it, was to keep Monica focused on completing her college degree. In the spring she returned to college to make up her final exams and to decide what her next steps might be. I held out the hope she would return there in the fall for her final year of studies. Back at home, Monica announced instead that she planned to transfer to a local university where she could major in dance. Her most confirming experiences in college, Monica confessed, had been her dance classes there. Her instructors assured her she had talent, and more important, she knew that dancing made her feel alive. What I was still too blind to see was the shape of Monica's new dream, already emerging in the sadness of her suffering.

Instead of taking time to reflect on what this decision meant to Monica, I put up resistance. As one would expect, our relationship suffered as I tried to move her in a direction that made more sense to me. Gradually, with the persistent help of a family friend who loves us both, I came to understand that Monica had been struggling with a learning disability. This realization has set us on a path toward understanding.

And gradually I was able to recognize—and to admit—the deeper loss I had been struggling with. Through these hard months of sadness and resistance I was grieving a dream at the heart of my identity as a mother: that I could protect my children from pain. Naming this loss opened me again to the mystery of life through death.

Standing with Monica in her search has helped me appreciate the very difficult work she has accomplished. With her suffering Monica has shown all of us in the family how significant our emotions are, how our fear and shame and anger often point the way to necessary change. Even our griefs carry gifts.

Respecting Painful Feelings

People need help dealing with grief's pain. As the initial shock and disbelief ebb, misery swamps us. A host of physical and emotional symptoms—irritability, anxiety, remorse, inability to sleep, lack of appetite, fatigue—signal our distress. These are common reactions during the acute phase of grief. Recognizing this distress as normal often helps people cope: "These dreadful feelings are not shameful, immature, or crazy; this is what loss feels like. Other sorrowing people have felt like this: I *should* feel this bad."

Finding ways to express these painful feelings helps us move toward acceptance. Grief alerts us to losses that threaten our sense of self and the stability of our established world. In the presence of a trusted listener, we find courage to explore our distress, testing the truth of grief's claims. A safe setting where we can voice our concern and confusion often eases the pain of bereavement. The struggle to put our feelings into words brings both insight and relief. In the midst of this struggle we come to appreciate—however slowly—that we will not feel this bad forever. One day we will be able to remember this beloved person, or this lost dream, or this experience of failure without being engulfed by the acute pain we experience now.

Gradually, we even come to recognize our pain as purposeful. Early on, grief shuts us down and threatens to close us in on ourselves. This withdrawal may be protective, providing the space we need for reflection or simply time to absorb the shock. But as grief's painful arousal continues, it brings us back to the present and compels us through the essential tasks of remembrance and reconciliation.

Holding the Loss in Memory

Effective grieving helps us gradually to accept the reality of our loss. But how are we to carry this loss into our future? Here we confront a central task of grieving: to create a cherishable memory. "There is an intimate connection between our capacity to hope and our capacity to remember," pastoral theologian Herbert Anderson insists. Remembering "may not be initially consoling—if by consoling we mean 'calming,' 'soothing,' or 'giving relief' from pain. However, remembering is consoling in a deeper sense because it makes it possible for people to hope." Revisiting the past so that we may honor what we have lost is not easy. But this arduous work brings transformation. Gradually, our loss becomes real to us in new ways, now in treasured and trustworthy memory. Without this transformation we are truly bereft. Until we have memories that we can cherish, pain is our only connection with what we have lost. Herb Anderson offers this good counsel to "any who wish to care for people when they have suffered a loss. Don't take their grief away. Even when we cannot bear their pain, we must honor their grief and their need to keep it. Until they have a memory, it is all they have."

But the effort of remembering forces us to face our mixed emotions about the past. Grief awakens a full range of ambivalent feelings: resentment over what has been taken away, regret for "what might have been," remorse about our own actions, even relief that an infirm loved one has finally died . . . followed by guilt for having these feelings! A common defense is to retreat into nostalgia, building up faulty images of a perfect family or an untroubled marriage or a career that was completely satisfying. But nostalgia only delays our movement through grief toward healing. Memories that help us heal are those that acknowledge the ambiguity of our losses and the ambivalence of our grief.

Reconnecting with Life on the Other Side of Loss

In the midst of the tasks of grieving, the tasks of living continue. In time, those who have suffered serious loss report a gradual—still unpredictable—return of energy and focus. The future can now be faced. As awareness of personal competence and confidence slowly return, the work of grieving shifts from reconciling with what has been lost to gathering resources for the journey ahead. Recommitting ourselves to the future includes its own delicate and necessary work. Just as we must clarify what needs to be left behind, we must also recognize the relationships and responsibilities—sometimes neglected in the heart of our grief—that continue to shape our life. These sources of stability can be crucial as we attempt to identify the risks the future holds and determine how these risks will be minimized. Finding support helps make risk reasonable. So strengthening the relationships that nurture our resolve and hold us accountable becomes crucial.

Effective grieving helps us acknowledge that we are not just victims of our losses. We participate in this movement; we are agents in the entry back into life now. Often in grief we feel deprived of our sense of *active mastery*—the competence and control that mark so much of adult maturity. But a complementary strength becomes familiar. Emerging from the dark tunnel of mourning, we can appreciate the experience of *receptive mastery*—as we have learned to let go, we have "been delivered" from our pain; we have "come through." And we are able to honor the return of hope, with its promise for the future.

Spirituality and Grief—How We Hold Our Hurt

Grief hurts. And because grief is so painful we are tempted to hold it off, to hold it down, to hold it out of sight. We do not want this loss; we cannot face this disappointment. So in an effort to deny our grief, we divert our attention. Intent that our grief remain hidden, perhaps even from ourselves, we hold our pain out of view. We turn instead for available remedies—overwork or alcohol, pharmaceuticals or pornography—for short-term relief. Catching ourselves in these patterns, we recognize this is not God's design. Refusing our grief seldom leads us to new life.

Sometimes we cling to grief by holding our hurt in chronic complaint. Then, instead of privatizing our loss, we publicize it—repeatedly. We complain and assign blame, but no healing results. The Bible provides a good example of this strategy. Soon after our ancient ancestors had escaped from Egypt, their exhilaration gave way to criticism. The desert, devoid of food and shelter and a sense of direction, seemed not much of an improvement on captivity. The text reports that some of the people gathered at the doors of their tents and "murmured against Moses and their leaders." They made their pain public, even if their grumbling might not quite reach the people in charge. This pattern continues many places in contemporary life: we find fault, we complain, nothing changes. The strategy does vent some frustration, but most often it proves ineffective. If we are alert, we come to see quickly that this form of grieving brings little relief.

A classic example of chronic grief comes as a parent's response to the loss of a child through illness or accident. Some parents determine to keep the child's room exactly as it was, attempting to create a shrine that freezes time. Here too, the effort to look away from the loss delays the healing dynamics of grieving.

But another path of grieving lies open to us: holding our losses up to God and turning our pain into prayer. This is the robust response that our biblical ancestors knew as lamentation. "Since I have lost all taste for life, I will give free rein to my complaints; I shall let my embittered soul speak out" (Jb 10:1). "All you who pass this way, look and see: Is there any sorrow like the sorrow that afflicts me, with which Yahweh has struck me on the day of his burning anger?" (Lm 1:12). This strategy for grief is exemplified in the Wailing Wall in Jerusalem; it also is shown in the tradition of "singing the blues" among African Americans, mindful of the history of slavery and the continuing indignities of discrimination. In both these public lamentations, those who suffered found a rhythm that revealed their pain; their losses found a voice. Released into the light of day—and thus shared—suffering does not destroy us. Instead, our grief is humanized.

Kathleen O'Connor underscores the power of grief's lament:

Lamentation can shred the heart and spawn despair, but, paradoxically, by mirroring pain it can also comfort the afflicted and open the way toward healing. It can affirm the dignity of those who suffer, release their tears, and overcome their experience of abandonment.

Biblical scholar Walter Brueggemann sums up the strategy of such prayer: "The daring speech of earth, when done with passion and shrillness, can change the affairs of heaven," and the hope that "pain brought to speech and made available in the community . . . is the mediator of new life."

The Role of Ritual

Lived in a vital community, Christian faith becomes a school of the emotions. Part of Christianity's vocation is to proclaim the life of Jesus as the model for us to follow in pursuit of a passionate life. Theologian William Spohn reminds us that the texts of sacred scripture "do not directly dictate what to do." Instead, by tutoring the imagination, these stories invite us to experience life as deeply and strongly as Jesus did. Gospel memories, stories of saints, liturgical devotions, shared prayer—these resources show us how to feel, how to respond to our delight and our depression, how to honor both our gratitude and our grief. For many in the community of faith, religious rituals play a privileged role in our seasons of grief.

Rituals are bodily gestures that call attention to some part of life. Rituals—whether a marriage ceremony or a funeral procession—offer ways to hold our powerful emotions. As Thomas Driver has remarked, "Ritual controls emotion while releasing it and guides it while letting it run." Rituals provide boundaries within which we can give full rein to our feelings. These communal boundaries, provided by the believers who stand with us, are strong enough to protect us in a time of great loss. Here we can fall apart, because we will be held. Here it is safe to feel as bad as we feel.

Ritual's second gift is to fold our pain into a larger narrative. The force of our loss—"surely no one can know how bad this feels"—heightens our sense of isolation. The gift of religious ritual reminds us of the larger story that, on better days, we have embraced: Jesus, too, has come this way. He has fallen and failed; he knew misunderstanding and betrayal and death. For him, grief became the door to life. This gospel story, reverently recalled, resonates with our own journey. Even now, in this terrible time, we are following Christ. Could our present troubles be part of the plot?

The third gift of ritual is to provide the pacing that leads us through loss toward renewed life. Grief stops us in our tracks, freezing us in the past or bending us into circles of chronic complaint. In rituals of grieving we step aside from our ordinary routines, but life does not come to a halt. In recognition of our loss, we slow our activities but we do not remain rooted in the past. The funeral procession provides a vivid example: the measured pace of our movement is a public display of our grief. But the ritual itself provides a momentum that carries us into the future.

A hospital chaplain shared this story of a ritual of grieving, spontaneously performed, that helped a grieving family move through a tragic loss.

The chaplain was called to a room where a ten-year-old girl lay dying from a massive and ravaging infection. The parents and siblings stood around her bed, numbed by the disaster. To the chaplain they seemed frozen in their grief. When the chaplain mentioned the dying girl's beautiful hair, the mother nodded, adding that her daughter loved to take special care of her hair. From this cue, the chaplain suggested that the whole family help to wash and shampoo her hair one last time. A basin of warm water and towels were brought in. Together, the family took turns stroking the dying girl's face as they lavished shampoo and conditioner on her hair. A hair dryer appeared and the mother dried and shaped her daughter's hair "just the way she liked it." Through all the gestures of this simple but profound ritual, the family members allowed themselves to touch the girl with affection. With this ritual accomplished, they seemed more ready for the inevitable task of turning off the machinery of artificial life support.

Graceful grieving, then, is a question of holding: a very special kind of embrace. Learning to grieve in ways that heal relaxes our grip on our losses. We resist the temptation to hold our hurt away or out of sight; we refuse the inclination to hold our injuries in endless, chronic complaint. Instead we struggle to bring our distress before God, praying that our losses may be honored and transformed. Praying our losses, we respect our pain even as we resist it; thus begins the process of grieving. Theologian David Power has said it best: "What is remembered in grief is redeemed, made whole, renewed." Now our loss finds its voice. Rather than holding distress at a distance, prayer becomes a way we say yes to our grief.

Along this painful journey we learn to honor what has been lost, to welcome what continues, and to open ourselves to the promise the future holds. On the way we come to embrace a deeper truth: grief is a salutary emotion, a necessary virtue that guides us through treacherous times. Its arousal ignites the dreadful feeling that something essential is perishing. The process of grieving prompts us to evaluate what we must let go. It stirs us to lamentation, with its cleansing if scalding effect. Finally, grief's energy impels us toward the future, uncharted but full of God's promise.

Reflective Exercise

Bring to mind a memory of loss from your own life; be sure to focus on an experience in which the process of grieving has already begun.

And take care of yourself as you move through this reflection, honoring the power of the emotions that may be evoked.

Prayerfully placing yourself in the presence of God's consoling spirit, recall some of the circumstances of this loss . . . who, what, when, how, why, with what result?

Then let the questions that are part of the grieving process arise: Can you identify what has been lost? Have you been able to express the feelings that are part of your grief? How do you hold this loss in memory now? What rituals—formal or spontaneous—have been part of your journey in grieving this loss?

Additional Resources

Experienced counselors provide both information and support for those experiencing grief: see Deborah Coryell, *Good Grief: Healing through the Shadows of Loss;* Thomas Ellis, *This Thing Called Grief: New Understandings of Loss;* Elisabeth Kubler-Ross and David Kessler, *On Grief and Grieving: Finding the Meaning of Grief through the Five Stages of Loss.*

Pastoral theologian Herbert Anderson continues to make significant contributions in clarifying the psychological dynamics of grieving and in describing effective ministry responses; see, for example, his now classic discussion in *All Our Losses, All Our Griefs: Resources for Pastoral Care,* co-authored with Kenneth Mitchell. We quote here from his later essay "What Consoles?" page 378.

Kathleen O'Connor examines the healing dynamic of lamentation in *Lamentation and the Tears of the World.* Walter Brueggemann explores grieving in his *The Prophetic Imagination.* In *Love and Loss: The Roots of Grief and Its Complications,* Colin Murray Parks provides an integrated perspective on the psychological issues that surround the grieving process. In *Healing through the Dark Emotions: The Wisdom of Grief, Fear, and Despair,* Miriam Greenspan offers an insightful consideration of role of the painful emotions in personal growth; this volume includes valuable exercises to guide readers in further reflection on each of these "dark emotions."

David Power's comment on grieving appeared in his "Households of Faith in the Coming Church," page 253; see William Spohn's discussion entitled "Jesus and Christian Ethics"; we quote from page 104. We quote Thomas Driver from page 156 in *The Magic of Ritual.*

11

Learning from Loneliness

My God, my God ... why have you forsaken me?
                                        —Mark 15:34

Loneliness is our response to the anguish of being alone. Separated from those we love, we experience sorrow, longing, helplessness. We may be angry or resentful; we are likely to sense frustration, even bitterness. Most of all, we feel abandoned. Our distress becomes especially acute in the face of personal loss—the death of a spouse, betrayal by a trusted colleague, the gradual erosion of a friendship that was once strong. These experiences deepen our dismay. A relationship that was of great significance to us is now gone. Confronted by this searing absence, we respond in the pain and panic of loneliness.

Loneliness passes judgment on our interpersonal world, signaling that our links with other people are not sustaining us. Sometimes our difficulty comes in making contact—reaching out to another person, even when we want to, is hard. Sometimes we feel distant from those who are nearby: we do not fit in, we do not belong. Often loneliness arises from a painful conflict, some significant disagreement that separates us from one another.

Loneliness questions our connections with other people. Perhaps our ties are too few, perhaps they are too superficial. Maybe we are asking too much from people, or maybe we are settling for too little. Paradoxically, this painful feeling can be a special ally of intimacy. The distress that loneliness brings can serve a good purpose by challenging the illusions we harbor about the place of other people in our lives.

Loneliness, then, is a bad feeling about something good—relationships. Our distress announces that something is wrong. The pain that grabs our attention points beyond itself to an important area of our life that demands scrutiny. By facing this uncomfortable emotion, we can discern the source of our distress.

Times to Be Lonely

Feelings of loneliness are common, but the circumstances that give rise to these feelings differ in important ways. During a quiet evening alone we may feel a twinge of sadness or a stirring of regret. But this mood does not overpower us. We are familiar with this feeling, so we can be patient and simply turn our attention elsewhere. Sociologist Robert Weiss estimates that as many as one quarter of the population feels "extremely lonely" at some time during any given month. For most of us, this experience passes without much disruption. But sometimes when loneliness stirs we are tempted to take the emotion too seriously. Making too much of this melancholy mood, we sink into self-pity. And feeling sorry for ourselves, we are easily distracted from the insight loneliness brings: a richer appreciation of the separateness of our lives and the incompleteness of our relationships.

Other experiences of loneliness are familiar, too. Changing circumstances may trigger *situational* loneliness. These instances of loneliness are sometimes easier to deal with because we can identify the cause. A dear friend dies, leaving an enormous gap in our life; but in our grief we at least know why we feel lonely. Or a job transfer moves us across country to a new city. As our initial excitement subsides, the realization suddenly dawns—we have left old friends behind! Panic assaults us. Will we be able to make any friends in this new location? In both of these examples a significant change has seriously altered our network of sustaining relationships. We have experienced a clear rupture in our interpersonal world.

Other experiences of loneliness are more *developmental*, triggered by the necessary losses in life. When young adults leave home, both child and parent are likely to be lonely. But this loss is more than situational. In this separation each person leaves behind something significant, a part of his or her life that will not be regained. The young adults experience the loneliness of being strangers in a strange land. Suddenly they must rely on themselves in new and unfamiliar ways. On some days this experience of independence is exhilarating. But often they feel alienated from past relationships and even from an earlier sense of self, as they test new identities. The loneliness of both young adult and parent is tinged with nostalgia for the "good old days." For both, maturity demands a leave taking in which loneliness is a normal companion.

Developmental loneliness often emerges in midlife. A husband in his early forties feels a growing dismay. He shares a house with his wife and two teenagers, but he feels strangely alone. Questions plague him about his job: "Is this really what I want to do for the rest of my life?" He wonders about his relationship with his wife: "What will our life together be like when our children are gone?" These questions frighten him and may isolate him from his family. A painful mood of loneliness often accompanies these important midlife reevaluations. He needs to face these questions, not flee them. By finding his own rhythm of letting go and recommitment, he can recover the energy and affection he has lost.

Psychologist Robert Kegan suggests that these experiences of developmental loneliness accompany us across the life span. In his influential model of cognitive development, Kegan describes the path by which our capacity to deal with diversity and change matures. He identifies a range of strategies along this path, marked by an expanding capacity to make sense of the complexity that confronts us in everyday life. Each strategy moves us "beyond" the comfort of an earlier cognitive style. Each step in this developmental movement places us outside a previously familiar context, a formerly satisfying way of making sense of life. This break forces us to reinterpret our self-understanding and values and our way of being with other people. This is a lonely experience of maturity, provoking a sense of separation—even alienation—from much that previously was comfortable and familiar. Happily, this developmental loneliness diminishes as the new level of cognitive complexity becomes more firmly established. Once again, we are at home in our world.

But sometimes loneliness becomes *chronic*. We fall into a mood of alienation and sorrow that seems to have no apparent cause. No special situation, no identifiable challenge is involved. We have just slipped into a pervasive mood of estrangement. This devastating mood moves us into self-doubt and self-contempt. When we are lonely for a long time, we typically start to blame ourselves rather than our circumstances. We conclude, "I am alone because I am unattractive and unlovable. I deserve to be lonely!" This self-castigation further depletes our energy to do anything to change the situation. We can see no way out, since our wretched self—not the situation—is at fault. A sense of unworthiness limits our attempts to establish more satisfying contacts. In a mood of chronic loneliness we may develop unrealistic expectations about friendships and intimacy. As we long for the ideal partner who would rescue us from this crippling mood, we overlook the familiar companions who could support us now. Often unrecognized dynamics of shame fuel this kind of chronic loneliness.

Lonely Men; Lonely Women

Both men and women experience a need for closeness, a sense of personal vulnerability, the desire to be able to depend on others. But many men have learned that these feelings are unacceptable for the "real" man. This conflict between personal needs and gender demands often leads to an ambivalence about relationships. Afraid to appear vulnerable, a man may hesitate to admit, to himself or others, that he needs other people. This reluctance generates a cautious interpersonal style; he acts somewhat diffident, a bit distant, emotionally cool.

The distress of loneliness can shatter these illusions of self-sufficiency. For the man who has been pursuing the cultural ideal of the autonomous and self-sufficient male, the pain reminds him of how much he wants and needs other people in his life. Loneliness may energize him to change the way he deals with other people, especially those close to him. This emotion can make a man more respectful of his companions along the journey, more grateful for their friendship. Loneliness benefits a man when it encourages him to acknowledge his need for other people and readies him to respond to the requirements of real mutuality.

For women, loneliness sometimes provokes a different purification. Both men and women learn much about themselves from the responses of people who are close to them; women and men alike depend on relationships for solace and support. But many women rely in a special way on their relationships to nourish an adult sense of identity and self-worth. This reliance on relationships does not mean that competence and career are meaningless to women. Rather, it signifies that the public world of work is not as exclusive a source of personal identity for women as it is for many men.

Typically, then, women develop self-esteem and a sense of security in the give and take of their interpersonal world. Taken to an extreme, this dependence on relationships may leave a woman unsure whether her own resources are sufficient. Psychic survival is more the issue here than economic survival. If her sense of self relies too heavily on her relationships, a woman's deeper question is how—or even if—she can thrive outside these connections. So relationships hold her captive. In a troubled marriage, for example, she cannot risk making demands because she cannot face the possibility that the relationship will end. Even an unhappy association—physically violent or emotionally arid—will seem better than no relationship at all.

For a woman like this, the distress of loneliness presents an opportunity to examine her relationships more critically, to reassess the imbalance between what she gives and what she receives, to challenge her conviction that she cannot survive on her own. Loneliness then becomes an ally, because not until a relationship disappoints her is she able to question her assumptions. Let down by a relationship upon which she is overly dependent, a woman initially feels lonely. But if she can face her panic and resist self-destructive behavior, the woman may begin to question her basic assumption that she cannot find these essential strengths within herself.

"I can survive on my own!" For many women this affirmation is a gift of loneliness. With this new strength comes a sense of freedom, as a woman recognizes choices: "I may choose the give-and-take of close relationships, with the personal accommodation and sacrifice that are often required. But I do this because a life of intimacy is worth the trouble; it is rewarding and life-giving even as it is demanding. But I have a choice, since I know that if I have to, I can survive on my own." This brings more freedom into a woman's relationships. She can be less demanding and more flexible, since her very survival is not at stake.

Loneliness, as a special ally of intimacy, invites us to purify our expectations of other people. This purification equips us for genuine interdependence. For some (men), loneliness helps us become more open to the risks and demands of genuine interdependence. Admitting our vulnerability, we can let others know how important they are to us and how much we need them. For some (women), loneliness helps us become more confident in our ability to stand apart from the demands of relationships. Acknowledging our strength, we realize that we can care for and sustain ourselves. Recognizing the legitimacy of our needs, we approach those close to us in ways that support genuine mutuality.

Exploring Our Interpersonal World

Loneliness sometimes seems unjustified. "How can I have this empty feeling," we ask ourselves, "when my life seems to be going so well? I have friends, my family appreciates me. So why do I feel so alone?" We can be well loved and still feel lonely. This paradox reminds us of the complexity of our social world. Different kinds of relationships make different contributions to our lives. For example, we all need people we can count on, no matter what. Whether or not they are blood relatives, these folks are like family to us. Other relationships bring other benefits: the acceptance we receive from a trusted confidant, the sense of solidarity we feel with people who share our values, the delight we experience as we enjoy an evening with friends. We are nurtured by the unwavering devotion of our intimates. However, we also need more objective colleagues who can recognize our competence and appreciate our skills. The support of a mentor, the love of our spouse, the affection of our children, the respect of co-workers— each of these gifts comes from a *particular* kind of relationship. These benefits, however, are not interchangeable. A friend's devotion enriches our life, for example, but does not cancel out the isolation we may feel at work.

Loneliness signals a relationship in pain. Relationships come "in the particular," each with different benefits and burdens. When we are lonely, our distress points to inadequacy in a particular part of our relational world.

To be sure, our anguish over a failed marriage differs from our disappointment that none of our friends shares our passion for political reform. But both these experiences can provoke the unease of loneliness—the sense that we are adrift, without the bonds that effectively link us with other people. To deal effectively with loneliness, we must identify where the pain is pointing. The remedy is easier to find when we know where the hurt is.

Invitations to Solitude

In the many separations that mark a life, we face being alone. Parents die, jobs end, our children or our friends move away. We are further tutored in our separateness as curiosity or anger or grief sets us out on journeys that lead us far from home: But what does our being alone signify: adventure? abandonment? blessed relief?

In loneliness we are not at ease with ourselves. Our inner world is a realm of many inhabitants—memories good and bad, consolations along with disappointments, guilt, and regrets. Confronted with this discomforting array, we are tempted to flee. Anything to avoid these painful recognitions! But if we remain uncomfortable with the inhabitants of our heart, we will have a difficult time being alone. Any absence—of friends or work or entertainment—will come as lethal emptiness, opening space into which sad or guilty memories flood. Learning to live with some of the limits and mistakes that are part of life, we are more "at home" with ourselves. There is less need to hide from our own history, even marked as it is by the scars of our personal past.

In loneliness we feel separated from valued others; we seem alienated from our own interior resources. At times like this, being alone is especially painful. So we busy ourselves with more work or turn up the music or pour another drink. But a different possibility exists: the invitation to solitude. In solitude, being alone does not panic or punish us. More comfortable with quiet, we come to treasure time apart. Solitude is not just another name for self-sufficiency; instead it signals integrity.

Solitude helps us befriend absence. The absence that accompanies the death of a friend invites us to accept the loss even as we hold this memory precious. Here absence generates both gratitude and hope. Anyone who prays must befriend absence; some days God's absence is louder than our prayer. But if we have become familiar with absence, God's occasional silence does not discourage us. We recall God's presence in our past, and we look forward in hope to God's return. In the time between, we can tolerate the stillness.

A Christian Script for Solitude

Christians find their script for solitude in the scriptures—particularly in the stories and memories of Jesus and his companions. The gospel account of Jesus' life is framed by two incidents of searing solitude. At the beginning of his public life, after his baptism by John, "the Spirit immediately drove him out into the wilderness" (Mk 1:12). Matthew and Luke enhance Mark's memory with the detail of Jesus' fasting that left him, at the end of these forty days, "famished" (Mt 4:1; Lk 4:1). The desert serves solitude, both symbolically and literally, by stripping away everyday activities and ordinary company. Stilling these social activities invites the "deserted" Jesus to search inwardly for motivation and to assess his resources for the journey ahead.

As Jesus approached his death, the Gospel of Mark records a briefer, more terrible aloneness. Separated from his friends and suspended on a cross, Jesus cries out, "My God, my God, why have you abandoned me?" (Mk 15:34). This alarming sense of abandonment startles the believer. How could Jesus, beloved son of God, feel so wretched? How could he experience such disorientation and desolation? But there it is, recorded in sacred scripture . . . and significant for Jesus' life and our own.

Between these two memories—aloneness in the desert and the desolation of approaching death—other stories of solitude fill out the Christian script. Jesus is informed of the death of his mentor, John the Baptist. "Now, when he heard this, he withdrew from there in a boat to a deserted place by himself." Stunned by grief, Jesus needed to get away, to be alone for a time. But his hope for solitude was thwarted; the crowds would not leave him. Only after speaking with them is he able to get away. Finally he "went up the mountain by himself to pray. When evening came he was there, alone" (Mt 14:23).

Like us, Jesus needed periods of quiet and retreat, time to think things over, opportunities to savor events that cannot be digested on the run or in a crowd. Like Jesus, we need to develop the disciplines of intimacy and solitude, learning how to live with other people and, at times, how to live apart from them. The Christian script alerts us to expect loneliness. This painful experience may teach us to embrace life in even richer ways.

Alone in the Presence of Another

Psychologists have long been intrigued by the maturing process that begins in the infant's painful discovery that its mother is not an extension of itself. British psychologist D. W. Winnicott directed a series of now-famous studies of children as they tentatively explored their separation from their parents. In one corner of a room Winnicott placed a small child, supplied with new toys and other unfamiliar objects to play with. In another corner the child's mother sat, having been instructed not to offer direction or otherwise interfere with the child's activities. With the parent present in this "detached" way, Winnicott observed that children would quickly become absorbed, displaying curiosity, initiative, and delight in deciding what to do with the novel objects around them.

Winnicott identified this setting as a "holding environment" significant in the child's cognitive and emotional development. The child recognized the mother in the room as a protective presence, available—in Winnicott's words—to "cover the risks." But her presence was not obtrusive; she neither hovered over nor directed the child's actions. With the parent present, but at a distance, the child experienced a special kind of "aloneness." In this context the child learns to concentrate and to play. Winnicott described this developmentally significant experience as being "alone in the presence of another." In the open space of this setting, the child explores its own resources. The child is gaining the capacity to be alone; the child is practicing solitude.

Winnicott found that children deprived of this early experience— those who have not benefited from being "alone in the presence of another"—have greater difficulty learning to concentrate, to play, and to risk. They have more difficulty in finding comfort in being alone. Spiritually observant people may recognize links between this psychological state of separate-while-connected and their relationship with God. Apart from those privileged moments when we feel God's palpable presence, we often experience our prayer as being "alone in the presence of another." Gradually we grow familiar with a loving God who is not always immediately evident in the circumstances of our life, but who remains nonetheless present "to cover the risk."

Learning from Loneliness

Loneliness invites us to purify our expectations, letting go of those that no longer fit. But for loneliness to serve us, we must learn to appreciate its arousal as an ordinary part of life. This emotion is not an automatic sign of our deficiency, nor is it always terrible and debilitating. It is simply loneliness.

Appreciating loneliness also alerts us to its physical demands. Being lonely takes a toll on us, body and spirit. A mature response to loneliness includes the effort to be good to ourselves. The suggestion here is not that we overeat or drink to excess or go on a sexual binge. Being good to ourselves means that we spend time in activities we enjoy; that we pleasure ourselves with a warm bath or comforting massage; that we prepare a special meal; that we contact an understanding friend. In these small "feasts" we balance the unavoidable fasting that loneliness brings.

Appreciating loneliness, we recognize a potential ally. Loneliness can teach us better ways to be close—ways more appropriate to who we really are, more suited to the people in our life, more expressive of our own deepest values, more rewarding for us and for our partners.

Loneliness urges us to action. Moved by this strong emotion, we take steps to expand our range of effective behavior: learning skills of self-disclosure and empathy; finding the courage to face conflict more assertively.

And loneliness also instructs us in patience. Psychologist Erik Erikson devoted his life to the study of those developmental crises "that make patients of us all." Genuine patience has little to do with passivity or self-pity. A hardier resource, patience steadies us to pay attention to our passion and our pain. The virtue of patience readies us to tolerate our distress long enough to discern its message. At one time or another, the emotion of loneliness "makes patients of us all." Learning to be patient, we can embrace this feeling as an ally of our affections.

Seasons of Solitude

Developing our capacity for mature interdependence includes the experience of solitude. But, as British psychologist Adam Phillips warns, "solitude is a . . . potentially fatal journey." On this journey, loneliness warns us that we do not thrive too far from others of our kind. Its arousal does not insist that we scurry back into the fold but reminds us that our separations—whether enforced or chosen—risk removing us from significant sources of nourishment.

As we muster courage to set out on adventures that take us far from home, we test our inner reservoir of strength. Our hope is that these resources will prove reliable along the way. We search for a solitude in which we can become comfortable with our own particularity. In Phillips's evocative vocabulary, solitude acknowledges those "withdrawals from human company" that move us "toward a replenishing privacy." Being alone will sometimes mean deprivation; on other occasions it can mark a privacy that nourishes us. As Christians we easily recall the words from Genesis: "It is not good for man to be alone." But life points to the paradox involved: there are times when it is very good to be alone, when it is necessary and salutary to separate ourselves from other people. This, too, is a lesson of loneliness.

Adam Phillips names adolescence, the often uneasy transition from child to adult, as a significant season of solitude. The increasing separation of the young child from the parent's enveloping presence now becomes the teenager's awkward and often rebellious stance. Adolescents may suddenly be embarrassed by their parents. They do not want to be seen in public with them, to receive their affectionate hugs and kisses. They feel the need to oppose their parents' values and interests, even if they as yet have none of their own to replace them. A common malaise of adolescents is boredom. Like loneliness, boredom serves as a social signal announcing our dissatisfaction with the present state of affairs (at home, at school, in the nation). Boredom carries the harsh judgment that there is nothing worth doing. Teenagers are often disgruntled with their elders' interests. Not yet knowing what they want to do, adolescents are often sure only about what they *do not* want to do. Their goodbyes to an earlier stage are spoken in the language of boredom.

In his therapeutic practice Phillips often met parents who seemed determined that their children would never be bored. Music lessons, ballet practice, and soccer camps filled their schedule, lest the parents suffer the indictment of their children's disinterest. Phillips urges parents to understand boredom not as a scandal but as the signpost of growth. The adolescent is setting out on the restless search for self-direction, an essential guidance system for adult life. In boredom adolescents announce that they are waiting—"waiting for themselves." In this difficult season parents are challenged not to "sabotage the boredom with distraction" but to provide a holding environment in which adolescents are allowed to wait for themselves, even with all the discomfort this waiting entails.

Surprises of Midlife Solitude

As psychologically savvy adults we expect adolescents' ambivalent attempts toward independence; we appreciate their sometimes awkward efforts to defend privacy and seek out solitude. But we are often surprised when, in the midst of the sober responsibilities of our own middle years, we suddenly find ourselves in an acute period of loneliness. Part of our dismay is that we feel so intensely alone, even as we remain surrounded by children, family, and friends. Loneliness seems all wrong, out of place. A participant in one of our courses reports her experience:

> When I get out of balance these days, it feels like loneliness to me. My stomach feels empty, my heart aches, and a sense of darkness envelops me. I feel overwhelmed by the needs of others, not fed by them. If I continue to give of myself, I start feeling alienated from who I am.

The clue to her midlife loneliness may lie in the two phrases "get out of balance" and "feeling alienated from who I am." In midlife, as elsewhere, loneliness serves as a signal, an alert that some significant relationship is in peril. For some, midlife loneliness is situational—following the death of a loved one or a geographic move that separates us from friends. Loneliness like this is painful, but at least it is easy to understand! We can identify the source of our distress. But there is a midlife loneliness that seems unrelated to our relationship with others.

Another course participant recounts his experience:

> When I was in my mid-thirties I was following my early dream, teaching in a foreign country for the Peace Corps. I was enjoying my work and liked my colleagues and friends. One day, while traveling by train to the capital city, I was struck with a terrible loneliness. Where did this come from? I had no clue. The mood lasted about two months and then lifted.

Looking back two decades later, he could see that the moment marked the beginning of a new direction in his life—an orientation that put him at odds with former ideals and commitments.

> Maybe my loneliness was a signal of the conflict inside me. Maybe it was telling me that I was moving away from a former self, an earlier arrangement in my life. Perhaps this painful feeling was warning me, telling me to be sure of the new direction I was about to choose.

These examples may be seen as developmental loneliness. A necessary disturbance erupts, alerting a now experienced adult to new hopes and expressing the tension these hopes provoke. This painful loneliness invites us to face the challenge of an interior reordering of values and commitments. It calls us to reintegrate our life.

Sometimes loneliness signals a slightly different developmental crisis. Many of us profit from the high ideals set out for us by our families and our religious heritage. "To give and not to count the cost." In our teens and early twenties this ideal expanded our life, challenging us to greater generosity. Years later, however, we may realize that "without counting the cost" we have nevertheless paid a high price. The ideals of our youth have continued to motivate us, but now they seem to function more as tyrant than as inspiration. This imbalance between caring for others and caring for myself sometimes registers as loneliness.

Midlife loneliness also occurs when a long-hidden wound reemerges in awareness, demanding attention now. This may be an experience of abuse that a person suffered in childhood, an injury so deep and so devastating that it had to be "forgotten." For decades this injury festered, out of consciousness but consuming considerable energy in denial. Now, in midlife, the person begins to aspire to something new and something more. The wounded child has matured into a more confident adult, strong enough to acknowledge the earlier abuse. This dawning awareness unsettles the "customary self" the person had learned to live with. This recovery, with all its threat and promise, often makes an initial appearance in an episode of intense loneliness.

These seasons of midlife loneliness often bring us to the threshold of integration. We are searching for a fuller and more honest relationship with the mystery of our own lives. Less at odds with ourselves, we are less driven in our work and less distanced from friends. The energy that had been consumed in self-protection is now freed. The journey from loneliness to solitude continues.

Aging and Solitude

"Home is where one starts from," T. S. Eliot suggests. "As we grow older, the world becomes stranger." Aging offers new invitations to solitude. Our relationships shift as we—or others close to us—move to new locations. Loneliness becomes more familiar as longtime friends are taken in death. Even as we reach out to meet new people, we recognize we cannot replace the bonds that have been crafted over years of shared experience. We cannot make new "old friends." For some of us there is the long loneliness of accompanying a loved one through the dark journey of dementia.

Many of the challenges that confront us in aging we have faced before. But in our senior decades these return in slightly different guises. As in adolescence, aging raises concerns about our body. Moving through our sixties, we recognize that muscles and joints have become less flexible; in our seventies we worry more about memory loss; in our eighties we are careful about conserving our energy. Questions arise: What accommodations must I make in response to the physical changes I am experiencing? Is my body reliable? Can it still be trusted?

Our seventies and eighties may surprise us with new experiences of boredom. Many interests that fascinate younger people now seem trivial or unimportant to us. We enjoy being with our grandchildren—briefly. But we especially enjoy returning home to the chosen routines shaped by our own interests. Growing preference for solitude suggests not alienation but a mellow quiet—a greater comfort, sometimes mixed with sadness, in being alone. This mellowness is not simply an experience of self-congratulation. Mature solitude brings not a denial of all the failed or incomplete parts of our past, but rather a deepening peacefulness with the particular—and peculiar—person we have turned out to be. In the words of poet Seamus Heaney, we acknowledge ourselves as both "world-scarred and world-skilled."

This journey of solitude is, of course, never completed. We never come to fathom fully who we have been and who we might still become. But, sufficiently blessed, we may come finally to trust ourselves and our world, to tolerate the discordant movements of our interior life, to appreciate ourselves and others for being simply human. As companions die and the world changes we will experience, again and more deeply, our uniqueness and even aloneness, but the mood will not be one of isolation or deprivation. Instead, we will be freed to cherish moments of replenishing privacy and to relish the quiet strength of solitude because we know ourselves to be in the presence of Another who is faithful into and through our death.

Reflective Exercise

Recall a recent time when you were keenly aware of your *aloneness*—perhaps just as a fleeting mood, perhaps as a growing concern in a troubled relationship, perhaps in an experience of "replenishing privacy." What thoughts were part of this awareness? What feelings? What decisions? What actions?

Now consider: How is solitude real in your own life these days? What practices or disciplines strengthen your experience of solitude? What gifts does solitude bring to you? What challenges does it carry?

Additional Resources

In *Loneliness: Human Nature and the Need for Social Connection,* John Cacioppo and William Patrick present evidence of the physical and emotional impact of loneliness on well-being and health. Ronald Rolheiser's reflections in *The Restless Heart: Finding Our Spiritual Home in Times of Loneliness* offer solace and support. In *Playing and Reality* D. W. Winnicott reflects on the significance of "holding environments"; see also Harriet Goldhur Lerner, *The Dance of Connection.*

Stephanie Dowrick discusses the psychological and spiritual significance of finding a balance between closeness and solitude in *Intimacy and Solitude: Balancing Closeness and Independence.* Adam Phillips explores connections between risk and solitude in *On Kissing, Tickling, and Being Bored,* chapter 3. Ester Buchholz examines the continuing need for solitude throughout the human life span in *The Call to Solitude: Alonetime in a World of Attachment.* In *Solitude: A Return to the Self* Anthony Storr examines the connections between solitude and creativity.

Robert Kegan sets out his schema of cognitive development in *In over Our Heads: The Mental Demands of Modern Life.* For a discussion of the role of solitude in developing the virtue of self-intimacy, see Evelyn Eaton Whitehead and James D. Whitehead, *Christian Adulthood: A Journey of Self-Discovery.*

The quotation from T. S. Eliot is from the poem "East Coker" in his *Four Quartets.* Seamus Heaney's observation of "world-scarred and world-skilled" appears in his *The Redress of Poetry;* we quote from page 114.

12

Finding Fear as a Friend

He is the Truth.
Seek Him in the Kingdom of Anxiety.
You will come to a great city that has
expected your return for years.

—W. H. Auden

Fear announces that danger may be near. Sometimes this foreboding serves us well, protecting us from genuine harm. But often our anxieties mislead us—closing off new possibilities, draining away our energy, and emptying life of joy.

As an early warning system, being afraid has considerable value. Fear predicts we are in harm's way while there is still time to seek protection or to avoid the threat. At heart, then, fear is an ally. But left unattended, fear starts to function as a barrier, closing us off from new possibilities and bringing life to a halt. Fear also leaves us vulnerable to false alarms, turning us away from experiences that mean us no harm.

Fear as an Emotion

Being afraid includes both physical and psychological reactions. While the underlying physiology of fear is common, people report different physical responses. Many of us identify a pounding heart, shallow breathing, sweaty palms. Some of us feel weak in the knees; others report butterflies in the stomach. Our muscles tense, causing our movements to be clumsy. We may become agitated or distracted, making it difficult for us to concentrate. And with these physical reactions come a host of distressing sentiments. We feel vulnerable to attack, helpless in the face of the danger, hostile toward the threatening force.

162

But fear's arousal is not always unpleasant; consider the commercial success of horror films and the long lines of eager paying customers at any amusement park's scariest ride. Fear charges the body with a physiological rush. Many people seek out and savor this physical excitement, especially in the protective setting of a movie theater or well-secured ride.

Risk gets our attention and gives us focus. Rather than distracting us, the agitation can sharpen awareness, making us more attentive to ourselves and our circumstances. Feeling afraid moves us beyond lethargy, bracing us for action. In the grip of this arousal, mind and body are charged—we feel alive! Fear fuels our escape from danger. Our response may be to hide or to flee the scene in an attempt to avoid the risk. Or we may reach out to confront or overcome the threat. In either case the goal is the same: to protect ourselves (or something that we value) from imminent harm.

Fear is future oriented, anticipating what lies ahead. But fear's prediction is always negative; it forecasts the future will be painful. Preparing us to avoid real danger, fear's advance warning serves us well. But fear serves us poorly when it misinterprets the world—anticipating greater harm than actually awaits or underestimating our strength to deal with the threat.

Fear issues a dual warning: the setting is not safe, and our resources are not adequate. This interpretation can become habitual; we start to anticipate that anything unexpected or unfamiliar will be dangerous. Now we *expect* the future to be painful. Harboring anxiety in this way makes fear our dominant mood. No longer an emergency response, apprehension becomes our characteristic stance toward life.

The physical arousal of fear is meant to energize our bodies, supporting action that will protect us in a time of peril. But the arousal itself can so overwhelm us that we lose contact with the genuine information our fears carry and lose focus for any appropriate response.

In the evolutionary scheme, then, fear is an emergency emotion, provoked by sudden threat and resolved in swift response. Like being angry, being afraid is a self-protective response to a threatening environment. And often the two emotions are experienced together. But they bring different interpretations. Anger carries a sense of entitlement (I deserve better), power (I can act to remedy this unacceptable situation), and vindication (what I am doing here is right). Fear more often carries the sense of vulnerability (I am at risk), helplessness (my own resources are not sufficient), and impotence (there is nothing I can do).

What Gives Rise to Fear?

When our familiar world is disrupted, when our strength seems no longer sufficient, then we are afraid. At the root of both of these experiences is the issue of control. A sense of control is essential to psychological maturity. Recognizing we are more than simply victims of circumstances, appreciating that we are responsible for our actions, being willing to take charge of situations and to influence events—these are important (and often not easily won) achievements. Without the confidence that comes from personal effectiveness, the dilemmas of daily existence can seem overwhelming.

A sense of control includes an awareness of personal strengths: "My resources are sufficient to meet the expectable challenges of my life. I know I am not omnipotent; regularly I face realities that outstrip my courage and talent and skill. But on balance I am strong enough to manage well."

Fear arises whenever this balance of power seems at risk. The danger may be physical. Walking alone at night in a strange city, we are concerned about our safety. Confronted by the damage in the wake of a flash flood or an earthquake, we are overwhelmed by the random force of nature. The freak accident we witness on the highway seems to mock our puny attempts to make our own life secure. In each case we sense our own resources are not sufficient to protect us. The balance of power goes against us. We are not really in control.

Threats to physical safety make fear a daily companion of millions of people throughout the world. Media reports bring us the brutal evidence from places where disease and famine spread unchecked, where ethnic hatred fuels the atrocities of civil war, where terror and torture restrain dissent. Even at a safe distance the violence that rules these faraway places alarms us. But an increasing number of Americans recognizes that fear of physical harm stalks us closer to home. National evidence shows women and children at risk of domestic violence; elderly persons who suffer physical abuse from family members or caretakers; an upsurge in hate crimes against immigrants, lesbians, and gays. And the national response—the proliferation of guns held for self-protection—is now itself a major cause of the increased fear for their physical safety that many Americans report.

While fear of bodily harm is a frequent concern, the anxieties that most threaten us arise in our interpersonal world. Here it is not physical *safety* but psychological *security* that is at risk. The pioneering work of British psychologist John Bowlby has illumined this significant distinction in how we learn the meaning of fear.

As Bowlby uses the terms, *safety* gives a reading of the objective risks we face, so we are *safe* when our environment holds no actual danger. *Security* assesses our sense of personal vulnerability, our awareness that we are likely to be hurt. So we are *secure* when we know that the resources available to us are stronger than the threat we face. Using these words as Bowlby does, then, we can be *secure* even in settings that are not *safe.* (And, of course, we can be insecure in settings where in fact our safety is not threatened.)

Take the example of a small child playing alone in the yard of the family home. Her parents are both at home and take turns coming to the door to check that she is content. The neighbor's yard, securely fenced, is usually empty. But this weekend their young adult son has returned from college for a brief visit, bringing along his newly acquired pet—a very large and friendly dog. While the small child is engrossed in play at some distance from the fence, the neighbor releases his dog into the yard. Bounding to the barrier that separates the yards and barking its greeting, the huge dog surprises the child and sets her crying in alarm. Her father rushes outside, cradles his tearful daughter in his arms to console her, and quickly assesses the situation. The toddler has not been hurt, the neighbor's son has rushed outside to calm his pet's exuberance, the dog is well secured and obviously friendly. Now, walking toward the fence, the father speaks to the child in his arms: "See the nice doggy? Such a big doggy! Let's go and say hello! Maybe the dog wants to be our friend." The child, comforted in her parent's presence, glances tentatively toward the fence. As they approach more closely, she smiles at her father and turns herself in his arms to give full attention to the dog. Now intrigued by the animal, she stretches out her hands in excitement. "Would you like to touch the nice doggy?" her father asks. "Let's ask our neighbor if we can pet the good dog." The setting is now transformed. The child, no longer alarmed, reaches out eagerly to make contact with the boisterous animal that only moments ago frightened her.

What has happened here? In Bowlby's analysis we are witnessing an important lesson: the child is learning that even in the presence of danger, she need not be afraid. Even when the environment seems unsafe, she can be secure. The crucial difference is the presence of a protective person who has her welfare at heart.

While we may not all agree with Bowlby's definition of these two words, we can appreciate the truth behind the distinction. As psychiatrist Willard Gaylin states it, "The abiding lesson of the first year of life is that he who is loved is safe. . . . The most dangerous thing is not to be weak but to be unloved." This is a lesson confirmed throughout adult life as well: the scariest thing is not to be in danger or even to be weak. What we fear most is to be abandoned—to be alone.

Psychologists confirm the continuing significance throughout adult life of mature attachments, close relationships in which we can acknowledge our vulnerability and count on one another's protective care. Without relationships like this, we do not thrive. Without relationships like this, the world is a scarier place.

No wonder, then, that relationships generate such concern. Interpersonal threat arises whenever we feel separated from loving protectors. A serious disruption—betrayal or desertion or death—wounds us deeply. But even smaller hints of trouble set us trembling: a disapproving look, reluctance to offer us support, a mocking joke at our expense.

We fear being separated from those we love because without them we stand weaker in the world. This threat of separation reminds us of an even deeper human vulnerability—that even those who love us cannot always protect us from harm.

Internal Threat—Changes in the Self

But danger does not always come from the outside. Some risks arise within, when our accustomed sense of "who I am" is threatened. Sometimes a colleague's accurate criticism forces us to recognize that our work falls short of expectations. Or we catch ourselves behaving in ways we're ashamed of—letting racist remarks go unchallenged or spreading malicious gossip or using someone else's misery to our advantage. Confronted by evidence that does not fit our "ideal self," most of us respond defensively. The risk is loss of self-esteem; we dread learning that we are, in fact, less than we hoped. Living with this diminished sense of self would leave us vulnerable—to guilt, to shame, to responsibility for change. So we defend against self-knowledge because we are afraid.

Positive personal change can be threatening, too. Paula returns to school after fifteen years at home as a full-time mother. Her initial objective, shared by her husband, is to complete her degree so that she can find a job to help pay their children's college expenses. But this move back to studies expands her horizon in unexpected ways. Learning more about herself leads Paula to reinterpret many of her earlier motives and decisions. New hopes for her future emerge as she recognizes talents and interests previously unexplored: "I am no longer the woman I once was!" Some days she is simply exhilarated by the changes; other days these new insights worry her.

Paula's fears have much to do with her adequacy—"Will I really be able to make it in the bigger world available to me now?" But some of her fears focus closer to home. No longer "the woman I once was," Paula herself is threatened. The roles and responsibilities and daily routines that shaped her earlier identity no longer fit. Paula is different now, in ways puzzling to her and mysterious to those around her.

Significant personal change disconcerts us and makes demands on other people, too. Expectations must be renegotiated as our priorities shift. Those closest to us, who matter most, are most directly affected. And we are susceptible to how they respond. When family and friends register displeasure—blaming us for being different or withdrawing support at any hint of change—risk escalates. The familiar solace of "how I used to be" urges caution lest more be lost than will be gained.

Fear that the new self being born may be orphaned holds us back. But when people who matter most stand with us through the change, they provide an environment that supports both continuity and growth. Personal change may still cost us dearly, but the price need not be paid in lost relationships.

Existential Threat—Meaning and Mystery

Natural disasters remind us there are forces over which we have no control—wildfires, hurricanes, drought, floods, epidemics. The evil humans do to one another scars the social imagination even more: the mushroom cloud over Hiroshima, the scent of the gas chambers at Auschwitz, the smoke arising on 9/11 in New York, the sight of refugees facing famine and disease in the wake of ethnic cleansing. Globally, worries over growing terrorist threats are matched by concerns about ecological destruction. Our own culture's addiction to drugs and pornography spreads unchecked, putting every family at risk. And each of us, heir to humanity's lot, knows that death surely awaits.

These fears acknowledge how vulnerable we are as a species, how puny our defenses, how frail our illusions of control. Problem-solving strategies we sometimes use to allay our anxieties seem insubstantial here. The mystery we confront provokes a deeper response, closer to awe than to understanding, less self-confident but more open to hope.

Fears That Destroy, Fears That Save

Fear is not always an accurate predictor of what will bring us harm. Distortions may be introduced into our interpretation of the danger we face. Sometimes the distortion comes from other people's judgments of what is harmful; sometimes the distortion comes from our own experiences in the past.

The fears that destroy and defeat us are those that prevent our responding adequately to reality. Some of our fears are illegitimate, arising more from unresolved parts of our past than from real dangers confronting us now. An earlier defeat leaves a mark. Rather than learning from this experience, we simply become afraid. This fear leads us to protect ourselves in advance. When new situations like this arise, we *expect* to be hurt, so we wince before we are hit.

Such generalized fear blinds us to the facts of our actual situation. If our parents were inconsistent or distant when we were children, we are likely to carry into adulthood a certain suspicion of persons who hold authority in our life. This fear of authority can become a dominant factor in our behavior—at work, in our church, in the civic community. As psychologist Michael Cowan reminds us, the "there-and-then" can overshadow the "here-and-now"—preventing us from seeing the ways in which powerful people in our life now are *different* from our parents. We can hold on tenaciously to our hostility and distrust, even when the current evidence contradicts our earlier fears. But when we do this, we are closed in on ourselves, no longer able to learn from new experience. The old battle continues, even if there are different players cast in the adversary role.

The fears that *save* us are those that help us deal with the real dangers we face. Our legitimate fears carry the wisdom of our past into the present, helping us to evaluate the danger and devise our response before the harm is upon us. The fears that save us draw on our past successes and help us learn from our past failures, rather than simply repeating them. These are the fears that fuel our courage.

Discerning the Fears That Save Us

Being afraid confronts us with a dilemma: how to sort out the fears that would save us from those that would bring us down. We know that our anxieties do not always tell the truth about our actual situation. How can we determine when our distress is trustworthy? John Bowlby's research has shown that, in humans, fear is not simply an innate instinct. Newborn infants display an "alarm response" in the face of *present* pain, but they do not show fear, that is, a distress reaction in *anticipation* of pain. Human beings have to *learn* to avoid what will bring them harm.

Fear—the ability to anticipate danger—is an acquired response. Newborns, unable to anticipate danger, are at a severe disadvantage. Unless they learn quickly to avoid what is harmful, they are not likely to survive. Fear, then, is one of the most important gifts that parents give their children. First in our families and later in other settings—school, neighborhood, church—our culture teaches us when and how to be afraid. It is these "received fears" that we carry into adult life.

But, as most of us come to realize, the gift of fear is not without ambiguity. From our parents and others we learn to fear those things that *they* know to be dangerous. Again, this is an essential contribution they make to our growth and well-being. The problem, of course, is that it is not always easy to know what is dangerous for another person. If our fears—these learned survival responses—are to continue to serve us well, they must be purified as we mature.

Maturity demands that we question our received fears. The first question we need to ask: Is this dangerous *for me*? Parents and mentors teach us to fear what they judge can bring us harm. Using their road map of dangers is not a bad place to start the journey, but eventually we must map the terrain for ourselves—using our own experiences and goals as guides. We may make some mistakes as we try to do this, but an even greater mistake would be to live a life based unquestioningly on other people's fears. The fears that save will be our own fears.

The second question to ask: Is this *always* dangerous? Most of the things we have been taught to fear are dangerous only in certain contexts. Often our teachers do not spell out these contexts; their goal, especially early in our development, is to reinforce the danger so that we will avoid this source of harm. We befriend our fears as we become more discriminating, identifying the more limited settings in which we should be genuinely afraid.

A final question asks: Is it dangerous for me *now*? We learn many of our fears early, as young children in the family or when we are neophytes in our jobs. As we mature—growing in age and grace and wisdom—we must ask whether these same dangers continue to exist for us. As old as I am now, should I still be afraid? At my current stage of development, are the same things likely to cause me harm?

Responding to Fear

Fear leads to self-protective behavior, sometimes in useful ways, sometimes in ways that are themselves harmful. The spontaneous response to danger is some kind of fight-or-flight behavior. Fear's physical arousal prepares us to take quick action. Our muscles tense, adrenalin flows, and breathing quickens to bring oxygen to the brain and body. We are readied for the exertion required to defend ourselves from physical attack or to run away from the danger.

For most adults, however, our fears are not usually about physical attack. Our emotional security is at risk more often than our personal safety. In the face of emotional threat, our fight-or-flight reactions become more sophisticated. Fear still leads to efforts to protect ourselves from danger, but the behavior changes. Instead of physically running away, we learn other ways to hide. We mask our real opinions or deny our values or remain silent about what we need. Our hope is that by "hiding" in these ways, we will avoid the impending threat.

But avoidance is not our only option. Instead of running away, we can try to overcome the danger by confronting the threat directly. True, confrontation may be hostile, even when it does not involve physical attack, as we set out to belittle and embarrass those who frighten us. But confrontation is not always hostile. Anxious about increasing tension in our marriage, for example, we can approach our partner with concern as we seek better understanding and reconciliation.

Befriending Our Fears

Befriending our fear means learning how to use its power to help us rather than to harm us. The goal is not to banish our fears (that would surely weaken us!) but to tame them: to identify their truth, to focus their energy, to welcome them home.

The experience of fear includes both painful feelings (vulnerability, helplessness, physical distress) and an impetus to action—whether the primitive responses of fight or flight, or the more sophisticated options of confrontation or avoidance. Since the negative feelings of fear are so unpleasant and so immediate, these are often the first focus of our attention. "Dealing with fear," then, means the effort to get rid of these disturbing feelings. And sometimes this is useful. When our sense of helplessness is so strong that we panic, we need to moderate this intense feeling before we can deal effectively with the danger. Perhaps something as simple as several moments of deep breathing or a centering meditation may help. Or a brisk walk or conversation with a good friend could be our approach.

But responding to fear primarily by trying to eliminate its distressing feelings is risky. Preoccupied with this unpleasant arousal, we can lose sight of the real danger to which it may point; increasingly, then, we may try to avoid these disturbing feelings, rather than welcome them as signals that serve our survival.

A focus on eliminating painful feelings of fear can have even more negative long-term effects. We can try to live in a way that avoids anything that makes us afraid. But pursuing a life without fear results in a risk-free lifestyle, where change becomes an enemy and personal choice is constricted within the ever-narrowing boundaries of what seems safe. For most of us, this kind of pseudo-safety comes at too high a price.

Befriending fear readies us to use its energy rather than simply dispel its arousal. We take action—assess the threat, explore our options, mobilize our resources, confront the danger at hand. And as we begin to appreciate fear's painful arousal as part of the early warning system that helps us deal with danger, we start to welcome fear as a friend.

Mobilizing Our Resources in the Face of Fear

Uncertainty gives rise to fear, so accurate information is a primary resource. Getting the facts straight often shows that the situation is less dangerous than we thought. Even when the facts are less friendly, knowing the truth helps us prepare for the real risks we face. Medical practice has changed to reflect this realization. Previously many physicians would avoid discussing directly with their patients a diagnosis of terminal illness. Now medical personnel are directed to provide ample information to patients and their families—what to expect as the disease progresses, the range of treatment options, the available medication regimes and their possible side effects, the expected prognosis. Having this information—even of potentially dire consequences—diminishes uncertainty and restores some sense of personal control.

Increasing information lessens fear in other settings as well. Advance training can reduce the risks of moving into a new job; consulting more experienced colleagues may help us prepare for a difficult discussion with our boss. Keeping track of our own experience with fear provides good information, too. Here, as with other difficult emotions, keeping a daily log or devoting time to regular reflection helps us identify patterns. When do I most often feel afraid? What are the risks that most frequently disable me? Where do I "generalize" my fear, letting past experiences predict future pain? Recognizing these personal dynamics frees us to respond more effectively.

Feeling powerless provokes fear; feeling resourceful counteracts fear. So acquiring new skills lessens our sense of risk. So does acknowledging the resources we already have, resources that include our connections with supportive friends and potential allies. Expanding our competence and enhancing our confidence make us stronger; even in the face of danger, we have less to fear.

The goal of maturity, Overstreet suggests, is not that we live without fear, but that we learn to be wisely, responsibly, and productively afraid. We are *wisely* afraid when the threat is real. We are *responsibly* afraid when the fears are our own—reflecting our own evaluation of danger and risk. We are *productively* afraid when fear leads to effective response—to actions that protect from harm ourselves, those in our care, and the values we hold sacred. Then fear comes as our friend.

Reflective Exercise

To begin this reflection, spend a few moments in peaceful prayer or quieting meditation. Be ready to return to this prayerful awareness if the reflection becomes disturbing in any way.

In a mood of calm and presence, recall some of the fears that are currently part of your own life—perhaps a sense of physical threat, troubles in a relationship, shifts in your sense of yourself, or a deeper vulnerability in the face of life's uncertainties. Be gentle as you revisit these concerns.

Now focus on one of these anxieties that you have begun to befriend—where you have learned that fear can be an ally, where fear has become a resource in your life. Take time to bring these memories to mind. Then consider: What has helped you to face this fear in your life? What have you learned from this fear? What blessings have come through this experience of befriending your fear?

Additional Resources

In *Coping with Anxiety: Ten Simple Ways to Relieve Anxiety, Fear, and Worry,* Edmund Bourne and Lorna Garano offer a thoughtful and practical approach to dealing with the normal range of feelings of anxiety and fear. Jeffrey Brantley, in *Calming Your Anxious Mind,* suggests mindfulness and meditative practice as helpful strategies; see also Susan Piver's program for the daily practice of meditation in *How Not to Be Afraid of Your Own Life.* Bonaro Overstreet's early discussion of the psychological dynamics of fear, *Overcoming Fear in Ourselves and Others,* remains a valuable resource.

In *The Dance of Fear* experienced therapist Harriet Lerner examines ways in which fear inhibits personal growth and explores practical responses of healing and transformation. Angela Neal-Barnett discusses factors that contribute to anxiety and fear in African American women in *Soothe Your Nerves: The Black Woman's Guide to Understanding Anxiety, Panic, and Fear.*

Developmental psychologist John Bowlby offers a readable account of his research into children's experience of fear and anxiety and their consequences in adult life in *A Secure Base: Parent-Child Attachment and Healthy Human Development.* We quote from Willard Gaylin's discussion of fear in *Feelings: Our Vital Signs,* pages 30–31.

In *Feel the Fear and Do It Anyway* Susan Jeffers examines fear and the ways it can be managed in everyday life. Eric H. F. Law sets out communication guidelines to help overcome polarization provoked by prejudice and social fear in *Finding Intimacy in a World of Fear.* In *Comforting the Fearful: Listening Skills for Caregivers,* Leroy Howe makes pastoral connections with the life of faith as he examines strategies for ministry responses to fear.

The quotation that opens this chapter is drawn from W. H. Auden's poem "For the Time Being."

13

The Christian Script for Fear

The disciples' boat, battered by the waves, was far from land, and the wind was against them.
—Matthew 14:24

Fear is an important emotion in the Bible. In the Gospels we meet three quite different faces of fear. The first is the dread that warns us of imminent danger: as their boat flounders in a storm, the disciples cry out for Jesus' help to save them from drowning. A second face of fear is less dramatic but runs as deep: the anxiety that is registered in worry about the future. Sending the disciples on mission, Jesus alerts them to the difficulties they will encounter. And he encourages them: "Have no fear." The third face of fear is that mix of terror and amazement the grieving women experienced when they discovered an empty tomb. It is the frightened confusion felt by the disciples when they became aware of Jesus' presence among them after his death. Fear in the face of danger was our focus in Chapter 12. Here we will examine fear as worry, then explore the religious experience of apprehension and awe often named in our tradition as *fear of the Lord*.

Fear as Worry about the Future

In Matthew's Gospel, Jesus instructs the disciples as he sends them out to preach and heal in God's name. He warns them of the perils ahead: "I am sending you out like sheep into the midst of wolves." He counsels them to travel light and be ready to "shake the dust off your feet" and move on. Jesus encourages them: "Do not worry about how you are to speak or what you are to say; for what you are to say will be given to you at that time; for it is not you who speak, but the Spirit of

175

your Father speaking through you." Three more times in this passage, Jesus reassures them: "Have no fear . . . do not fear . . . do not be afraid" (Mt 10).

Anxiety about a threatening future is the central concern in the passage above. Earlier in Matthew's account the focus is worry: "Do not worry about your life, what you will eat or what you will drink, or about your body, what you will wear. Is not life more than food, and the body more than clothing?" (Mt 6:25). The disciples are reminded, "Can any of you by worrying add a single hour to your span of life?" Jesus' instruction concludes with the repeated plea: "Do not worry. . . . Do not worry about tomorrow."

Jesus' counsel—*Do not be afraid!*—shapes the Christian script for the emotion of fear. Jesus warns us that to follow him is perilous. We will meet difficulties; we should expect at times to be rejected. In all this we should keep our priorities straight: "Seek first the kingdom of God" (Mt 6:33), and remember that life is more important than food, and the body more important than clothing.

As evidence, Jesus points to the birds of the air and the lilies of the field. The sparrows "neither sow nor reap." This image holds the key. The guarantee is not that the birds will not die; the promise is that they are held by the Creator, both in life and in death. So too the promise of Jesus today: God is with us, in success and failure, in life and death. Embracing this promise, our anxiety about the unknown future will diminish. In this dangerous world we will never be completely safe, but we are secure.

Christian faith does not banish all dread and anxiety. Paul admitted as much when he recalled his worry about the new communities in his care: "I am under daily pressure because of my anxiety for all the churches" (2 Cor 11:28). Worry is a necessary byproduct of the concern we carry for vulnerable loved ones and cherished values. If we did not care, we would not worry. Trusting God does not banish all fear and anxiety. But growing in a sense of the Spirit's protective presence frees us for risks we would otherwise be unable to take.

Worry Faces Us toward the Future

Psychologist Adam Phillips describes worry as a way we hold the future. A mother watches her teenage daughter leave for college. She can no longer hold her child protectively in her arms as she once did years ago. But at least she can still hold her daughter close as she worries about her. Or during a sleepless night we mull over the troubles and challenges awaiting us in the coming week.

Phillips reminds us that the word *worry* was originally a hunting term. It described what dogs do to the prey when they catch it. *Worry* means the action of seizing and throttling; the dog holds the rabbit or fox in his teeth, shaking it back and forth. The original meaning of *worry* was "to kill by strangulation." In the mid-eighteenth century Samuel Johnson's dictionary expanded the meaning of the word to include "to harass or persecute others." Only in the nineteenth century did the active verb "to worry something" begin to be used in the passive tense, as in "I am worried to death." Now, it seems, our worries often prey upon us.

But worry is not always an act of self-punishment. Worry about the future is not always a disabling waste of time. The discomfort that worry evokes may impel us to plan for coming hazards. Phillips observes,

> Worrying is a form of thinking. At one end of some imaginary spectrum, there is something akin to creative rumination. At the other end, there is the stalled thought of obsession. If worrying can persecute us, it can also work for us, as self-preparation. No stage fright, no performance.

Worry can build into a spiraling anxiety, leading us nowhere even as it consumes our energy. But worry is an arousal that is meant to put us on alert, triggering action so that we might face the future well prepared. Worry urges us to pay attention to the tasks ahead.

Ingmar Bergman, the award-winning Swedish director of many dark films, describes his own lifelong relationship with anxious worry. "Anxiety is my life's faithful companion, inherited from both my parents, placed at the very center of my identity—my demon and my friend spurring me on." Film critic John Lahr comments on Bergman's singular taming of this emotion: "His gift lies in his access to dark feelings and in his ability to call them out into the open, where they can be seen and acknowledged and finally understood." For ordinary folk, troublesome worry can prompt fruitful planning. Bergman's genius was his ability to transform a usually crippling emotion into great art.

A Third Face of Fear—Astonishment and Awe

At the heart of religious life resides a complex emotion that is both deeply unsettling and strangely uplifting. This emotion is aroused when we stumble upon the Mystery that envelops and transcends us. The force of this experience may so disorient us that we identify the feeling as terror, but much more than fear is aroused. This mixed emotion has been variously named: wonder, awe, astonishment, transcendence, even fear of the Lord.

The Book of Job narrates a dramatic version of this experience. Job, sure of his own uprightness, demands of God an explanation for his suffering. Finally God tires of such presumption and staggers Job with an onslaught of questions: Where were you when the world was created? When have you ever caused the dawn? Or visited the storehouse of the snows? (Jb 38—41). Job is brought up short, humbled. He acknowledges his chagrin: "I have uttered what I did not understand, things too wonderful for me which I did not know. . . . I regret my actions and repent in dust and ashes" (Jb 42:3, 6).

Here fear arises as a mixed emotion, a blend of amazement, dread, and awe. This is neither the fear that warns of an immediate danger, nor is it worry about future threats. Instead, this emotion registers the astonishment and fascination that overcome us in certain bewildering circumstances.

Another glimpse of the complex emotion of fear-as-amazement comes in the intriguing story of the Transfiguration. The disciples suddenly experienced the profound disorientation that accompanied the startling awareness that Jesus stood among them as more than simply a holy man. The story is ornamented with the pyrotechnics of a mythic tale: they ascend a mountain (the traditional locus of revelation); Jesus' clothes turn dazzling white (signaling special illumination). Suddenly Jesus' appearance is radiant, and he is seen to be talking with ancient prophets. The disciples are filled with fear and display the physiological symptoms of befuddlement; for example, overcome, they experience a kind of stupor or drowsiness. Peter speaks, "not knowing what he was saying" (Lk 9:33). In Matthew's Gospel they lose their balance and fall to the ground (Mt 17:6). Jesus, sensing their confusion and astonishment, urges them not to be afraid (Mt 17:7).

A similar range of emotions floods the women who visit the tomb of Jesus after his death and burial. When they find the tomb empty they are astonished and frightened. What could this mean? Has someone stolen his body or has something yet more amazing taken place? In Luke's account we read that the women are "perplexed." Their hearts are jolted and, as Mark's Gospel reports, "They fled from the tomb, for terror and amazement had seized them; and they said nothing to anyone for they were much afraid" (Mk 16:8). Literally, the Greek words in the New Testament accounts suggest trembling and ecstasy. The women were beside themselves with a frightening and euphoric disorientation. In Matthew's Gospel, written some decades after Mark's stark account, the women at the tomb encounter an earthquake and lightning. An angel informs them that Jesus has risen, and they rush from the tomb "with fear and great joy" (Mt 28:8).

This bewildering emotion erupts again and again in the stories of the risen Jesus appearing to the disciples. Suddenly aware of his presence, they are "startled and terrified" (Lk 24:37). What can this mean? How can someone who has died appear to be present to us? To this quite reasonable amazement, Jesus responds, "Do not be afraid."

Psychologists today have turned to a study of the positive emotions, including awe and the sense of transcendence. Jonathan Haidt offers one definition: "Awe involves being in the presence of something powerful, along with associated feelings of submission. Awe also involves a difficulty of comprehension, along with associated feelings of confusion, surprise, and wonder." In Haidt's analysis two themes are at play in this experience: "The stimulus is vast and . . . requires accommodation." By "vast" he means something "much larger than the self"—whether this is a frightening storm, a somber diagnosis of a life-threatening disease, or—as in our reflection here—the startling awareness of God's powerful presence. By "accommodation" he means the need for "adjusting mental structures that cannot assimilate a new experience." The biblical experiences of Job, like that of the disciples at the transfiguration and before the empty tomb, demanded such a profound accommodation. Haidt concludes: "Awe can transform people and reorient their lives, goals, and values." Reading the scriptural accounts, we recognize that the astonishment experienced by Job and by the disciples of Jesus profoundly reoriented their lives.

This experience of astonishment and awe occurs in various ways in our lives. A summer electrical storm erupts suddenly and a dramatic lightning display fills the cosmic theater. Fascination and fear mingle in our response; we are reminded of our human frailty. Or, we learn that a close friend has terminal cancer. This announcement takes our breath away, even before we begin to ponder the dire implications. Confronted by impending death, we are frightened—for our friend, for his family, even for ourselves. But more than fear is involved. Something of profound significance commands our attention. We are likely to experience the astonished confusion felt by the disciples on the mountain of transfiguration. Our own daily schedule with its insistent agenda seems suddenly unimportant. Brought to acute awareness of the realities of life and death, we are stunned.

In these extraordinary moments we come up against the boundaries of our existence. Pressing against this barrier, we are gripped by a range of emotions. These feelings, however we name them, mark the place where our understanding and control reach their limit, and something greater, more mysterious begins. Standing at this sharp edge both excites and repels us. We fall silent—neither capable of nor eager for speech. These terrifying feelings humble us, but we are not humiliated. In a mood of reverence, we savor something that is within our vision but beyond our grasp. Without being open to these emotions, our lives would be less rich, and we would be less human.

Religion and Fear

"Be not afraid"—this encouragement echoes again and again through the Gospels. In moments of imminent danger, or when facing an uncertain future, or even when confronted with the terror of an empty tomb, we are instructed that we need not be afraid. Religious practices, designed to cultivate our trust in God, allow us gradually to let go chronic fears as well as excessive worries about the future. But every institution, perhaps especially religious institutions, is sorely tempted to deploy fear to enforce compliance and conformity. Old Testament images of an angry God can be transformed into warnings about a vengeful deity who is ever watchful for any misstep we might commit. Such mistakes—we learn to fear—may well merit our eternal punishment in hell. In such a toxic atmosphere, reinforced in stern doctrinal statements and fiery sermons, religious faith is made a co-conspirator in unhealthy emotional habits. Here religion serves not as vehicle of grace but of malpractice. Then religious belonging exaggerates our caution and diminishes our courage. Such malpractice instills a mood that defeats curiosity and cripples the ability to risk. Instead a constant low-grade fearfulness hedges our life with chronic anxiety. The humorist Garrison Keillor writes of the injuries that his own religious upbringing caused him:

> You taught me the fear of becoming lost, which has killed the pleasure of curiosity and discovery. In strange cities, I memorize streets and always know exactly where I am. Amid scenes of great splendor, I review the route back to the hotel.

Courage: How We Hold Our Fear

Fear is a necessary disturbance, an essential element in our repertoire of survival. How are we to hold this volatile feeling? By alerting us to real dangers, the emotion unsettles us. And fear easily escalates into a dread that brings us to a halt. Paralyzed by fear, we are tempted to abandon ideals and goals that hold the hint of threat. Then we rule out more and more worthwhile risks, as caution displaces courage.

Thomas Aquinas judged that courage arouses us "to face the dreadful." Courage does not mean fearlessness. As theologian Josef Pieper reminds us, courage assumes our vulnerability. Courage arises out of our acknowledgment of danger, and then it energizes us to respond *despite* our fear. We are en*couraged*—literally, "en-heartened"—to pursue an important value in the face of serious risk. The Chinese sage Mencius put this conviction most sharply:

> I love life, but there are things I love more than life;
> that is why I do not cling to life at all costs.
> I hate death, but there are things I hate more than
> death;
> that is why there are some dangers I do not avoid.

The stirring of courage is not unfamiliar. Our personal well-being is a great value, but we regularly honor other commitments that outweigh our own safety. The survival instinct that protects our life is matched by the moral recognition of yet more compelling values. And so we put ourselves at risk—for our children, for our nation in time of war, for other ideals that we esteem as important as life itself. Frightened of death, we still recognize that there are worse fates. For us, too, "there are some dangers I do not avoid."

Courage often requires weighing values as we face a conflict of goods. Personal reputation, financial reward, career advancement—these genuine benefits sometimes flow from our conscientious behavior. But single-minded pursuit of these advantages can dampen our courage. Fearful of losing these rewards, we may hold back, withdraw from challenges, abandon other values. Here John's Gospel alerts us: "Those who love their life will lose it" (12:25). Clinging to some of these good things of life, we risk losing touch with the deeper, life-giving values. In these situations courage empowers us to face the conflict of goods. No single "correct" response is immediately obvious as we weigh these complex decisions. But courage will support our effort to recognize the values at stake, to discern the likely consequences of our choices, and to act with conviction in the face of our anxious concerns.

Courage as Patience

The earliest cultural icon of courage was the warrior. The tribe survived because some members were willing to risk their lives for the common good. A culture survived by encouraging such bravery and heroism. Early in both the Greek and the Chinese languages, the word for courage included the word for "man," since courage was understood as an essential characteristic of manhood. Aquinas, in his reflection on courage, broadened the meaning of this virtue and altered its focus. Aquinas suggested that courage is less about attack (the focus of the warrior) and more about endurance. This interior resource's greatest gift is to empower us to pursue our best values, even in the face of difficulty and threat. To endure courageously, Aquinas judges that we will need the companion virtue of patience. Patience buttresses courage by not allowing us "to be made inordinately sorrowful" by difficulties.

The conflict of goods brings with it not only fear but sadness. We regret having to risk our successful career or our well-established reputation by standing up for a moral principle we deeply cherish. That one of our values puts another in jeopardy saddens us. Why should life demand such choices? As we experience these necessary losses, patience protects us. "Patience," Lee Yearley notes, "allows people to be properly saddened by their own and the world's state and yet also to remain unimpeded in their pursuit of and adherence to valuable goods." In a world of conflicting values, sadness is a fitting emotion. Regret and disappointment are unavoidable. It is patience—a form of courage—that helps us survive our sorrow, enabling us to hold our necessary losses without being defeated by them. Pieper summarizes Aquinas's thought: "Patience keeps man from the danger that his spirit may be broken by grief and lose its greatness."

Courage and Hope

Courage stirs in the midst of fear and anger, supporting our confidence that risks are worth taking. Yearley suggests that courage is rooted in hope—"an expectation that safety is close at hand." For the religious believer, courage arises from a confidence that God will prevail. This *prevailing* may not prevent our death, but we are convinced that there "are some things more loathsome than death, so there are dangers I do not avoid." This conviction, the bedrock of courageous hope, gives meaning and purpose to our actions in the midst of danger.

The hope that is the ground of courage lifts us out of narrow self-concern and centers our attention on God. Believing we belong to a Mystery greater than ourselves, we are set free to risk our lives in pursuit of goals that will outlive us. We are free even to fail in the eyes of the world because there are some things we love more than life.

Be Not Afraid!

"Do not be afraid." This encouragement echoes again and again through scripture. But if not in fear, how are we to respond? In moments of imminent danger, or when facing an uncertain future, or even when confronted with the disquieting awareness of transcendence—in each of these settings the gospel narratives offer a clue.

A first clue is found in Jesus' encouragement to the disciples who feared that their boat might capsize in a storm (Mt 8:25). Here "be not afraid" might be fittingly translated as "don't be so timid!" In the face of present dangers we are urged to be more courageous. Of course life is filled with threatening situations. Have courage, the Lord is with you.

A second clue addresses our worry about the future. The gospel counsel us to recall the birds of the air, held in existence by the Father's provident care. This confidence does not guarantee the success of all our endeavors or our protection from sorrow and loss. In fact, we are at risk. But the invitation here is to trust, to align ourselves with the movement of Life that is more powerful than death, a Presence revealed to us through Jesus as *agape* (faithful love).

The third clue responds to the astonishing experience of faith—recognizing the reality of God's Spirit in our lives. Breaking bread with a stranger in the village of Emmaus, the disciples suddenly recognize the presence of Christ (Lk 24:31). At daybreak of another morning, a figure appears before the disciples resting on the seashore; "none of the disciples dared to ask him, 'who are you?' because they knew it was the Lord" (Jn 21:12). The counsel here is reverent awe. Within and beyond our ordinary perception lies the wonderment of the divine: God is mystery beyond comprehension. Our fleeting, fragile apprehension of this reality can provoke bewilderment and confusion. But this is not fear in any ordinary sense. Here, be not afraid. Be amazed.

The world we inhabit today is truly fearsome. Suicide bombers, ethnic cleansing, domestic violence, terminal disease—there is no lack of reasons to be afraid. The final conviction in the face of all these experiences, from fear to worry to astonishment, is that we are not safe. But we are secure. In our living and in our dying we are held by the Spirit. Such confidence can release in us the courage to face immediate dangers and future risky ventures. Such confidence also opens us to the splendor that spills out of creation, surrounding us and—from time to time—taking our breath away.

Reflective Exercise

From your own life, recall an example of each of these expressions of fear: fright in the face of danger; worry about the future; astonishment in the presence of Mystery. For you, how are these experiences *similar?* How are they *different* from one another? Which of the "faces of fear" is most familiar to you?

Then spend some time in prayerful reflection: how have the consoling words of Jesus—"Be not afraid"—been part of your spiritual journey?

Additional Resources

Kathleen Fischer reflects on the spiritual dimensions of fear in *The Courage the Heart Desires: Spiritual Strength in Difficult Times,* especially chapter 6, "Praying When We're Scared," and chapter 8, "The Core of Courage." Kerry Walters examines fear, vulnerability, and insecurity in *Jacob's Hip: Finding God in an Anxious Age.* Rabbi Shmuley Boteach offers cogent suggestions for transforming fear into a resource for spiritual living in *Face Your Fears: Living with Courage in an Age of Caution.*

Adam Phillips explores the ambiguous dynamic of worry in *On Kissing, Tickling, and Being Bored;* we quote from page 57. Garrison Keillor describes his distress with his religious upbringing in *Lake Wobegon Days;* we quote from page 254. John Lahr discusses Ingmar Bergman's anxiety in "The Demon Lover"; we quote from page 67.

Lee Yearley compares the understanding of courage in Thomas Aquinas's thought and in the writings of Chinese philosopher Mencius; see *Mencius and Aquinas: Theories of Virtue and Conceptions of Courage,* especially pages 120–30. Josef Pieper draws on Aquinas's work in *The Four Cardinal Virtues;* we quote from the discussion of fear and courage found on pages 127–30.

Psychologist Jonathan Haidt has pioneered the study of *awe* as a moral emotion; see his essay "Approaching Awe: A Moral, Spiritual, and Aesthetic Emotion." We quote from pages 303, 297, 304, and 312, respectively. Dacher Keltner offers an expanded and more accessible discussion of these research findings in *Born to Be Good: The Science of a Meaningful Life.*

Conclusion

THE WAY OF THE PAINFUL EMOTIONS

The Chinese character for the Way *(Tao):* the mysterious path of be-friending our emotions, performing our passions, and becoming fully human.

14

The Way of the Painful Emotions

In the middle of the journey of my life I found myself inside
a dark forest, for the right way I had completely lost.
—Dante

Calamities befall us on the journey of our life, but there is no other route to our destination. Journeys figure prominently in many religious traditions. The exodus and the exile define the spiritual journey for Jews. Pilgrimages—to Mecca or Jerusalem or Fatima—move religious seekers across varied landscapes. The ultimate question of every quest is "how do we get there from here?" Often, the question arises "inside a dark forest," when we realize "the right way I had completely lost."

Finding Our Way

The way of the painful emotions, like the *Tao* of Taoism, is a mysterious dynamic through which our life unfolds. The *Tao* is "silent, vast, independent and unchanging" (*Tao Te Ching*, 25). Clues, rather than clear road signs, mark the path. Attempting to plumb our passions, we set off on a track without a finish line. If we endure, the way discloses harmful habits of our past and opens us to unexpected reservoirs of energy. The route seems cyclic, winding repeatedly past familiar haunts—but it is different at each passing because we have changed along the way.

Not everyone enters upon the mysterious way of the painful emotions. Instead, we may linger in a life of quiet desperation bound by boredom or hedged in by guilt. Conforming numbly to what is expected, we may never take leave, never launch out into the deep of our fathomless feelings.

189

When we do dare embark, we quickly detect the spiritual exercises required of us, especially those of presence and participation. Out of the "dark forest" we travel toward presence—becoming more attuned to the history that has molded our emotions and more aware of aspirations abandoned along the way. We bid farewell to the myriad techniques of distraction through which we had sought to absent ourselves from feeling. We journey, too, out of passivity toward participation. From the status of victims who bemoan our bad luck and dysfunctional families, we become actors in our interior life, acknowledging our complicity in the guilt or resentment we still harbor. Along the way we begin to shoulder the risks of a life both passionate and responsible.

The way of the painful emotions leads us toward participation in a second sense. We are not lone players in a private drama, attempting a solitary and heroic healing. As we were injured by unwholesome environments, so we are healed by compassionate companions and vital communities. The path of the negative emotions is a *way with*, a social adventure.

Learning Patience

This book opened with the Chinese character for patience, a knife suspended over a heart. The way of the negative emotions begins with the courage to hold still long enough to recognize what we are feeling. Such patience is not placid compliance but rather courageous attention to the turns and invitations of our life.

"A wild patience has taken me this far." Thus does poet Adrienne Rich describe her efforts to steer a course through the narrows of her life. "In this forty-ninth year of my life," she struggles to integrate the once conflicting energies of "anger and tenderness: my selves." To weave together life's disparate elements into a coherent story takes time and patience. To see our commitments through to fruition demands endurance.

Rich's patience is *wild*—not the passive submission in which women, the poor, and minorities have been instructed. The traditional virtue of patience earns a bad reputation where political and religious leaders encourage followers to submit to servitude and accept their fate. There patience is stripped of its courage and domesticated into docility. In her poem Rich reminds us that finding our way through the mystery of our life is a demanding exercise.

To receive the surprising gifts of the painful emotions, we need much patience. We will have to *suffer* them actively and in full consciousness. We will have to feel as bad as we feel. Patience trains us to live our life wide awake, to taste our painful emotions rather than simply swallowing them.

Paying Attention

The pain of a negative emotion gets our attention. Patience arrests our flight from feeling, helping us stay attentive. Ancient sages and contemporary social scientists agree on the value of this virtue. A central virtue in the Confucian moral armory was *ssu*: attentive awareness. Confucius believed that nine aspects of human interaction demand our special attention; for example, the eighth is "anger, for the difficulties it causes." The potentially dangerous emotion of anger must be carefully attended to. Arthur Waley, in his commentary on Confucius, observes that "we must think of *ssu* rather as *fixing attention* on an impression recently imbibed from the outside and destined to be immediately re-exteriorized in action."

For the sage Mencius, *ssu* was a matter of moral alertness. "If one attends [*ssu*], one achieves it; if one does not attend, one does not achieve it." Chinese scholar Lee Yearley defines *ssu* as "an inner ability to focus attention in a selective but concrete fashion." In his study of Mencius's vision of courage, Yearley links the skill of attention with nurturing *ch'i*—that physiological/spiritual energy that sometimes flowers in anger. If one pays no attention to this volatile source of energy, *ch'i* either withers into timidity or mushrooms into rage. Paying attention is a discipline that helps refine a person's vital energy into courage.

Complementing these Chinese convictions is Mihaly Csikszentmihalyi's research at the University of Chicago. In *Flow: The Psychology of Optimal Experience* he describes the experiences of work and leisure that make people feel most alive and give them "a sense of participation in defining the content of life."

At the core of people's experience of *flow*—feeling most alive and absorbingly engaged—is the phenomenon of attention. To enter the optimal experience of flow, people must concentrate in a particularly enriching way. A person absorbed in climbing a rocky cliff gives total attention to the moment. Distractions fall away and time stops. Wrapped in the present challenge, the climber enters the nourishing *flow* of the experience. Similarly, woodworkers or potters give rapt attention to their task. Fully concentrated on what they are doing, they enter into a focused, nourishing mood. Baseball players who find themselves in the middle of a hitting streak report that they are "seeing the ball clearly." During this brief period they are able to bring all their attention to what they are doing, without allowing distractions to intrude. Utterly focused, they perform with uncommon excellence.

Two characteristics of this experience are noteworthy. Absorbed in work or play, we are taken out of ourselves, lost in the activity that deeply refreshes us. Second, in the midst of these activities, our experience of time changes. We no longer watch the clock or calculate the finish line. Instead, time rushes by (we look up from an engrossing book to find the morning gone).

We call this ability *paying* attention because it is neither spontaneous nor free. Paying attention is a learned discipline, a developed skill. The ability to focus our attention on painful feelings sets us on the *way* of the negative emotions. As attention attunes us to the turmoil in our heart, we become aware of its acoustics.

In the Greek language, which has so influenced Western culture, *listening* and *obeying* share the same verbal root, *akouein*. In its most basic sense, *obedience* means not meek submission but careful listening. We cannot obey unless we first pay attention to what is being said. Patience and attention are ways that we listen to our life; they are modes of our obedience.

The Greek word for listening and obedience also gives us the word *acoustics*. Acoustics refers to the factors in an environment that allow us to hear what is going on. Some buildings have acoustics that distort music and muddle public announcements. Some hearts, too, have bad acoustics: crackling static and the feedback of judgmental voices make it almost impossible to attend to our own experience. In such a life, being patient and paying attention is difficult. To set out on the healing way of the painful emotions demands that we improve the acoustics of our heart. Only by listening well can we honor the laments and invitations being sounded there.

The way of naming our emotions is fraught with peril. We frequently fool ourselves by assigning the wrong name or naively believing that simply finding a name brings its cure. Yet naming is the only way through the thicket of emotion. Humbly, allowing for mistakes and self-deception, we continue to name the feelings that surge through us. Naming our emotions we are less their victims, even as we surrender the fantasy of becoming their masters. Gradually bringing these feelings to light, we see what we must do.

A Place to Listen—Sanctuaries

A sullen husband, a crying infant, and a barking dog were finally too much. Maria told her teenage son to watch the baby and ran from the house. Two blocks away she slipped into the back of a dark, empty church. Protected by this solitary space, at last she could cry. Fear and anger and regret spilled out into this quiet place. Finally, she could acknowledge to herself how bad she felt.

Religion has long provided sanctuary and safe haven in conflicted times. In medieval Europe church buildings functioned as legal asylums in which a fugitive could find protection. In the 1980s Christian groups in the United States formed a sanctuary movement to protect political refugees fleeing oppression in Central America and elsewhere.

Sanctuary is a place of safety. An emotional sanctuary is, by design, a place that allows us to fully experience our dangerous feelings. But just as words may distort emotions, sanctuaries can become places to hide. The rituals of a religious institution may provide us with a hiding place to avoid our painful emotions. Refusing the demanding tasks of naming and taming, we bask contentedly in the ready-made sentiments of empty ceremony instead.

To tame our negative emotions, we seek out sanctuaries where we can genuinely experience our feelings. Effective sanctuaries appear in many guises: the comforting quiet of a chapel, the privacy of a counselor's office, the safe shelter of a hospital room. We find haven in a support group's acceptance or in the solitude of confiding our thoughts in a personal journal. In the novel *A River Runs through It* a father and his two sons go frequently to a nearby stream for fly fishing. With little talk and much concentration, they occupy this privileged place together. During difficult times they bring their painful emotions to the river; it serves as their sanctuary.

Living with Passion

If the way of the painful emotions has no finish line, it does have a goal: to live with passion. The arduous disciplines of patience, naming, and taming teach us to trust our instincts. Knowing the difference between vindication and vengeance, we can afford to feel our anger. Having faced failure and discerned our grief, we can allow ourselves to mourn. No longer poisoned by toxic shame, we can dare to trust our emotional response.

Trusting our own responsiveness enables us, in Robert Bly's words, to "nurture tiny desires." Early in life much energy goes into defending ourselves or accommodating others' demands. In the crush of duties and distractions we lose track of our own best desires—deep longings still too fragile to make a claim on us. Grounded in no authority other than our slender hopes and tentative dreams, these "tiny desires" lie buried under the busy agenda of job and family and civic life.

Decades later a crisis or defeat or loss brings us to a halt. In the pause our gaze is altered. We recognize longings we have long ignored. We recall our early love of music; now at age fifty-five we want to learn to play a new instrument. But, of course, it's too late to take that up . . . or is it? Personal ambitions set aside, dreams forgotten for thirty years, return as hopes and hints for our future. In these fragile desires we remember what we really want.

Bly quotes William James's observation about the power of these *wants*:

> Man's . . . wants are to be trusted. . . . The uneasiness they occasion is still the best guide of his life and will lead him to issues entirely beyond his present power of reckoning.

Our wants often fly in the face of a familiar, well-developed social character, the solid shape of our responsible public persona. The uneasiness they cause reminds us of passions long ignored. As we tame our negative emotions, we gain confidence to listen again to tiny desires that show the way to a passionate future.

Embracing Our Shadow

Living more comfortably with passion helps us reconcile with our shadow. The metaphor of shadow refers, of course, to the underside of our personality. These are the conflicted humors and less than noble thoughts that we prefer to keep in the dark. Our shadow includes the petty jealousies, the habits of sarcasm, our reluctance to acknowledge an opponent's gesture of goodwill. The shadow is also the reverse side of our strengths. Good at initiating plans, we have difficulty following projects through to completion. Or we are able to see through unjust political structures quickly but have little tolerance for anyone questioning our opinions or our motives.

Each of us casts a long shadow. Often we push these unsavory parts outward, projecting the dark outline of what we dislike in ourselves onto others. If we remain unaware of these projections, they cloud our relationships and encumber our life.

The shadow in us has its own history. In the energetic idealism and enthusiasm of youth we fly, like Icarus, directly toward the sun. This assertive posture safely hides our shadow behind us. It is utterly out of our view as our eyes focus on the light ahead. As we mature, the shadow swings out from behind us. Now the sun no longer blinds us. Out of the corner of our eye we catch sight of our shadow. From the angle afforded at midlife we spot a somber outline that looks disconcertingly familiar. In a season of depression the sun swings behind us, leaving us face to face with our shadow. Our faults and limitations then loom large; we cannot put them in perspective. Our shadow stretches out in front of us, absorbing our attention and obscuring our path.

As we acknowledge the accumulated wounds of anger or guilt or shame, we begin the process of healing. A midlife executive recognizes his success has come precisely because he has been so driven. Working hard, he has pushed himself to achieve and pushed others away. Now he notices the shadow of this strength—his compulsiveness. Gradually he lets up on himself. He begins to embrace his shadow.

A woman, troubled by guilt all her life, realizes she cannot tolerate feeling beholden to anyone. Every debt must be quickly repaid; every gracious gesture received must be countered by a gift given in return. To help her relinquish guilt's grip on her life, she now consciously allows herself to savor her indebtedness, seeing how it links her life to others. She, too, begins to embrace her shadow.

Gradually we let go of what we no longer need. Since our shadow is part of us, we cannot completely jettison it. But gathering it back into ourselves we find—paradoxically—that our shadow strengthens us.

Holding Our Emotions

The way of the negative emotions brings us again to the metaphor of embrace. Before starting on the way, we aspired to "master" our emotions. But crossing the bridge of sadness, we let go of our ambitions of mastery. We learn—as the gospel predicts—that losing control brings surprising gains. In the words of Roberto Unger:

> You lose the world that you hoped vainly to control, the world in which you would be invulnerable to hurt, to misfortune, and loss of identity, and you regain it as the world that the mind and the will can grasp because they have stopped trying to hold it still or to hold it away.

Pledged to a God of desire, we do well to return to scripture to savor again Yahweh's anger and compassion, Jesus' disappointment and joy. Here we learn again how to hold the painful emotions, patiently in touch with the mystery that transforms our troublesome feelings into fruitful passions.

Reflective Exercise

In a final exercise, we invite you to consult your own journey on the way. Begin by considering a painful emotion that is familiar to you, sometimes even troublesome. It may be one of the several we have considered here: anger or fear, shame or guilt, loneliness or grief. Or it may be another feeling that is problematic for you at this time. Once you have made your selection, trace that emotion through the disciplines of the Way.

Start with *patience*. For example, have you gotten better at paying attention to the troublesome feeling as it arises? What helps you do this? How have you improved the acoustics in your heart? Don't rush the reflection. Other questions or insights may arise, helping you sense what *patience* means to you in this context.

Then move on to the other disciplines of the Way. How you have learned to *name* this emotion accurately; where you have been able to *tame* this feeling without losing its force; trace your growing confidence in *living with passion*. Spend time with each of these disciplines of emotional maturity, exploring what your past experience has been, what new hope you have now.

Bring the reflection to a close with a prayer of praise or gratitude or lament. When time allows, return to this exercise later with another emotion as your focus.

Additional Resources

See Adrienne Rich's poem "Integrity" in *A Wild Patience Has Taken Me This Far,* page 8. Thomas Moore examines the spiritual journey with gentleness and depth in *Care of the Soul;* a Jungian psychologist, Moore returns often to the theme of the shadow. In *The Wisdom of the Ego* George Vaillant demonstrates the positive function of the mind's defenses, which "like the body's immune mechanisms, protect us by providing a variety of illusions to filter pain and to allow self-soothing" (1).

Confucius's remarks on anger appear in book 16, chapter 10 of *Analects.* Arthur Waley comments on *ssu* in his translation of *The Analects of Confucius*, page 45. On Mencius's understanding of *ssu*, see Lee H. Yearley's *Mencius and Aquinas*, page 63. Mencius's observation is from 6a 15; see *The Works of Mencius*, translated by James Legge, page 885.

Robert Bly's evocative suggestions for "discovering tiny desires" appear on page 167 of *Iron John*. The William James quotation is from *The Will to Believe*, pages 131–32.

In *Flow: The Psychology of Optimal Experience*, Mihaly Csikszentmihalyi defines *flow* on page 4 and examines the role of attention on page 54. Roberto Unger's final quote is from *Passion: An Essay on Personality*, page 111.

Bibliography

All scriptural quotations are taken from *The New Revised Standard Version* (London: Collins, 1989), unless otherwise noted.

Albin, Rochelle Semmel. *Emotions*. Philadelphia: Westminster Press, 1983.

Anderson, Herbert. "What Consoles?" *Sewanee Theological Review* (1993): 378.

Angelou, Maya. "Interview with Maya Angelou." In *Writing Lives: Conversations between Women Writers*, ed. Mary Chamberlain. London: Virago Press, 1988.

Aquinas, Thomas. *St. Thomas Aquinas: The Treatise on the Virtues*. Translated by John Oesterle. Notre Dame, IN: University of Notre Dame Press, 1966.

———. *Summa Theologiae*. Latin text with English translation by the English Dominicans. New York: McGraw-Hill, 1963.

Aristotle. *Nicomachean Ethics*. In *The Basic Works of Aristotle*, ed. Richard McKeon. New York: Random House, 1941.

Auden, W. H. "For the Time Being." In *Collected Poems*. Modern Library Edition. New York: Random House, 2007.

Aurelius, Marcus. *The Meditations*. Translated by G. N. A. Grube. Indianapolis: Bobbs-Merrill, 1963.

Averill, James R. *Anger and Aggression: An Essay on Emotion*. New York: Springer-Verlag, 1982.

———. "Studies on Anger and Aggression: Implications for Theories of Emotion." *American Psychologist* (November 1983): 1145–60.

Bateson, Mary Catherine. *Composing a Life*. New York: Penguin, 1990.

Bausch, Richard. *Rebel Powers*. New York: Houghton Mifflin, 1993.

Berkowitz, Leonard. "On the Formation and Regulation of Anger and Aggression." *American Psychologist* (April 1990): 494–503.

Borysenko, Joan. *Guilt Is the Teacher, Love Is the Lesson*. New York: Grand Central Publishers, 1991.

Boteach, Shmuley. *Face Your Fears: Living with Courage in an Age of Caution*. New York: St. Martin's Press, 2004.

Bourne, Edmund, and Lorna Garano. *Coping with Anxiety: Ten Simple Ways to Relieve Anxiety, Fear, and Worry*. Oakland, CA: New Harbinger, 2003.

Bowlby, John. *A Secure Base: Parent-Child Attachment and Healthy Human Development*. New York: Basic Books, 1988.

Bradshaw, John. *Healing the Shame That Binds You*. Deerfield Beach, FL: Health Communications, 2005.

Brantley, Jeffrey. *Calming Your Anxious Mind.* Oakland, CA: New Harbinger, 2003.

Briggs, Kenneth. *The Power of Forgiveness.* Based on a film by Martin Doblmeier. Minneapolis: Fortress Press, 2008.

Brown, Peter. *Body and Society: Men, Women, and Sexual Renunciation in Early Christianity.* New York: Columbia University Press, 1988.

Broyard, Anatole. *Intoxicated by My Illness.* New York: Clarkson Potter, 1992.

Brueggemann, Walter. *The Prophetic Imagination.* Philadelphia: Fortress Press, 1978.

Buchholz, Ester. *The Call to Solitude: Alonetime in a World of Attachment.* New York: Simon and Schuster, 2000.

Buckley, Thomas. "The Seven Deadly Sins." *Parabola* (Winter 1985): 6.

Burns, David D. *Feeling Good: The New Mood Therapy.* New York: HarperCollins, 2000.

Bly, Robert. *Iron John.* New York: Addison-Wesley, 1990.

Cacioppo, John, and William Patrick. *Loneliness: Human Nature and the Need for Social Connection.* New York: Norton, 2008.

Callahan, Sidney. *In Good Conscience: Reason and Emotion in Moral Decision Making.* New York: HarperCollins, 1991.

Chambers, Edward, with Michael Cowan. *Roots for Radicals: Organizing for Power, Action, and Justice.* New York: Continuum, 2003.

Cheever, John. *Journals.* New York: Vintage, 2008.

Clement of Alexandria. *Le Pedagogue.* Edited by M. Harl with Introduction by H. I. Marrou. *Sources Chretiennes.* Vol. 158. Paris: Editions du Cerf, 1970.

———. "Stromata," In *Alexandrian Christianity.* Vol. II. Edited by Henry Chadwick. Philadelphia: Westminster Press, 1954.

Confucius. *The Analects of Confucius.* Translated by Arthur Waley. London: Allen and Unwin, 1983.

Coryell, Deborah. *Good Grief: Healing through the Shadows of Loss.* Rochester, VT: Healing Arts Press, 2007.

Csikszentmihalyi, Mihaly. *Flow: The Psychology of Optimal Experience.* San Francisco: HarperCollins, 1990.

Curran, Charles. *Faithful Dissent.* Kansas City: Sheed and Ward, 1986.

Damasio, A. R. *Descartes' Error: Emotion, Reason, and the Human Brain.* New York: Putnam, 1994.

———. *Looking for Spinoza: Joy, Sorrow, and the Feeling Brain.* Orlando, FL: Harcourt Brace, 2003.

Dowrick, Stephanie. *Forgiveness and Other Acts of Love.* New York: Penguin Global, 2005.

———. *Intimacy and Solitude: Balancing Closeness and Independence.* New York: Norton, 1998.

Driver, Thomas. *The Magic of Ritual.* Harper San Francisco, 1991.

Earle, Ralph, and Gregory Crow. *Lonely All the Time.* New York: Pocket Books, 1998.

Ekman, Paul. *Emotions Revealed: Understanding Faces and Feelings.* 2d edition. New York: Henry Holt, 2007.

Eliot, T.S. "East Coker" in *Four Quartets.* New York: Harcourt, 1943.

Ellis, Thomas. *This Thing Called Grief: New Understandings of Loss.* Minneapolis: Syren Books, 2006.

Erikson, Erik. *Identity and the Life Cycle.* New York: Norton, 1980.

———. *The Life Cycle Completed—A Review.* New York: Norton, 1982.

Erikson, Erik, Joan M. Erikson, and Helen Q. Kivnick. *Vital Involvement: The Experience of Old Age in Our Time.* New York: Norton, 1994.

Fairlie, Henry. *The Seven Deadly Sins Today.* Notre Dame, IN: University of Notre Dame Press, 1979.

Ferrucci, Piero. *What We May Be.* New York: Jeremy Tarcher, 1982.

Fischer, Kathleen. *The Courage the Heart Desires: Spiritual Strength in Difficult Times.* San Francisco: Jossey-Bass, 2006.

———. *Transforming Fire: Women Using Anger Creatively.* New York: Paulist Press, 2000.

Fossum, Merle, and Marilyn Mason. *Facing Shame.* New York: Norton, 1986.

Gaylin, Willard. *Feelings: Our Vital Signs.* New York: Harper and Row, 1989.

———. *Hatred: The Psychological Descent into Violence.* New York: Public Affairs Press, 2003.

———. *The Rage Within: Anger in Modern Life.* New York: Penguin Press, 1989.

Gentry, W. Doyle. *When Someone You Love Is Angry.* New York: Penguin, 2002.

Gerner, Christopher. *The Mindful Path to Self-Compassion: Freeing Yourself from Destructive Thoughts and Emotions.* New York: Guilford Press, 2009.

Goldberg, Carl. *Understanding Shame.* London: Aronson, 1991.

Goleman, Daniel. *Healing Emotions: Conversations with the Dalai Lama.* Boston: Shambala, 2003.

———. *The Destructive Emotions: A Scientific Dialogue with the Dalai Lama.* New York: Bantam Books, 2004.

Gondreau, Paul. *The Passions of Christ's Soul in the Theology of St. Thomas Aquinas.* Munster: Aschenndorff Verlag, 2002.

Greenspan, Miriam. *Healing through the Dark Emotions: The Wisdom of Grief, Fear, and Despair.* Boston: Shambala, 2003.

Haidt, Jonathan. "Approaching Awe: A Moral, Spiritual and Aesthetic Emotion." *Cognition and Emotion* (2003): 297–314.

Hanh, Thich Nhat. *Anger: Wisdom for Cooling the Flames.* New York: Berkeley Group, 2002.

Harper, James, and Margaret Hoopes. *Uncovering Shame.* New York: Norton, 1990.

Harrison, Barbara. "The Place of Anger in the Works of Love." In *Making the Connections: Essays in Feminist Social Ethics,* ed. Carol S. Robb. Boston: Beacon Press, 1985.

Heaney, Seamus. *The Redress of Poetry.* New York: The Library of America, 1988.

Hillard, Erika. *Living Fully with Shyness and Social Anxiety.* New York: Marlow, 2005.

Howe, Leroy. *Comforting the Fearful: Listening Skills for Caregivers.* New York: Paulist Press, 2002.

Jack, Dana Crowley. *Silencing the Self: Women and Depression*. Cambridge, MA: Harvard University Press, 1991.

James, William. *The Will to Believe*. New York: Longmans, Green, and Company, 1907; first edition 1897.

Janeway, Elizabeth. *Improper Behavior: When and How Misconduct Can Be Healthy for Society*. New York: William Morrow, 1989.

Jeffers, Susan. *Feel the Fear and Do It Anyway*. New York: Ballantine, 2008.

John Paul II. *The Splendor of Truth (Veritatis Splendor)*. *Origins* (October 14, 1993).

Johnson, Hiram. *Tragic Redemption: Healing Guilt and Shame*. Austin, TX: Langmarc, 2006.

Kaufman, Gershen. *The Psychology of Shame: Theory and Treatment*. 2d edition. New York: Springer, 2004.

Keen, Sam. *Inward Bound*. New York: Bantam, 1992.

Kegan, Robert. *In over Our Heads: The Mental Demands of Modern Life*. Cambridge, MA: Harvard University Press, 1998.

Keillor, Garrison. *Lake Wobegon Days*. New York: Viking, 1985.

Keltner, Dacher. *Born to Be Good: The Science of a Meaningful Life*. New York: Norton, 2009.

Kubler-Ross, Elisabeth, and David Kessler. *On Grief and Grieving: Finding the Meaning of Grief through the Five Stages of Loss*. New York: Scribner, 2007.

Lahr, John. "The Demon Lover." *The New York Times,* May 31, 1999.

Law, Eric H. F. *Finding Intimacy in a World of Fear*. St. Louis: Chalice Press, 2007.

Lazarus, Richard S. *Stress and Emotion: A New Syntheses*. New York: Springer, 2006.

Lee, Bernard. *Jesus and the Metaphors of God*. New York: Paulist Press, 1993.

Lerner, Harriet Goldhur. *The Dance of Anger*. New York: Harper and Row, 2005.

———. *The Dance of Connection*. New York: HarperCollins, 2002.

———. *The Dance of Fear*. New York: HarperCollins, 2004.

Levine, Marvin. *The Positive Psychology of Buddhism and Yoga: Paths to a Mature Happiness*. Boca Raton, FL: Taylor and Francis, 2009.

Lewis, C. S. *A Grief Observed*. New York: Seabury, 1961.

Lewis, Michael. *Shame: The Exposed Self*. New York: Free Press, 1995.

Lilla, Salvatore. *Clement of Alexandria*. New York: Oxford University Press, 1971.

Lorde, Audre. *Sister Outsider: Essays and Speeches by Audre Lorde*. Freedom, CA: The Crossing Press, 1984.

Lynd, Helen Merrill. *On Shame and the Search for Identity*. New York: Harcourt, Brace, 1958.

MacIntyre, Alasdair. *After Virtue*. Notre Dame, IN: University of Notre Dame Press, 1981.

———. *"Sophrosune: How A Virtue Can Become Socially Disruptive."* In *Ethical Theory: Character and Virtue*, ed. P. A. French, T. E. Uehling, and H. K. Wettstein. Notre Dame, IN: University of Notre Dame Press, 1988.

Magai, Carol, and Jeannette Haviland-Jones. *The Hidden Genius of Emotion: Lifespan Transformations in Personality.* New York: Cambridge University Press, 2007.

May, Gerald. *Addiction and Grace: Love and Spirituality in the Healing of Addiction.* San Francisco: HarperOne, 2007.

McKay, Matthew, Peter Rogers, and Judith McKay. *When Anger Hurts: Quieting the Storm Within.* 2d edition. Oakland, CA: New Harbinger Publications, 2003.

McKenzie, John. "Anger." In *The Jerome Biblical Commentary.* Englewood Cliffs, NJ: Prentice-Hall, 1968.

McNeill, John. *Sex as God Intended.* Maple Shade, NJ: Lethe Press, 2008.

———. *Taking a Chance on God.* Boston: Beacon Press, 1996.

McNish, Jill. *Transforming Shame: A Pastoral Response.* New York: Haworth Press, 2004.

Mencius. *The Works of Mencius.* Translated by James Legge. New York: Dover, 1970.

Mitchell, Kenneth, and Herbert Anderson. *All Our Losses, All Our Griefs: Resources for Pastoral Care.* Philadelphia: Westminster, 1983.

Moore, Thomas. *Care of the Soul.* New York: Harper Perennial, 1994.

Narramore, Bruce. *No Condemnation: Rethinking Guilt Motivation.* Portland, OR: Resource Publications, 2002.

Nathanson, Donald L., ed. *The Many Faces of Shame.* New York: Norton, 1987.

———. *Shame and Pride: Affect, Sex, and the Birth of the Self.* New York: Norton, 1992.

Neal-Barnett, Angela. *Soothe Your Nerves: The Black Woman's Guide to Understanding Anxiety, Panic, and Fear.* New York: Simon and Schuster, 2003.

Norman, Elizabeth. *Women at War: Studies in Health, Illness, and Caregiving.* Philadelphia: University of Pennsylvania Press, 1990.

Nussbaum, Martha. *Upheavals of Thought: The Intelligence of Emotions.* New York: Cambridge University Press, 2001.

O'Connor, Kathleen. *Lamentation and the Tears of the World.* Maryknoll, NY: Orbis Books, 2003.

Overstreet, Bonaro. *Overcoming Fear in Ourselves and Others.* New York: Collier, 1964.

Parks, Colin Murray. *Love and Loss: The Roots of Grief and Its Complications.* London: Routledge, 2008.

Patteson, Stephen. *Shame: Theory, Therapy, Theology.* New York: Cambridge University Press, 2000.

Peck, Scott. *The Road Less Traveled.* New York: Rider, 2003.

———. *A World Waiting to Be Born: Rediscovering Civility.* New York: Bantam, 1993.

Pembroke, Neil. *The Art of Listening: Dialogue, Shame, and Pastoral Care.* New York: T&T Clark, 2002.

Peurifoy, Reneau. *Anger: Taming the Beast.* New York: Kodansha America, 2002.

Philippot, Pierre, and Robert Feldman, eds. *The Regulation of Emotions.* Mahwah, NJ: Lawrence Erlbaum, 2004.

Phillips, Adam. *On Kissing, Tickling, and Being Bored: Psychoanalytic Essays on the Unexamined Life*. Cambridge: Harvard University Press, 1998.

Pieper, Josef. *The Four Cardinal Virtues*. Notre Dame, IN: University of Notre Dame Press, 1966.

Piver, Susan. *How Not to Be Afraid of Your Own Life*. New York: St. Martin's Press, 2007.

Potter-Efron, Ronald, *Angry All the Time: Emergency Guide to Anger Control*. 2nd edition. Oakland, CA: New Harbinger Publications, 2005.

———, and Patricia Potter-Efron. *Letting Go of Anger: Common Anger Styles and What to Do about Them*. Oakland, CA: New Harbinger, 2006.

———. *Letting Go of Shame*. San Francisco: Harper Collins, 1989.

Power, David. "Households of Faith in the Coming Church." *Worship* (May 1983): 237–55.

Rich, Adrienne. "Integrity." In *A Wild Patience Has Taken Me This Far: Poems 1978–1981*. New York: Norton, 1981.

Ricoeur, Paul. *The Symbolism of Evil*. Boston: Beacon Press, 1967.

Rieff, Philip. *Freud: The Mind of the Moralist*. New York: Doubleday, 1959.

Rogers, Mary Beth. *Cold Anger: A Story of Faith and Power Politics*. Denton: University of North Texas Press, 1991.

Rohrer, Norman, and Philip Sutherland. *Facing Anger*. Minneapolis: Augsburg, 1981.

Rolheiser, Ronald. *The Restless Heart: Finding Our Spiritual Home in Times of Loneliness*. New York: Image Books, 2006.

Rosenthal, Norman. *The Emotional Revolution: Harnessing the Power of Your Emotions for a More Positive Life*. New York: Kensington, 2002.

Schillebeeckx, Edward. *Ministry: Leadership in the Community of Jesus Christ*. New York: Crossroad, 1981.

Schneider, Carl. *Shame, Exposure, and Privacy*. New York: Norton, 1992.

Sharansky, Natan. *Fear No Evil*. New York: Random House, 1988.

Sheehan, Neil. *A Bright Shining Lie*. New York: Random House, 1988.

Smedes, Lewis B. *Forgive and Forget: Healing the Hurts We Don't Deserve*. San Francisco: HarperCollins, 2007.

———. *Shame and Grace: Healing the Shame We Don't Deserve*. San Francisco: Harper Collins, 1998.

Solomon, Robert. *The Passions: The Myth and Nature of Human Emotions*. 2d edition. Indianapolis: Hackett Publishers, 1993.

Sorabji, Richard. *Emotions and Peace of Mind: From Stoic Agitation to Christian Temptation*. New York: Oxford University Press, 2000.

Spohn, William. "Jesus and Christian Ethics." *Theological Studies* 56 (1995).

Stegner, Wallace. *All the Little Live Things*. New York: Penguin, 1991.

Storr, Anthony. *Solitude: A Return to the Self*. New York: Free Press, 2005.

Stringfellow, William. *A Simplicity of Faith: My Experience of Mourning*. Eugene, OR: Wipf and Stock, 2005.

Svitil, Kathy A. *Calming the Anger Storm*. New York: Alpha Books, 2006.

Swinburne, Richard. *Responsibility and Atonement*. New York: Oxford University Press, 1990.

Tangney, June Price, and Ronda L. Dearing. *Shame and Guilt: Emotions and Social Behavior*. New York: Guilford Press, 2003.

Tavris, Carol. *Anger—The Misunderstood Emotion*. New edition. New York: Simon and Schuster, 1989.

Theodosius, Catherine. *Emotional Labor in Health Care*. New York: Routledge, 2008.

Tournier, Paul. *Guilt and Grace: A Psychological Study*. New York: Harper and Row, 1985.

Trible, Phyllis. *God and the Rhetoric of Sexuality*. Philadelphia: Fortress Press, 1978.

Unger, Roberto. *Passion: An Essay on Personality*. New York: Free Press, 1984.

Vaillant, George. *The Wisdom of the Ego*. Cambridge, MA: Harvard University Press, 1993.

Villaseñor, Victor. *Rain of Gold*. New York: Dell Publishers, 1991.

Walters, Kerry. *Jacob's Hip: Finding God in an Anxious Age*. Maryknoll, NY: Orbis Books, 2003.

West, Cornel. *Race Matters*. Boston: Beacon Press, 2001.

"When Health Workers Stop to Mourn." *New York Times.* June 25, 1992.

Whitehead, Evelyn Eaton, and James D. Whitehead. *Christian Adulthood: A Journey of Self-Discovery*. Liguori, MO: Liguori Press, 2005.

———. *Community of Faith: Crafting Christian Communities Today*. Mystic, CT: Twenty-Third Publications, 1992.

Whitehead, James D., and Evelyn Eaton Whitehead. *Holy Eros: Pathways to a Passionate God*. Maryknoll, NY: Orbis Books, 2009.

———. *The Promise of Partnership: A Model for Collaborative Ministry*. San Francisco: Harper Collins, 1993.

Williams, Bernard. *Shame and Necessity*. 2d edition. Berkeley and Los Angeles: University of California Press, 2008.

Wilson, James Q. *The Moral Sense*. New York: Free Press, 1993.

Winnicott, D. W. *Home Is Where We Start From*. New York: Norton, 1986.

———. *Playing and Reality*. Chatham, Kent: Tavistock, 1971.

Yearley, Lee. *Mencius and Aquinas: Theories of Virtue and Conceptions of Courage*. Albany: State University of New York Press, 1990.

Index

abandonment, 124–25

abuse, response to, 87–89

achievement: compensating for shame, 88–89; reaching for, 100

acoustics, 192

active mastery, 142

addiction, 99; linked with unmanageable negative emotions, 6

adolescence, as season of solitude, 157

adolescents, handling painful feelings, 6

aggression, 46

aging, solitude and, 159–60

agon, 71

Albin, Rochelle, 39, 55

Alinsky, Saul, 58

All the Little Live Things (Stegner), 43

alone in the presence of another, 154–55

Anderson, Herbert, 141

Anderson, John, 71

anger: ability of, to expose, 70; acquiescing to, 53; addressing, through humor, 59; appraisal of, 43–47; arenas of, 38–43; assertive response to, 45–46; attentiveness to, 191; avoiding, 22–23; befriending, 51, 53, 54; benefits of, 5; channeling into effective action, 56–57; children learning about, 54–55; Christian spirituality of, 74–75; chronic, 42–43; cold, 58; consequences of, 3; courage related to, 72–74; discerning appropriate responses to, 54–55; distinguishing from other emotions, 37; doomed responses to, 51; enabling the facing of difficulty, 36; evaluating, 52–54; as experience of arousal and interpretation, 37–38; expressing, 55–56; forgiveness in, 59–61; generating energy, 46–47; harboring, 44; honing, to achieve virtuous action, 72; honoring, 51–52; inability to experience, 36; increased by angry expression, 56; instigating change, 71; intimate, 38–39, 66, 67; justice, 41–42; leading to destructive sentiment, 7; leading to hope, 46–47; learning from, 52–54; letting go of, 58–59; linked with reason, 69–70; as most frequent of the negative emotions, 35–36; necessity of, 47; optimistic view of, 36–37; outlawing of, in the church, 68; passion of, 73; physiological arousal resulting from, 37–38; positive vision of, reclaiming, 69–70; provocation of, 44; public, 39–40; in pursuit of justice, 72; reappraising, 59; related to shame, 70; resulting from frustration, 44; scriptural accounts of, 64–66; signaling social transformation, 47; as sin, 67–68; social, 67; standing in for shame, 88

apatheia, 29

Aquinas, Thomas, 30, 36, 69, 181, 182

Arendt, Hannah, 60

Aristotle, 36, 42, 69–70

arousal: naming of, 37–38; stemming from emotions, 11

attentiveness, 191–92

Augustine, 64, 99

207

authority, fear of, 168
Averill, James, 44, 46
avoidance, 22–23, 170, 171
awe, 179–80

Bateson, Mary Catherine, 71
Bausch, Richard, 3
befriending emotions, 15, 18; anger, 51, 53, 54; fear, 171; loss, 137
belittling, 124–25
belonging, 81; boundaries of, religion redrawing, 127; enforcing the rules of, for children, 82
Bergman, Ingmar, 177
Berkowitz, Leonard, 52
Bernardin, Joseph, 74
blame, related to anger, 44–45, 51
Bly, Robert, 86, 194
body, one's own, feeling shame about, 111–12
Body and Society (Brown), 29, 73
boredom, 157
Borysenko, Joan, 95
Bowlby, John, 165–66, 169
Bradshaw, John, 25, 89, 90
bridge of sadness, 24–28
Bright Shining Lie, A (Sheehan), 89
Brown, Peter, 29, 73
Broyard, Anatole, 26–27
Brueggemann, Walter, 143
Buckley, Michael, 24–25, 28

Callahan, Sidney, 82, 115
caregivers, code of silence for, 4, 25
chastity, 73, 117–18
Cheever, John, 9
ch'i, 35, 73, 191
childhood, perils of, 86–87
children, separating from parents, 154–55
Christians: arguing over role of passion, 63; harboring suspicions about negative emotions, 28–30
chronic anger, 42–43

chronic grief, 143
City of God (Augustine), 64
civility, 74–75
Clement, 29
code of silence, for health professionals and caregivers, 4, 25
cold anger, 58
Communities Organized for Public Service (COPS), 58
community of faith, imaged as body of Christ, 112
community organizing, 47, 57–58
Composing a Life (Bateson), 71
composure, 110–11
conflict: difficulty with, 36; facing, 40; role of, in religious heritage, 71
conformity, 122
confrontation, 170–71
Confucius, 82, 191
conscience, 103–5
control: essential to psychological maturity, 164; loss of, bringing gains, 196
coping, as part of grieving process, 138, 140
Cortez, Ernesto, 57–58
courage, 190; fear as component of, 5; hope and, 183; as patience, 182–83; related to anger, 72–74; use of, to hold fear, 181–82
covenant, 96–97, 126
Cowan, Michael, 168
cross, taking up, 27
Crow, Gregory, 6
cultural messages, reinforcing consequences of negative emotions, 4
Csikszentmihalyi, Mihaly, 191

death: confronting, 26–27; effect on, of Jesus' death, 129–30
demoniacs, 18–19
denial: mastery leading to, 14; as part of grieving process, 138, 140; as response to anger, 51; stemming from emotional arousal, 13

dignity, 116, 117; arising from bond with the Creator, 127; emerging from shame, 5

Dignity/USA, 116–17

distress, concentration on, risk of, 22–23

Driver, Thomas, 144

dualism: of emotion and reason, 10, 29; as reason for holding off emotions, 14

Earle, Ralph, 6

Eliot, T. S., 7, 159

embarrassment, 85

embrace, at base of Christian life, 13–14

emotions: as actions we take, 9; A-I-M approach to (arousal/interpretation/movement), 11–13; as alerts to trouble, 8; ambiguous approach to, 14; burying, effect of, 13; deeper themes underlying, uncovering, 20–21; embrace of, 14–15; harboring, 23–25; holding, 14–15, 196; as instruments of rationality, 10; mastering, 14; naming, 18–21, 192–93; passivity of, 8–9; personifying, 18–19; private nature of, 8; providing energy for change, 21–23; puzzle surrounding, 3–4; recognizing origins of, 19–20; as social realities, 8

empathy, 101–2

Erikson, Erik, 85, 103–4, 114, 156

expectations, 53–54

exposure, threat of, 123

expulsion, threat of, 124

Fagan, Jeffery, 40

Fairlie, Henry, 68

fear: as acquired response, 169–70; anticipating pain, 163; avoiding, 22; befriending, 171; benefits of, 5; from changes in the self, 166–67; Christian script for handling, 176, 183–84; consequences of, 4; destructive nature of, 168; different psychological interpretations of, 163–64; as emotion, 162–64; from existential threats, 167–68; future-oriented nature of, 163; in the Gospels, three faces of, 175; holding, with courage, 181–82; leading to astonishment and awe, 178–80; as mixed emotion, in Book of Job, 178, 179; mobilizing resources in face of, 172; paralysis from, 181; physical response to, 162–63; range of emotions stemming from, in New Testament stories, 178–79; religion and, 180–81; response to, 170–71; saving nature of, 169–70; sorting out, 169–70; sources of, 164–66; standing in for shame, 88; value of, 162; as worry about the future, 175–77

fight-or-flight behavior, 12, 170, 171

flow, 191–92

Flow: The Psychology of Optimal Experience (Csikszentmihalyi), 191

forgiveness: holding guilt in check, 102–3; replacing vengeance, 128; used in reinterpreting anger, 59–61

Freud, Sigmund, 104

frustration, 53

Gaylin, Willard, 8, 10, 21, 36–37, 93, 94, 166

gender slurs, 123

genuine guilt, 94, 95, 96

God: breaking the covenant with, 96–97; immersed in all the passions, 63; impassibility of, 64; stirred by anger and compassion, 64–65; as unmoved mover, 64

grief: acute phase of, 140; addressing, ritual's role in, 143–45; awakening ranges of ambivalent feelings, 141; benefits of, 5; chronic, 143; holding losses up to God, 143; holding on to, 142–43; leading to destructive sentiment, 7; many emotions accompanying, 135; personal and social nature of, 135; refusal of, 137; as salutary emotion, 145; spirituality and, 142–43; strategies for, 143

grieving: grace in, 145; identifying healing process of befriending loss, 137; process for, 137–42

guilt, 82; addressing correctness, 115; avoiding, 23; benefits of, 5; as companion of commitment, 93–94; consequences of, 4; cultural metaphors of, 96–98; destructive, 98–99; devolving into self-punishment, 93–94; genuine, 94, 95, 96; inauthentic, 95–96; internalizing, 82; keeping, in bounds, 100–103; leading to destructive sentiment, 7; men's feelings of, 97; original, 105–6; as price of belonging, 93; as response to anger, 51; responsibility's relationship to, 100–102; shame linked to, 82–83; Western culture's experience of, 96–97; women's feelings of, 97

Haidt, Jonathan, 179
harboring emotions, 23–25
Harrison, Barbara, 8, 55
Harrison, Beverly Wildung, 37
health professionals, code of silence for, 4, 25
Heaney, Seamus, 160
Homer, 81
honor, as measure of our worth, 121
honoring anger, 51–52
hope: courage and, 183; emerging from anger, 46–47; grief opening to, 5
humility, 115–16, 117
humor, addressing anger with, 59
hunger, using, to address emotions, 12, 13

Iliad (Homer), 81
impermanence, 28
inauthentic guilt, 95–96
incest, 88

indifference, as enemy of reconciliation, 47
Industrial Areas Foundation (IAF), 57–58
initiative, 103–4
injury, related to anger, 43–44
injustice, anger as response to, 41–42
integrity, supported by guilt, 5
interpretation, stemming from emotions, 11–12
intimacy: loneliness allied with, 151; loneliness prompting search for, 5; resulting from expressed anger, 55–56
intimate anger, 38–39, 66, 67
Intoxicated by My Illness (Broyard), 26
irony, habitual use of, 43

Jack, Dana Crowley, 39, 71
James, William, 194
Jesus: anger of, 65–66; confronting death, 129; experiencing full range of emotions, 63; humbled but not destroyed, 130; as model for crossing the bridge of negative emotions, 27; moved by grief, 137; overturning authority of traditional clan lines, 127; solitude of, 153–54
Johnson, Samuel, 177
Journals (Cheever), 9
justice, pursuit of, resulting from anger, 5
justice anger, 41–42

Kant, Immanuel, 7–8
Kegan, Robert, 149
Keillor, Garrison, 181
King, Billie Jean, 98
Kundera, Milan, 110

Lahr, John, 177
laughter, belittling function of, 125
Lerner, Harriet, 47
Lewis, C. S., 135
listening, 192

loneliness, 147–48; aging and, 159–60; benefits of, 5; Christian script for, 153–54; chronic, 149–50; developmental, 148–49, 158–59; different responses to, for men and women, 150–51; experiencing, times for, 148–50; as invitation to solitude, 152–53; learning from, 155–56; seeming unjustified, 152; signaling a relationship in pain, 152; sinking into, 148; situational, 148, 158

Lonely All the Time (Earle and Crow), 6

loss: acceptance of, 138–40; befriending, 137; holding, in memory, 140–41; life after, reconnecting with, 141–42

loyal opposition, 74

MacIntyre, Alasdair, 71, 72

magnanimity, 70

Marcus Aurelius, 28–29, 67, 137

mastery, 14; active, 142; receptive, 142

maturity, goal of, relative to fear, 172

Meditations (Marcus Aurelius), 28–29, 67

Mencius, 72–73, 181, 191

missing the mark, 96–98

modesty: false, 110; modeling, 111

mourning, 26

movement, stemming from emotions, 11, 12–13

mystery, 7

naming, as strategy of social shame, 123–24

negative emotions, 3; addiction linked to, 6; attracting our attention, 191; befriending, 27 (*see also* befriending emotions); benefits of, 5; Christians' suspicion of, 28–30; consequences of, 3–4; desire to understand, 4; leading to destructive sentiment, 7; leading to embrace of mystery, 7; linked to inadequacy and weakness,

4; message of, discerning, 22–23; prompting self-examination, 6–7; revelations resulting from, 10; shaping a spirituality from, 6; taming, 21–23; virtuous response to, 23

Obama, Barack, 74

obedience, 192

O'Connor, Kathleen, 143

On Kissing, Tickling, and Being Bored (Phillips), 110

original guilt, 105–6

outcasts, welcoming of, 127

Overstreet, Bonaro, 172

pain: avoiding, 22; as bad feeling about something good, 21; publicizing, 142; respecting, 22; taming, 21–23; transforming into suffering, 25

painful emotions, way of, 189–96

painful feelings, respecting, 140

pars pudenda, 111, 112

participation, as spiritual exercise, 190

passion: living with, 194; performance of, 9; as price of love, 63. *See also* emotions

Passions, The (Solomon), 9

passive aggression, as outlet for anger, 43

patience, 30–31, 156; courage as, 182–83; learning, 190–91

Peck, Scott, 25

people pleasing, 86–87

perfectionism, 99

personal will, 112, 113–14

Phillips, Adam, 110–11, 156, 157, 176–77

physical activity, used to deal with emotions, 13

Pieper, Josef, 72, 74, 181, 183

Plutarch, 111–12

Power, David, 145

presence, as spiritual exercise, 190

prophecy, institution of, disappeared, 68

prophets, reliance of, on anger, 65
public anger, 39–40
public lamentations, 143

rage, 50–51
Rain of Gold (Villaseñor), 50
reason, informed by emotion, 10
Rebel Powers (Bausch), 3
receptive mastery, 142
recognition, 123
reconciliation, 128
reflection, leading to proper mood regulation, 52
relaxation, used to deal with emotions, 13
religion, contribution of, to healing social shame, 126
religious malpractice, 180–81
resentment, 42–43
respect, 120–22, 123
responsibility, 100–102
restitution, 103
revenge, 121
Rich, Adrienne, 190–91
Rieff, Philip, 104
righteousness, 73
rituals, role of, in addressing grief, 143–45
River Runs through It, A, 193
Road Less Traveled, The (Peck), 25
Rogers, Mary Beth, 57–58

sacred, recognition of, as dangerous terrain, 128–29
sadness, bridge of, 24–28
safety, 165–66
sanctuary, 193
Schneider, Carl, 84, 90, 117
security, 165–66
self-condemnation, as response to anger, 51
self-control, balancing, with self-esteem, 114
self-examination, resulting from pain, 6–7

serenity, 28
service, ideals of, 100
seven deadly sins, 68
sexuality, feeling shame about, 111–12
sexual slurs, 123
shadow, embracing, 194–95
shame: addressing worth, 115; avoiding, 23; benefits of, 5; in childhood, reacting to, 86; composure as aspect of, 111; conscience linked to, 81–82; consequences of, 3–4; economy of, 120–22; as element of child development, 113–14; as element of the story of Jesus' death, 129; as erotic virtue, 111–12; as exposure, 84–86; expressing, through other emotions, 88; as grace and disgrace, 83–84, 85–86; guarding boundaries of the bodily self, 111; guilt linked to, 82–83; healing from, 89–90, 125–26; healthy, 90, 112–15; leading to destructive sentiment, 7; learned nature of, 89–90; many meanings of, 120; as more than an emotion, 108–9; naming, as strategy of, 123–24; personal responsibility linked to, 82; as positive resource, 108–9; positive sense of, 117–18; related to anger, 70; role of, in socialization, 113–15; and seeing God face to face, 128–31; social, 120–31; social dynamics surrounding, 120; used as attempt to enforce conformity, 122; virtues of, 115–17
Sharansky, Natan, 116
Sheehan, Neil, 89
shock, as part of grieving process, 138, 140
shyness, 110
silencing, 125
sin, New Testament approach to, 96–97
social anger, 67
social shame, 120–22; healing of, and Christianity, 126–31; strategies of,

122–25; success of, ensuring its survival, 131; transformation of, 125–26

socialization, 122

solitude: aging and, 159–60; invitation to, 152–53; journey of, never completed, 160; midlife, 157–59; seasons of, 156–57

Solomon, Robert, 9, 42

Sopranos, The, 121

spirit, as link to a passionate Creator, 15

spiritual exercises, 190

Spohn, William, 143–44

ssu, 191

Stegner, Wallace, 43

Stoicism, 28–29, 67–68

stress, calming, 22

Stringfellow, William, 25–26

struggle, as means of finding one's way, 71

suffering, pain transformed into, 25

suffering servant, 130–31

Summa Theologiae (Aquinas), 69–70

systemic injustice, 41

tact, 109

Tao, 189

Tavris, Carol, 56

temperance, 73–74

terrible two's, 112–15

thinking/feeling, dualistic approach to, 10

transcendence, 179–80

Unger, Roberto, 10, 196

urban unrest, 40, 41

value, personal, arising from bond with the Creator, 127

Vann, John Paul, 89

victimhood, 27

Villaseñor, Victor, 50

voice, as metaphor for conscience, 104–5

Waley, Arthur, 191

weight gain, as defense, 87

Weiss, Robert, 148

West, Cornel, 41

will, 112–15

Williams, Bernard, 111, 115

Winnicott, D. W., 154–55

wonder, as response to emotions, 13

worry, 175–77, 183–84

wrath, 74–75

Yearley, Lee, 35, 73, 182–83, 191

Zullo, James, 11, 13